The New Gas Grill Gourmet

THE NEW
GAS GRILL
GOURMET

GREAT GRILLED FOOD

FOR EVERYDAY MEALS

AND FANTASTIC FEASTS

A. Cort Sinnes

The Harvard Common Press ✳ Boston, Massachusetts

For Tim and Gene,

the best grinning,

swilling, laughing,

lying, dominoes-playing,

Friday-night friends

a person could ask

for—thanks for

your help.

The Harvard Common Press
535 Albany Street
Boston, Massachusetts 02118
www.harvardcommonpress.com

Printed in the United States of America

LIBRARY OF CONGRESS CATALOGING-IN-PUBLICATION DATA
Sinnes, A. Cort.
   The new gas grill gourmet: great grilled food for everyday meals and fantastic feasts / A. Cort Sinnes.
       p. cm.
Includes index.
ISBN 1-55832-281-7 ((hardcover) : alk. paper) — ISBN 1-55832-282-5 ((pbk.) : alk. paper)
1. Barbecue cookery. I. Title.
TX840.B3S565 2005
641.5'784—dc22   2004024277

Special bulk-order discounts are available on this and other Harvard Common Press books. Companies and organizations may purchase books for premiums or for resale, or may arrange a custom edition, by contacting the Marketing Director at the address above.

10 9 8 7 6 5 4 3 2 1

Interior design by Richard Oriolo
Illustrations by Chris Van Dusen
Cover design by Night & Day Design
Cover photograph © StockFood / Leigh Beisch

Contents

Acknowledgments   vi

Introduction   vii

1 The Basics of Gourmet Gas Grilling   1

2 Appetizers   13

3 Fish and Shellfish   47

4 Poultry and Game Birds   105

5 Beef   165

6 Lamb and Veal   215

7 Pork, Ham, and Sausage   243

8 Vegetables and Vegetarian Main Dishes   279

9 Fruits and Desserts   325

10 Off-the-Grill Side Dishes   339

Measurement Equivalents   364

Index   365

Acknowledgments

I am happy to thank the kind folks at several gas grill manufacturers for providing me with some wonderful cooking equipment; the Barbecue Industry Association for facts about the history of gas grills and trends in their use; Gina, Jorge, and Matt of Sunshine Foods in St. Helena, California, for stocking the kind of food that makes cooking such a joy; Aunt Patty and the adventurous Miss Odette for their help in the fish department; Sean and Laura and their family of good eaters, Tom, Jeanne, Mike, Deezie, Ruthie, Jennifer G., Jack, Michelle, and all the other late-night, drive-by taste-testers; and Scout and Spot, who kept us entertained. Special thanks go to John Puscheck, a natural-born chef, whose culinary skills and knowledge always amaze.

Introduction

A lot has happened in the sphere of home cooking since 1996, the year the first edition of *The Gas Grill Gourmet* was published. Americans have become far more adventurous grillers, willing to try more and different foods and flavors than ever before. In addition to delving ever deeper into the regional traditions of France, Italy, and China, seemingly all of a sudden we've become exposed to the cuisines of Cuba, the Caribbean, Southeast Asia, Japan, India, the Middle East, and South America, to name just a few. The recipes in this revised and expanded edition of *The Gas Grill Gourmet* reflect this new culinary spirit—an international invitation for enjoyment, from the grill to your table.

A generation ago, outdoor grilling typically meant hamburgers, hot dogs, chicken, and, on special occasions, steaks. Take a peek into American backyards today and you're likely to find the cook of the house grilling lamb in a spicy yogurt marinade, teriyaki steak, fish tacos, or pork satays. America has always been a melting pot, but it appears we've finally been together long enough to break out of our respective culinary traditions and sample foods our parents and grandparents couldn't even imagine. Salsa has now outstripped sales of that perennial favorite ketchup; supermarkets everywhere regularly stock items like hoisin sauce, wasabi paste, and peanut sauce; and what you can't find around the corner, you can find a few clicks away on your computer, delivered right to your door a few days later.

And with the ever-increasing popularity of gas grills, the grills themselves have improved significantly. Manufacturers have been listening to the marketplace, resulting in better heat distribution, less likelihood of flare-ups, more useful accessories, and better and longer-lasting construction. It's a good time to be grilling over gas!

As the most primitive form of cooking, grilling over a live fire is the most adaptable cooking technique known to humankind. Dig deep enough into any of the world's culinary histories and you'll find a grill, a fire, and some tasty food waiting to be turned into a meal. All of which means that each time you light up your gas grill and prepare something you've never tasted before, you're continuing in an age-old tradition, no matter whose culinary tradition you're trying.

Welcome to the wide world of grilling. Enjoy!

1

The Basics of Gourmet Gas Grilling

The first gas grills were introduced to consumers in 1961 by Charmglow. The earliest models were meant to be permanently installed, fueled not by an LP gas cylinder but by a direct link to a residential gas line. They were large and quite costly, and considered luxury items. * Local gas-utility companies, quick to spot an up-and-coming trend (not to mention increased use of their product), took an interest in promoting gas grills to their residential customers. When the gas crunch hit in the early 1970s, the utility companies reversed themselves, issuing a moratorium on all nonessential natural gas-burning appliances such as pool heaters and, of course, gas grills.

Manufacturers of gas grills were quick to switch to LP gas cylinders as a source of fuel, resulting in the sophisticated—and smaller, more mobile—units we see in the marketplace today. Interestingly, there now is a trend toward outfitting new residential homes with permanent natural gas hookups for gas grills, proving, once again, that what goes around comes around.

Each year, consumers are offered increasingly sophisticated gas grills. Accessories range from multiple main and side burners, rotisseries, and warming racks to built-in fish grids, smoking drawers, and containers for water to make steaming or moist cooking possible. A choice of radiant materials, including lava rocks, ceramic briquettes, and metal plates, is now available. Although the majority of grills sold today are in the $150 to $400 range, there has been a significant increase in the premium gas grill market, with some grills selling for $2,000 and even up to $5,000 and beyond!

What should you look for when buying a gas grill? As with any piece of equipment, sound fundamentals are more important than the number of flashy extras. For starters, do not skimp on the size of the cooking surface. As you gain more experience at gas grilling, you are likely to want to cook several dishes simultaneously, not just the entrée but also appetizers, side dishes, and desserts. I recommend a minimum cooking area of 350 square inches and, preferably, 400 square inches or more.

Look for a grill made of a relatively heavy-gauge metal that either resists rust or has a rust-resistant coating. Some grills have a rust-resistant main unit but the other parts (legs, wheels, supports for swing-up racks, burners, and so on) are not rust protected. If this is the case with your unit, spend the extra money for a first-rate, snug-fitting weatherproof covering from your grill's manufacturer. When your neighbors replace their grill after two or three years while yours still looks new, you will appreciate the investment you made.

Although every experienced griller learns that his or her grill has "hot spots," where the heat is highest, the less you need to think about them, the better. Therefore, you should ask your dealer about how quickly and evenly the grill spreads heat. This is a function of the quality of metal in the main grill box, the grill's shape, the radiant material (lava rocks, ceramic briquettes, or metal plates) that spreads the heat around, and the placement of the burners relative to the radiant material. Most gas grillers will advise you to steer clear of grills that use lava rocks as a radiant material, as they are notorious for allowing flare-ups.

One of the first things you will learn about any grill is the number of British thermal units (BTUs) it delivers. Do not fall prey to the illusion that more BTUs are always better.

Like a high-horsepower car, a grill with a particularly high number of BTUs may have you burning fuel at a hefty clip, a wasteful and expensive proposition. For a typical-size gas grill, you will want somewhere between 20,000 and 50,000 BTUs, and you might opt for the higher end of the scale if you think you will be grilling often in cold or windy weather. But what is more important than the gross number of BTUs is the efficiency with which the grill heats and cooks. Ask your dealer to make a case to you for the efficiency of the unit you are considering, and, if a particularly efficient unit means an extra $50 or so up front, know that you will eventually save more than that in fuel costs over the long haul.

Two or three main burners are desirable, especially for indirect cooking (see page 4), and three is the standard number available on most grills sold today. Buy a one-burner grill only if you need a particularly small and portable one. Side burners are good for boiling marinades and keeping them hot, for keeping finished food warm, and for cooking off-the-grill side dishes. They will, however, add a not insignificant amount to the cost of the grill. If your grill is situated at a fair distance from your kitchen, a side burner or two may be a good idea. Side burners should always come with sturdy metallic covers to protect them when they are not in use.

Swing-up or fixed side shelves and worktables are nice, but even on the largest units they rarely give you all the working space you will need. I highly recommend having a separate, freestanding auxiliary table—preferably one with a heatproof surface—near your grill for laying out utensils, cutting boards, and bowls of rubs or marinades. In addition, you can use the table as a place to serve hot-off-the-grill appetizers. If you opt for side surfaces, make sure any wood they include is waterproofed well, either by the manufacturer or by you.

Many modern grills come with one or more of the following: condiment racks, towel bars, and utensil hooks. These accessories add little to the cost of the grill, so there is no reason to avoid them. I would not, however, make any of them the deciding feature, especially if you keep a separate table nearby. Chances are you'll have more utensils than you can hook up to your grill, and many of them won't hang from hooks anyway!

Your best and simplest rule of thumb when shopping for a gas grill is to be what car dealers call a "tire kicker." Lift and lower the lid a few times to see if the hinges are wobble-free and smooth, and make sure that when the lid is completely open it stays in place. If you are on the short side, try the following test: Grab the lid handle with your hand, swing the lid completely up, and make sure that once the lid is up the metal front edge does not bump up against your wrist or forearm—an inconvenience you will definitely want to avoid when the grill is very hot.

Lift and lower any swing-up shelves, too, and put some pressure with your hand on all shelves and work surfaces to make sure they are sturdy, steady, and flat. Roll the unit back and forth a little to see if the wheels work well. Stand by the grill and check to see if the various knobs, handles, racks, and shelves are at a convenient height for you. Stand a few feet back from the grill to see if all the surfaces that are supposed to be parallel to the ground really are.

If you get less-than-satisfying results on any of these tests and your dealer tells you it is because the stock clerk did not assemble the grill properly, take *that* as a sign of potential trouble. It may mean that you, too, will have difficulty assembling the grill, and it almost certainly means that if you choose to pay the dealer to assemble the unit for you, it will not be done right.

Finally, if you are replacing an old gas grill with a new one and you use propane rather than natural gas, get yourself a new main and spare tank, even if they do not come with the grill and you have to pay extra. Propane tanks tend to develop rust, and the purchase of a new grill is a good occasion for replacing them. You may need new tanks, in any case, because gas fittings have changed in recent years and your old tanks may not hook up correctly to a new unit.

Direct and Indirect Cooking

Direct cooking on a gas grill means cooking directly over the heat. Indirect cooking means placing the food to be cooked over a burner that has been turned off, leaving the other one or two burners on low, medium, or high. (All but the smallest gas grills are equipped with more than one burner.) In indirect cooking, the lid of the grill is kept closed.

In most of the recipes in this book, indirect cooking is recommended. The reason for this is twofold. First, indirect cooking virtually ensures that the food being cooked will not burn. Second, indirect cooking greatly reduces the incidence of fat dripping onto the burners and returning to the food via flare-ups and smoke.

Almost all experienced gas grill cooks prefer the indirect-cooking method. Indirect cooking may take a little longer, but once you give it a try you will appreciate the improvement in the quality of your grilled food and the greater control it gives you while you grill. For some foods you may want to place the foods directly over the heat at the very beginning of the cooking time to sear them, and for others you may want direct heat at the very end for just a minute or two to develop a nicely browned exterior. In most instances—and in most of the recipes in this book—even these brief periods of direct-heat cooking are unnecessary, because the food will be sufficiently browned using the indirect method.

If your gas grill has only one burner, you can approximate indirect cooking by turning the burner on low. Or if your one-burner grill is large enough, you can try covering half of the lava rocks or other radiant material with a double thickness of heavy-duty aluminum foil and placing the food over this covered half. With this latter method, you may be able to keep the burner at medium.

Note that whether you are using the direct- or the indirect-cooking method, your grill will need to be preheated, with all of the burners on high and the lid closed, for approximately ten minutes. Preheating helps to burn off any food residue from previous meals that has adhered to the cooking grate or the radiant material, and it brings the grill up to a temperature that will cook food properly, without sticking.

Cooking Times

Many, many variables affect the cooking time of gas grilled food. The outside air temperature and the level of wind will change the temperature in the grill, in the directions you would predict but, in my experience at least, more dramatically than you might expect. Just as much variation comes from your grill itself: the types of burners and radiant material in your particular model; the shape and size of the grill; the distance from the burners or radiant materials to the cooking grate; and, especially, the differences from one manufacturer or model to another in what the settings high, medium, and low mean.

Therefore, all of the cooking times given on the following pages are, by necessity, approximate. As many people do with their indoor ovens, you will get a feel for whether your grill cooks "hot," more quickly, or "cool," more slowly, relative to the recipe instructions that follow, and you can make adjustments accordingly. Feel free to note your adjustments in the margins; just don't do so in a copy you have borrowed from a friend or the local library!

To avoid adding even more variability in cooking times, try to keep to a minimum the number of times you open the grill's lid when you are cooking. Every time you do so, you lose heat and add to the cooking time. A good instant-read thermometer for testing the doneness of meats will help.

Keep in mind that it is always better to err on the side of undercooking rather than overcooking. Any food can easily be returned to the grill for more cooking, but there is little you can do if you have overcooked your food.

General Grilling Guidelines

Always start with the best possible ingredients, whether it's a tomato, a salmon fillet, or a beef tenderloin. Grilling is a very simple form of cooking and, as such, there is little to mask or improve the flavor of less than the best and freshest of ingredients. Here are some tips I've found particularly helpful:

* Allow food to come to room temperature before grilling. Generally speaking, this means removing it from the refrigerator 20 to 30 minutes prior to cooking.

* Always preheat your grill for approximately 10 minutes prior to grilling. Preheat with the burners on high and the lid down.

* As a rule, do not partially cook vegetables before grilling them. Parboiling, steaming, or microwaving produce prior to grilling will result in a mushy, inferior texture.

* When in doubt, use a meat thermometer. It offers the easiest and most reliable way of determining the doneness of any meat or poultry.

Safety

Gas grills are remarkably safe to use, but only if they are used properly. Take the time to read through the owner's manual that came with your gas grill, making special note of any safety precautions specific to your equipment. For whatever grill you own, the following guidelines are worth keeping in mind:

* Gas grills are intended for outdoor use only. Do not use your grill in a building or garage, in a screened or unscreened porch, in a semi-enclosed area, on a balcony, or under a ceiling, overhang, or other cover. Do not install gas grills on a recreational vehicle or boat. Always keep the area around and under the grill clear of any combustible materials.

* Do not locate the grill on an uneven or unstable surface. Do not place the grill on a sidewalk or path.

* Do not store or use flammable vapors and liquids, such as gasoline, near your gas grill.

* LP gas cylinders should be stored outdoors, in an area where the temperature never exceeds 125°F. If exposed to high temperatures, the relief valve may open, allowing flammable gas to escape.

* Do not store an auxiliary LP gas cylinder in the vicinity of the gas grill, and do not store it in a building, garage, or other enclosed or semi-enclosed area.

* Always transport, store, and use LP cylinders in an upright position.

* Do not disconnect gas fittings or valves while the grill is in use.

* Make sure the lid of the grill is open before lighting the burners.

* Do not leave the grill unattended while it is in use.

* Do not move the grill while it is lit.

* Do not block air to the grill or to the ventilation openings. Do not use lump charcoal in your grill; it will break down and plug the ventilation holes.

* Do not wear loose-fitting clothes (sleeves, especially) when you grill.

* Do not let children play near the grill. It's a good idea to keep pets away from a hot grill, too.

* If you smell gas, shut off the gas to the grill, extinguish any open flame, and open the lid to the grill. If the odor continues, immediately call your gas supplier or your local fire department.

* Never check for gas leaks with a lighted match or open flame. A good way to test for leaks is to keep a spray bottle full of soapy water on hand; spray the joints or fittings, and if you can see bubbles forming, you have a leak. Repair or replace the leaking parts promptly. Test for leaks the first couple of times you use a new grill, and on a regular basis as your grill gets up in years.

* If a burner does not light, turn off the gas, wait five minutes, and try again. The problem may be a blockage in your grill's venturi tube. Check your owner's manual for instructions on cleaning it out.

* Always make sure the LP cylinder valve is closed when the grill is not in use.

* Have dented or rusty gas cylinders inspected by your propane dealer. If the rust or dents are severe, replace the tank.

* If you are discarding and not refilling an old tank, do so according to the safety and waste-handling regulations in your community. Remember that while an empty tank may have no more liquid in it, it does have flammable vapors.

* To avoid bacterial contamination, use different cutting or carving boards and different platters for raw foods and cooked or finished ones. Any marinade that will be reused in a finishing or table sauce must first be boiled fully.

Accessories

Great grilling starts with a solid, reliable grill. Beyond that, the list of accessories most grillers find truly useful is mercifully short:

* Spatula Get one with a long handle and a thin and flexible but not too floppy blade, which will be ideal for sliding under delicate foods like vegetables and fish. Offset spatulas, with the blade lower than the handle, work particularly well in grilling.

* Basting brushes For fast and easy basting, paintbrushes from the hardware store work great, especially ones about $2^1/2$ inches wide. Because it is not easy to clean brushes on the fly, I recommend you keep at least two on hand, for meals with different sauces for different dishes. Otherwise, your sauces may get mixed together.

* Forks You will need a large chef's or carving fork or two if you will be grilling larger roasts or birds. Find the best quality ones you can—long handled, extra sturdy, and with sharp tines. Do keep the tines sharp. With dull ones you will have to force the fork farther into the meat to get a grip, and that will lead to the draining of flavorful juices.

* Spring-loaded tongs Again, get the best-quality and heaviest-duty ones you can find. Although long tongs are useful, the laws of physics say that the longer the tongs, the more effort you will have to expend when you use them to lift something heavy, like a roast. I prefer using medium-length (12 inches or so) tongs, along with a great pair of gloves or mitts.

* Gloves Of all the grilling and barbecue accessories available these days, heat-resistant gloves are the ones that most commonly disappoint the experienced griller. Grilling

suppliers typically offer what are standard kitchen mitts with an extra couple of inches of length, barely covering the wrist and with scarcely any extra heat protection. If you live in or near a large city, do what Cheryl and Bill Jamison, authors of the definitive books on smoke-cooked barbecue, *Smoke & Spice* and *Sublime Smoke*, recommend: Stop by a firefighters' supply store and get yourself a pair of truly protective, elbow-length neoprene gloves. If you cannot find these, do get the longest and most heat-resistant gloves you can find.

* **Instant-read meat thermometer** This is an indispensable tool if you will be cooking larger items like roasts or whole birds. Get one that is sturdy and has a sharp insert.

* **Skewers, both bamboo and metal** Have plenty on hand, especially if you entertain, and do not forget to soak bamboo ones for 30 minutes before you use them to keep them from scorching. Some kebab pros favor two-pronged skewers, which keep the skewered food from spinning around when you turn them. These come in metal but not disposable bamboo, so if you opt for these, you will have to wash them after meals.

* **Grids, racks, baskets** Grill grates are designed for the big, sturdy old standards, like burgers and steaks. For smaller or more delicate foods, you will want to own a separate grid or rack with smaller openings. The rack will simply sit atop your built-in cooking grate. Wire baskets, with hinges and a handle, will serve you well if you cook whole fish or fish fillets; you can turn the fish and remove it from the heat without fear of it sticking to the grate or breaking apart and falling into the grill. Fish baskets are indispensable if you will be cooking any skin-on fish.

* ***Two* large cutting boards** Save yourself cleanup trips to the kitchen by keeping one board for cutting raw foods and one for finished dishes.

* **Marinating bowls** Make sure these are made of glass or another nonreactive material. Have at least one on hand that is quite wide and deep.

* **Cleaning brush** Get one with stiff bristles, such as brass. Do follow your grill manufacturer's recommendations, particularly if you own a model with a cooking grate made of porcelain-coated steel, which can chip. Grill dealers sell brushes that are designed for cleaning porcelain.

* **Lighting** If you have not yet outfitted your cooking area with an overhead light for cooking at night, a clip lamp or a flashlight will come in handy.

* **Lots of heavy-duty aluminum foil** You will find this useful, especially if you do not own separate racks or baskets, for holding small and delicate foods in place on the grill. If your grill has a warming rack for foods that are done cooking, an extra layer or two of foil under or around the food will keep it moist and give you more insurance against overcooking. Foil is also helpful for containing wood chips or other aromatics. Some grilling aficionados swear that the best cooking-grate cleaner is crinkled-up foil; it certainly works well, but the catch is that the easiest time for cleaning a grate is when it is still hot, and you will need to be careful if using foil.

* **Spare gas tank** If there is one immutable law of gas grilling, it is that the most likely time for you to run out of propane is on a Sunday evening, when there's a small horde of hungry guests waiting to eat and no propane dealer is open for business.

Wood Chips

One of the easiest ways to add flavor to gas grilled food is to add wood chips to the inside of the grill when you cook. As the chips smolder in the heat, they will infuse your food with a smoky flavor reminiscent of old-fashioned barbecue. But while in traditional smoke-cooked barbecue wood is both a flavor enhancer and a fuel, in gas grilling it is solely a flavoring agent. In a gas grill, the gas burners are the primary heat source.

The recipes in this book do not call for using wood chips or other smoke-producing aromatics. The marinades, herb and spice combinations, and sauces in the recipes will yield full-flavored dishes without the need for extra help. Although wood chips now are widely available at gourmet stores and grill dealerships and by mail order, I have also avoided calling for them because the chances are fair that on a given night you will not have on hand the particular type of wood that pairs with the food you are cooking. Many grocery stores and supermarkets do not carry chips, so it is possible that you would be in for an extra shopping expedition if the recipes demanded them.

Nonetheless, using wood chips is a fun way to expand your grilling skills. Use wood chips only when you are cooking indirectly, with the lid closed. Wood chips can ignite, of course, so always check your owner's manual first for directions on how to use them safely with your grill. You must soak the chips beforehand, for 30 minutes or so. You must contain them, too, either in a special aluminum or cast-iron box—usually called a "smoker box"—sold as an accessory by grill dealers, in a similar box or drawer that is built into your grill, or by wrapping them in a double thickness of heavy-duty aluminum foil (perforate the foil numerous times with a fork to create holes through which the smoke can escape).

Some grills will accommodate a box that holds larger chunks of wood; again, check your manual to see if using wood chunks is recommended. Chips provide a sufficient amount of smoke for smaller foods or foods that cook in shorter times. Larger chunks, which last longer, come in handy for more substantial pieces of food, such as roasts or whole birds, with longer cooking times.

If you do decide to experiment with wood-smoke flavoring, you'll add a whole new dimension to your grilling repertoire and, with practice, you'll even be able to approximate the skills of a venerable Southern pitmaster. To get you started, here are the more common types of wood available, along with the foods with which they go best:

* **Alder** Traditionally pairs with seafood, especially salmon, but is also excellent with pork and chicken.

* **Apple** Its sweet flavor is very good with ham, sausage, and other pork dishes, as well as with poultry and game birds.

* **Cherry** Great with duck and very good with chicken and turkey; it pairs handsomely with lamb and venison, too.

* **Hickory** This is the traditional wood for Southern-style pork barbecue, but perfectly appropriate for beef and poultry, as well.

* **Maple** Traditional, of course, with cured or cold-smoked ham; it is very fine, too, with grilled ham, and a good complement for turkey and some vegetables, such as squash.

* **Mesquite** Not a traditional barbecue wood, but popular in recent years, to say the least. Use it sparingly and not over a long cooking time, to avoid a bitter flavor. It goes well with pork or lamb chops, beefsteaks, swordfish, and, used modestly, vegetables.

* **Oak** Great with steaks and other beef dishes, it does nice things for duck and all manner of pork.

* **Pecan** Subtle, mild, and versatile, it's good with poultry, pork, and beef.

* **Sassafras** Used sparingly, it provides a nice, sweet touch for poultry, pork, and seafood.

Always avoid softwoods, such as pines and other evergreens, which are too bitter for smoke flavoring, and by all means avoid chemical-laden chips derived from pressure-treated lumber or any wood that has ever been finished or painted.

Some grilling aficionados get tasty results with grapevines, nutshells, cinnamon sticks, tea bags, citrus peels, and herbs, both leaves and twigs. As with wood chips, you must soak any of these items thoroughly and contain them in a smoker box or foil packet. Experimenting with materials like these makes for an interesting way to recycle what otherwise might be kitchen waste. Start with small quantities used over a short portion of the grilling time, so that you do not overwhelm the flavor of your food.

2

Appetizers

Grilling involves a little bit of theater. There's something about cooking over an open fire that makes people want to be part of the action. Maybe it's because most grilling takes place outdoors, or because cooking over live heat has a primal appeal, or simply because grilling is a relaxed, informal activity that invites camaraderie. Whatever the reason, why not reward your family and friends for their good company with a little something while they're waiting for the main course? As your guests stand around the grill and watch you prepare these tasty tidbits, they will feel as if they're really part of the event. After all, inviting family and friends to your home for a meal isn't called *entertaining* for nothing.

The following recipes take little time to prepare and even less time to grill. Some, like Grilled Cheese on a Skewer, will appeal to everyone, young and old alike. Others, like Grilled Oysters with Fresh Ginger Vinaigrette, will attract those with more sophisticated palates.

Appetizers made with grilled bread, like the Italian bruschetta, are universally popular. Indeed, more home cooks should try grilling breads on their gas grills. A simple grilled bread can be the perfect starter for an excellent meal.

Any type of bruschetta is best made with a coarse-textured Italian or French bread, which is becoming more widely available in all parts of the country. Don't worry if the bread isn't as fresh as possible: there's something about the grilling process that makes even slightly stale bread taste great. If a bruschetta recipe calls for olive oil, always use the best extra-virgin olive oil you can find. In recipes with only a few ingredients and such simple preparation methods, each ingredient must be a standout.

Whatever you choose to serve as an appetizer, remember that it should tease the appetite, not sate it. It's a good idea to serve only a small amount of any appetizer to guarantee that everyone will have room for the delicious meal still to come.

Grilled Pizza	16
Grilled Garlic Bread	17
Bruschetta with Shaved Parmesan	18
Tomato-Basil Bruschetta	19
Gorgonzola Toasts	20
Grilled Cheese on a Skewer	21
Cheese-Stuffed Grape Leaves	22
Raclette in a Bowl	23
Asparagus Wrapped in Provolone and Prosciutto	24
Marinated Mushrooms and Cherry Tomatoes	25
Mixed Grilled Vegetables with Feta Cheese Dip	26
Grilled Scallop Ceviche	27

Scallops on Endive with Pickled Ginger	29
Grilled Shrimp Cocktail	30
Prosciutto and Basil-Wrapped Lemon Shrimp	31
Garlicky Skewered Shrimp	32
Mussels Bordelaise	33
"Barbecued" Oysters	34
Grilled Oysters with Fresh Ginger Vinaigrette	34
Exotic Grilled Oysters— Two Ways	35
Skewered Chicken Livers with Fresh Lime and Cilantro	37
Rumaki	38
Red Wings	39

Grilled Chicken "Sashimi"	40
Fresh Ginger-Garlic Chicken Satay	42
Hot Peanut-Sesame Beef Satay	43
Hoisin-Chili Pork Satay	44
Spicy Asian Lamb Chops	45
Lamb Riblets with Garlic and Rosemary	46

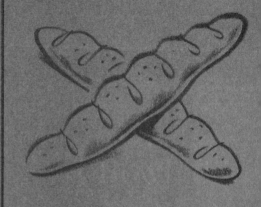

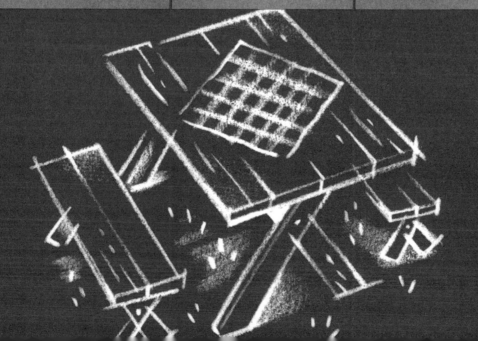

Grilled Pizza

Here's a fast appetizer or a good way to keep the kids happy before grilling the adults' food. I was a little skeptical of premade pizza dough in a tube, but it's really very good. Covering the work surface with cornmeal makes the dough a lot easier to work with and, just as important, keeps the dough from sticking to the hot grill. *Note:* Keep the pizza dough in the refrigerator until just before rolling it out; cold dough is much easier to handle.

2 tablespoons cornmeal

One 10-ounce tube premade pizza dough (available in the refrigerator case)

One 15-ounce jar pizza sauce

Your favorite toppings: sliced or shredded cheese, crumbled or sliced precooked or smoked sausage, sliced salami, olives, sliced tomato, onion, or bell peppers, etc.

1. Preheat the grill with all the burners on high for 10 minutes and the lid down.

2. Sprinkle the cornmeal evenly over your work surface. Open the pizza dough and unroll on top of the cornmeal. The dough will be rectangular in shape. Cut the dough into two easy-to-manage squares. Top the dough with a thin layer of pizza sauce and whatever other toppings you desire. Using a couple of metal spatulas or your hands, slide the pizzas onto a cookie sheet without sides.

3. Leave the back burner on high; turn the other burners to low.

4. Slide the pizzas off the cookie sheet and onto the grill over the burners on low. Close the lid and grill until the cheese has just melted, 7 to 8 minutes. Serve hot off the grill cut into wedges.

MAKES 2 MEDIUM-SIZE PIZZAS

Grilled Garlic Bread

It's hard to find anyone who dislikes garlic bread. These crusty slices are also good as an accompaniment to a main course.

1 large loaf coarse-textured Italian or French bread

About 1/4 cup extra-virgin olive oil

4 to 6 garlic cloves, to your taste, pressed

1. Preheat the grill with all the burners on high for 10 minutes and the lid down.

2. While the grill is preheating, cut the bread in half lengthwise. Combine the olive oil and garlic and lightly brush the mixture onto the cut sides of the bread.

3. Once the grill is hot, turn all the burners to low. Place the bread halves on the grill cut side up and grill, with the lid down, until toasted on both sides, turning it once. Watch closely, because the toasting will take only a few minutes.

4. Transfer the toast to a cutting board and cut into individual slices. Serve warm.

SERVES 4 TO 6

Bruschetta with Shaved Parmesan

Bruschetta starts with a rustic loaf of high-quality, coarse-textured bread. The bread is brushed lightly with olive oil, then toasted on the grill. In this version, the bread gets a topping of Parmesan. This is about as simple as food gets, and about as good. All that's necessary are the finest possible ingredients: crusty Italian or French bread, Parmigiano-Reggiano, and a first-rate extra-virgin olive oil. Serve with a dry red wine for a real taste treat. One small loaf will yield about 12 slices; a baguette about 16 slices.

1 loaf coarse-textured Italian or French bread

About $1/4$ cup extra-virgin olive oil

One 6-ounce chunk Parmesan cheese

1 large garlic clove, cut in half lengthwise

1. Preheat the grill with all the burners on high for 10 minutes and the lid down.

2. While the grill is preheating, cut the bread into $1/2$-inch-thick slices and lightly brush both sides of each slice with olive oil. Using a vegetable peeler, shave the Parmesan very thin—it may crumble somewhat—and set it aside. Alternatively, you can grate the cheese on the coarse side of a box grater.

3. Once the grill is hot, turn all the burners to low. Place the bread on the grill and toast both sides, with the lid down, turning once. Watch closely, because the toasting will take only a few minutes. Once the slices are toasted, rub each quickly on one side with the cut garlic.

4. Arrange the toasted bread on a platter, top with the Parmesan, and serve warm.

SERVES 6 TO 8

GRILLED CRUDITÉS

JUST ABOUT ANY VEGETABLE THAT RETAINS A LITTLE SNAP AFTER GRILLING CAN BE SERVED AS AN APPETIZER WITH A DIP. TRY ASPARAGUS, CARROTS, OR EVEN POTATO WEDGES. SEE CHAPTER 8 FOR MORE INSTRUCTIONS ON GRILLING THESE AND OTHER VEGETABLES.

Tomato-Basil Bruschetta

At the height of summer, when vine-ripened tomatoes are at their peak, try this bruschetta, with its simple but absolutely delicious topping of ripe tomatoes and sweet basil. One small loaf will yield about 12 slices; a baguette about 16 slices.

1^1/$_2$ pounds ripe red tomatoes

^{1}/$_2$ cup extra-virgin olive oil

1 cup minced fresh basil or parsley (or a combination of both)

Kosher salt and freshly ground black pepper to taste

Balsamic vinegar to taste

1 loaf coarse-textured Italian or French bread

1 large garlic clove, cut in half lengthwise

1. Preheat the grill with all the burners on high for 10 minutes and the lid down.

2. While the grill is preheating, prepare the tomato-basil topping. Chop the tomatoes into small chunks and transfer to a medium-size bowl. Add ^{1}/$_4$ cup of the olive oil and the basil and season with salt, pepper, and a dash of balsamic vinegar to taste. Let stand at room temperature until serving time.

3. Cut the bread into ^{1}/$_2$-inch-thick slices and brush both sides of each slice with the remaining ^{1}/$_4$ cup olive oil.

4. Once the grill is hot, turn all the burners to low. Place the bread on the grill and toast both sides, with the lid down, turning once. Watch closely, because the toasting will take only a few minutes. Once the slices are done, rub each quickly on one side with the cut garlic.

5. Place the toasted bread on a platter. Using a slotted spoon, top each slice with some of the tomato-basil mixture. Serve immediately—and be prepared to make more!

SERVES 6 TO 12

Gorgonzola Toasts

This is a variation on a wonderful hors d'oeuvre originated by the great Italian-cookbook author Marcella Hazan. It's a real crowd-pleaser, so make plenty.

$1/2$ cup crumbled Gorgonzola cheese

$1/2$ cup finely shredded mozzarella cheese

2 tablespoons pine nuts, toasted in a dry skillet over medium heat until golden, about 3 minutes

1 garlic clove, pressed

Freshly ground black pepper to taste

1 loaf coarse-textured Italian or French bread

About $1/4$ cup extra-virgin olive oil

1. Preheat the grill with all the burners on high for 10 minutes and the lid down.

2. While the grill is preheating, combine the cheeses, pine nuts, garlic, and pepper in a small bowl, toss lightly with a fork, and let stand at room temperature until needed.

3. Cut the bread into $1/2$-inch-thick slices and lightly brush both sides of each slice with the olive oil.

4. Once the grill is hot, turn all the burners to low. Place the bread on the grill and toast on one side only, with the lid down. Watch closely, because the toasting will take only a minute. Turn the bread and top each one with the cheese mixture, pressing down on it slightly with a fork. Close the lid and bake the toasts for a few minutes, until the cheese mixture has melted.

5. Serve the toasts hot off the grill.

SERVES 6 TO 8

Grilled Cheese on a Skewer

These bite-size, skewered grilled cheese sandwiches are simple but satisfying. If you feel like taking the recipe a step further, you can insert small slices of smoked ham or prosciutto between the slices of bread and cheese for a variation on the French specialty *croque monsieur.*

1 large loaf coarse-textured French or Italian bread

About $1/2$ pound Gruyère, Emmenthaler, or Monterey Jack cheese

6 bamboo skewers, soaked in water for 30 minutes and drained

About 2 tablespoons extra-virgin olive oil

1. Preheat the grill with all the burners on high for 10 minutes and the lid down.

2. While the grill is preheating, prepare the bread and cheese. Remove the crust from the loaf of bread, cut the bread into $3/4$-inch-thick slices, and then cut each slice into pieces about 2 inches square. Cut the cheese into slices that are $1/4$ inch thick and about 2 inches square. Thread the bread and cheese squares onto the skewers: Begin with bread, add cheese and bread in turn, and end with bread. Brush the skewered bread and cheese with the olive oil.

3. Once the grill is hot, turn off the center burner and turn the others to medium. Position the skewered bread and cheese over the center burner. Close the lid and grill the skewers, turning them several times, until the bread is lightly toasted on all sides and the cheese has melted, 8 to 10 minutes.

4. Transfer the skewers to your work surface and pull out each skewer. Place the "loaves" of grilled bread and cheese on a platter. Tear off individual slices, and pass the Dijon mustard, please!

SERVES 6 TO 8

TONGS ARE THE TOPS

GET YOURSELF THE STURDIEST PAIR OF SPRING-LOADED TONGS YOU CAN FIND. THEY ARE THE BEST TOOL FOR HANDLING ANY FOOD ON THE GRILL.

Cheese-Stuffed Grape Leaves

Around the world, wherever grapes are grown, cooks wrap a variety of foods in grape leaves before grilling: everything from meat and rice to fish or cheese. Not only do the leaves keep what's inside them from falling apart, but they also impart their own unique, piquant, somewhat lemony flavor. If you're fortunate enough to live within picking distance of a grapevine, use fresh leaves. Just be sure to remove their stems and blanch them in boiling water for 4 to 5 minutes. When finding fresh leaves is out of the question, use bottled grape leaves, which are readily available at specialty food shops and easy to work with. This recipe makes an unusual and delicious appetizer certain to elicit lots of comments.

One 8-ounce jar grape leaves in brine

About 1 pound cheese, such as Monterey Jack, fontina, brie, or Teleme

About 3 tablespoons extra-virgin olive oil

Balsamic vinegar to taste

1 baguette (optional), thinly sliced

1. Rinse the grape leaves, drain well, and blot dry. Discard any very small or torn leaves. Cut the cheese into rectangles about $1^1/2$ x 2 inches and $3/8$ inch thick.

2. Preheat the grill with all the burners on high for 10 minutes and the lid down.

3. While the grill is preheating, stuff the grape leaves. To begin, place a grape leaf on your work surface, vein side up. Place a piece of cheese in the center of the leaf. Wrap the leaf around the cheese as if you are wrapping a package, folding in the stem side first. Then place the stuffed leaf on another leaf and make a secure bundle. Repeat with the remaining cheese and leaves. Finally, brush each bundle with olive oil.

4. Once the grill is hot, turn off the center burner and turn the others to medium. Put the grape leaves in a hinged grill basket and place the basket over the center burner. Close the lid and cook, turning the grill basket once or twice, until the cheese has melted, about 15 minutes (taste one stuffed leaf to check).

5. Transfer the stuffed leaves to a platter. Douse them with balsamic vinegar and serve by themselves or on top of thin slices of crusty bread.

SERVES 8 TO 12

Raclette in a Bowl

Traditional raclette is a Swiss cheese that has been melted in a special broiler unit and is served with boiled new potatoes, pickled onions, and gherkins. This variation requires nothing more than your gas grill and four to six small, shallow, heat-proof bowls.

2 pounds small new potatoes, well scrubbed (or substitute about 2 dozen small pieces of toasted, crunchy French or Italian bread)

1¹/4 pounds raclette, Swiss, Emmenthaler, Gruyère, or fontina cheese, finely shredded

Pickled onions and cornichons or gherkins

1. Boil the potatoes in enough salted water to cover until tender, about 15 minutes. Drain and cut them in half. (If you're substituting bread for the potatoes, proceed to step 2.)

2. Preheat the grill with all the burners on high for 10 minutes and the lid down.

3. While the grill is preheating, divide the cheese among 4 to 6 small bowls. Cover each with aluminum foil.

4. Once the grill is hot, turn off the center burner and turn the others to medium. Place the covered cheese-filled bowls over the center burner, close the lid, and cook until the cheese melts, about 10 minutes. Once it melts, remove the foil and continue to cook just until the cheese starts to bubble at the edges.

5. Serve the cheese in the bowls hot off the grill, using the potatoes or the bread to dip. Accompany with the onions and pickles.

SERVES 4 TO 6

Asparagus Wrapped in Provolone and Prosciutto

There's a restaurant here in the Napa Valley called Bistro Don Giovanni, a favorite with locals and visitors alike. Chef/owner Donna Scala (along with her husband, Don Giovanni) is a wizard in the kitchen, cooking up really tasty real food, and often amazingly simple combinations of flavors. This recipe was inspired by one of her dishes, only Donna's has a light coating of bread crumbs and is sautéed rather than grilled. I was curious whether or not I could re-create the flavors on the grill and, to my surprise, it turned out great. More than one person has said after the first bite: "I could make dinner out of just a plateful of these!" Thanks, Donna.

12 fat spears fresh asparagus, tough skin from bottom half peeled with a vegetable peeler

12 thin, long strips prosciutto, about as wide as the asparagus

12 thin, long strips provolone cheese, about as wide as the asparagus

2 tablespoons sherry vinegar

Freshly ground black pepper to taste

1. Bring a large skillet of water to boil over high heat. Add the asparagus and blanch for $1^1/2$ to 2 minutes. Immediately place in a large bowl of ice water for about 3 minutes. Drain and dry on a large towel or several thicknesses of paper towel.

2. Preheat the grill with all burners on high for 10 minutes and the lid down.

3. Place a slice of prosciutto on the work surface, and lay an asparagus spear on top of one end of the prosciutto. Place a piece of provolone next to the asparagus spear. Tightly wrap the prosciutto around the spear and provolone; the prosciutto will hold the cheese in place. Repeat with the remaining prosciutto, asparagus, and provolone.

4. Turn off the center burner and turn the other burners to medium. Place the spears over the center burner and grill, with the lid up, for a total of 5 to 6 minutes, $2^1/2$ to 3 minutes per side.

5. Place grilled asparagus on a platter. Douse with the sherry vinegar and a few grinds of black pepper, then serve. Delicious!

SERVES 4 TO 6

Marinated Mushrooms and Cherry Tomatoes

Grilled marinated mushrooms and cherry tomatoes are delicious hot or cold, by themselves or as a topping for Grilled Garlic Bread (page 17). Any way you serve them, they make a wonderful snack.

RED WINE AND THYME MARINADE

$1/2$ cup dry red wine

$1/4$ cup extra-virgin olive oil

Juice of $1/2$ lemon

1 large garlic clove, pressed

2 teaspoons dried thyme, crumbled

1 teaspoon kosher salt

$1/2$ teaspoon cracked black peppercorns

1 pound mushrooms, wiped clean and stems trimmed

1 pound cherry tomatoes

12 bamboo skewers, soaked in water for 30 minutes and drained

Slices of toasted bread (optional)

1. Combine the marinade ingredients in a 1-gallon zippered-top plastic bag and mix well. Toss the mushrooms and the cherry tomatoes in the marinade, seal, and refrigerate for 1 to 2 hours.

2. Preheat the grill with all the burners on high for 10 minutes and the lid down.

3. While the grill is preheating, thread the mushrooms onto 6 skewers and the cherry tomatoes onto the remainder.

4. Once the grill is hot, turn off the center burner and turn the others to medium. Position the skewers over the center burner, close the lid, and cook for 8 to 10 minutes, turning the skewers a few times. The mushrooms should be tender and the tomatoes heated all the way through and soft to the touch.

5. Serve the mushrooms and tomatoes hot off the grill, or toss them together in a bowl and serve at room temperature on slices of crunchy, toasted bread if desired.

SERVES 6 TO 8

Mixed Grilled Vegetables with Feta Cheese Dip

This variation on the ubiquitous raw-vegetables-and-dip platter can be served warm or cold. Grilling intensifies the flavors of the vegetables, and the feta cheese dip is fresh tasting and relatively low in calories and fat.

FETA CHEESE DIP

1 cup sour cream

3/4 cup crumbled feta cheese

2 cloves garlic, pressed

2 tablespoons minced fresh parsley

1 tablespoon red or white wine vinegar

Freshly ground black pepper to taste

1 red bell pepper, seeded and cut into 1-inch squares

1 green bell pepper, seeded and cut into 1-inch squares

2 medium-size onions, cut into 1-inch cubes

18 cherry tomatoes or 9 yellow pear tomatoes, cut in half

18 white mushrooms, wiped clean and stems trimmed

1 small to medium-size zucchini or other summer squash, cut into 1-inch cubes

12 bamboo skewers, soaked in water for 30 minutes and drained

About 1/2 cup extra-virgin olive oil

Kosher salt and freshly ground black pepper to taste

2 tablespoons chopped fresh thyme or 2 teaspoons dried thyme

1. In a medium-size bowl, combine the dip ingredients and mix well. Cover and refrigerate until needed.

2. Preheat the grill with all the burners on high for 10 minutes and the lid down.

3. While the grill is preheating, thread the vegetables onto the bamboo skewers in an alternating pattern. Make sure to pierce the mushrooms through the cap, so they don't fall apart, and to skewer the zucchini through the skin, so all the cut sides face outward. Coat the vegetables with a liberal amount of olive oil, season with salt and pepper, and sprinkle with the thyme.

4. Once the grill is hot, turn off the center burner and turn the others to medium. Position the brochettes over the center burner, close the lid, and cook until the tip of a sharp knife easily pierces the vegetables but they still have a little crunch, 8 to 12 minutes, turning them a few times.

5. Serve the vegetables hot off the grill, accompanied by the feta cheese dip.

SERVES 6 TO 12

Grilled Scallop Ceviche

Ceviche—raw fish or shellfish "cooked" in a highly acidic marinade usually composed of citrus juices—is a popular appetizer in Mexico. Besides "cooking" them, the marinade imbues the fish and shellfish with very distinct and piquant flavors. It takes at least 4 hours to fully "cook" the fish and shellfish in the marinade; in this recipe, the scallops marinate for a maximum of 2 hours and finish cooking on the grill. It's a delightful combination of cooking techniques and flavors. You can also serve these scallops as an alternative filling for Fish Tacos (page 92).

CEVICHE MARINADE

$1/4$ cup fresh lime juice

$1/4$ cup fresh lemon juice

$1/4$ cup fresh orange juice

1 small onion, diced

3 tablespoons light vegetable oil, such as canola

$1/4$ cup minced fresh cilantro

$1/2$ teaspoon hot pepper sauce

$1/4$ teaspoon dried oregano

$1/4$ teaspoon kosher salt

2 pounds sea scallops

12 bamboo skewers, soaked in water for 30 minutes and drained

Lemon wedges and chopped fresh cilantro for garnish (optional)

1. Combine the marinade ingredients in a 1-gallon zippered-top plastic bag and mix well. Wash the scallops in cold water and blot dry with paper towels. Add the scallops to the marinade, seal, and refrigerate for no more than 2 hours.

2. Preheat the grill with all the burners on high for 10 minutes and the lid down.

3. While the grill is preheating, thread the scallops, with their sides touching, onto the skewers.

4. Once the grill is hot, turn all the burners to medium-high. Place the skewered scallops on the grill and cook, with the lid down, just until they turn opaque white on all sides, 2 to 3 minutes, turning once.

5. Serve immediately, with lemon wedges and a sprinkling of cilantro if desired.

SERVES 6 TO 8 GENEROUSLY

Scallops on Endive with Pickled Ginger

I believe this probably qualifies as a "fancy" appetizer. Be that as it may, it is very tasty and a great combination of textures, with the silken scallops and the crunchy endive. The lemon-flavored mayonnaise doesn't hurt, either. Cook the scallops whole, then cut them into quarters before assembling on the endive. Look for the pickled ginger in the Asian section of your supermarket.

2 heads green endive

$1/4$ cup mayonnaise

$1/2$ teaspoon grated lime zest

$1/2$ teaspoon fresh lime juice

2 large sea scallops

1 teaspoon toasted sesame oil

Ground white pepper to taste

8 pieces pickled Japanese ginger

1. Cut the root end off the endive. Carefully separate the individual leaves; there will only be 4 or 5 leaves on each head that are large enough for this presentation.

2. Preheat the grill with all the burners on high for 10 minutes and the lid down.

3. While the grill is heating, in a small bowl combine the mayonnaise and lime zest and juice. Place the endive leaves on a platter. Place about $1/2$ teaspoon of the lime mayonnaise on the large end of each endive leaf. Set aside.

4. Keep the back burner on high; turn the other burners to medium.

5. Coat both sides of the scallops with the sesame oil and a dusting of white pepper. Place the scallops over the burners on medium and cook, with the lid up, for a total of about 3 minutes, $1^1/2$ minutes per side. Do not overcook.

6. After removing from the grill, slice each scallop into quarters. Place one scallop piece on top of the lime mayonnaise on each endive leaf, then top the scallop with a small slice of pickled ginger. Serve immediately.

MAKES 8 INDIVIDUAL APPETIZERS

Grilled Shrimp Cocktail

This is a delicious twist on the more common bay shrimp cocktail, loosely based on the way shrimp are served in Baja, Mexico. Not only are the shrimp grilled, but the sauce is also much lighter than the typical stateside cocktail sauce. Serve well chilled.

MEXICAN-STYLE COCKTAIL SAUCE

1 cup Spicy Hot V8 juice

1 cup cherry tomatoes, quartered

1 cup peeled, pitted, and diced ripe avocado

$1/2$ cup diced red onion

$1/2$ cup diced celery

2 tablespoons chopped fresh cilantro

Juice of 1 lime

$1/2$ teaspoon kosher salt

4 to 5 large shrimp per person

Vegetable oil

Kosher salt to taste

Chopped fresh cilantro for garnish

Lemons, cut into thin rounds, for garnish

Waverly Wafers or saltine crackers

1. Combine the sauce ingredients in a medium-size bowl. Refrigerate until needed.

2. Peel the shrimp, leaving the tails on. Rinse under cold running water and blot dry with paper towels.

3. Preheat the grill with all the burners on high for 10 minutes and the lid down.

4. Turn all the burners to medium-low, place the shrimp on the grill, and cook, with the lid up, for a total of 3 minutes, $1^1/2$ minutes per side.

5. Remove the sauce from the refrigerator. Add about $1/3$ cup of the sauce to individual bowls or glasses (stemmed wineglasses make for a nice presentation). Place 4 or 5

shrimp around the edge of each glass, with the tails pointing up. Garnish with chopped cilantro and a lemon slice on the edge of the glass. Serve with Waverly Wafers (like they do in Mexico) or saltines.

Prosciutto and Basil-Wrapped Lemon Shrimp

This appetizer is a triple threat if there ever was one: three simple main ingredients that add up to much more than the sum of their parts. Eat these hot, hot, hot off the grill—they'll disappear so fast it'll make your head spin.

8 large shrimp, peeled, with tails left on

8 large fresh basil leaves

8 thin slices prosciutto

Juice of 1 fresh lemon

Freshly ground black pepper to taste

1. Preheat the grill with all the burners on high for 10 minutes and the lid closed.

2. While the grill is preheating, rinse shrimp in cold water after peeling. Blot dry with paper towels. Wrap each shrimp with a basil leaf, followed by a slice of prosciutto: The natural stickiness of the prosciutto will hold the basil in place.

3. Turn all the burners to medium-low, place the shrimp on the grill, and cook, with the lid up, for a total of 3 minutes, $1^1/2$ minutes per side.

4. Place the grilled shrimp on a platter; squeeze the lemon juice over them, and sprinkle with a few grinds of pepper. Enjoy!

SERVES 2 TO 4

Garlicky Skewered Shrimp

On their own, these shrimp make an outstanding (and hearty) appetizer. On top of pasta tossed with a little garlic, olive oil, and chopped fresh parsley, they make a tangy, tasty main dish. Add some warm, crusty bread and a glass of white wine and you've got yourself a meal-size treat.

GARLIC AND WINE MARINADE

1/2 cup dry white wine

1/2 cup minced fresh basil

1/3 cup extra-virgin olive oil

2 tablespoons fresh lemon juice

3 large garlic cloves, pressed

Freshly ground black pepper to taste

2 pounds large or jumbo shrimp, peeled, deveined, and rinsed in cold water

2 dozen bamboo skewers, soaked in water for 30 minutes and drained

1. Combine all the marinade ingredients in a 1-gallon zippered-top plastic bag and mix well. Add the shrimp, seal, and let marinate in the refrigerator for about 1 hour.

2. Preheat the grill with all the burners on high for 10 minutes and the lid down.

3. While the grill is preheating, skewer the shrimp by threading them on two parallel skewers. This will keep them from spinning around when you turn them on the grill.

4. Once the grill is hot, turn off the center burner and turn the others to medium. Place the shrimp over the center burner, close the lid, and cook just until they turn opaque on both sides and feel firm, 6 to 8 minutes, turning once. Do not overcook. Serve immediately.

SERVES 8 TO 10

SKEWERING FOR SUCCESS

TO HELP ENSURE UNIFORM COOKING, MAKE PIECES OF FOOD DESTINED FOR SKEWERS AS UNIFORM IN SIZE AS POSSIBLE.

Mussels Bordelaise

I'm dead set against wrapping any food in foil and then "grilling" it: I mean, what's the point? Why not just cook it inside on the stove, right? This is the one exception you'll find in this book, simply because it's so good, fast, and delicious. Mussels make a great appetizer, or you can turn this dish into an entrée with the addition of a crisp green salad and some warm, crusty bread. Mussel lovers will be able to eat a dozen or more as an appetizer without blinking. Rinse the mussels first, pulling off their beards and discarding any that won't close (a live mussel will slowly close its shell when handled).

FOR EACH DOZEN MUSSELS

$^1/_3$ cup dry white wine

1 clove garlic, pressed or minced

Juice of $^1/_2$ lemon

1 tablespoon finely chopped fresh parsley

$^1/_4$ teaspoon kosher salt

Freshly ground black pepper to taste

1. Preheat the grill with all the burners on high for 10 minutes and the lid down.

2. While the grill is preheating, place the mussels on the center of a rectangle of aluminum foil about 24 inches long. Form into a bowl-like shape and add the wine, garlic, lemon juice, parsley, salt, and pepper. Fold up the sides of the foil and crimp the top and sides to make a sealed foil packet.

3. With the burners still on high, place the foil packet on the grill and close the lid. The mussels will open in 4 minutes.

4. Remove the packet from the grill, open carefully (watch out for steam), and pour into a large shallow bowl. Discard any mussels that haven't opened. Eat immediately. Be sure to provide some warm, crusty bread for sopping up the liquid. Simple and absolutely delicious!

MAKES ABOUT 1 SERVING PER DOZEN MUSSELS

"Barbecued" Oysters

Grilled oysters are great party food, especially when you need some entertainment out by the grill, because that's exactly where these appetizers should be enjoyed. Be forewarned: The world is divided between those who will try one oyster just to be a good sport and those who can down a couple of dozen without thinking twice. So when it comes to figuring out how many oysters to buy, caveat emptor.

About 2 dozen fresh oysters, or more

Bottled barbecue sauce of your choice, heated

1. Scrub the oysters under cold running water and store them, flat shells up, in a cool place until you are ready to grill.

2. Preheat the grill with all the burners on high for 10 minutes and the lid down.

3. With all the burners still on high, place the oysters, flat shells up, on the grill, close the lid, and cook just until the shells pop open slightly, 2 to 3 minutes; some may take a little longer to open than others. Discard any oysters that do not open.

4. Transfer the oysters to your work surface. Using an oyster knife, remove the top shell of each oyster and discard. Pour a dab or two of warm barbecue sauce on top of each oyster. Put the oysters back on the grill just until the sauce starts to bubble at the edges. Serve immediately, on the half shell.

SERVES 4 TO 6

Grilled Oysters with Fresh Ginger Vinaigrette

Grilled fresh oysters are about as festive as an appetizer can get. When you grill them directly over the fire, the oysters even pop open on their own, so you don't have to pry those tight shells apart. Although lemon juice, grated horseradish, and bottled hot sauce are traditional—and delicious—accompaniments to oysters, this recipe offers a fresh alternative.

3 dozen fresh oysters

FRESH GINGER VINAIGRETTE

1/2 cup rice vinegar

Juice of 1 lemon

1/4 cup peeled and grated fresh ginger

Tabasco sauce to taste

1. Scrub the oysters under cold running water and store them, flat shells up, in a cool place until you are ready to grill.

2. In a small, nonreactive bowl, combine the vinaigrette ingredients and mix well. Cover and refrigerate until needed.

3. Preheat the grill with all the burners on high for 10 minutes and the lid down.

4. With all the burners still on high, place the oysters, flat shells up, on the grill, close the lid, and cook just until their shells pop open slightly, 2 to 3 minutes; some may take a little longer to open than others. Discard any oysters that do not open.

5. Transfer the oysters to your work surface. Using an oyster knife, remove the top shell of each oyster and discard. Serve the oysters immediately with the bowl of fresh ginger vinaigrette close by.

SERVES 6 TO 9

Exotic Grilled Oysters— Two Ways

Thanks to Sean Behrens for these exotic flavor explosions! Sean's folks were the original owners of the legendary Folie Douce restaurant in Arcata, California. These recipes were actually recommended by their loyal diners. Prepare them at your own risk: They're habit-forming. Count on 4 to 6 medium-size oysters per person. Both variations require the following preliminary steps:

1. Scrub the oysters under cold running water and store them, flat shells up, in a cool place until you are ready to grill.

2. Preheat the grill with all the burners on high for 10 minutes and the lid down.

3. With all the burners still on high, place the oysters, flat shells up, on the grill, close the lid, and cook for about 3 minutes; then take a peek. The oysters will be done as soon as their shells pop open slightly; some may take a little longer to open than others. Discard any oysters that do not open.

4. Transfer the oysters to a flat work surface. Using an oyster knife, remove the top shell of each oyster and discard. Add either of the Japanese-style or Mexican-style ingredients listed below. Put the oysters back on the grill just until the sauce starts to bubble at the edges, about 1 minute. Serve immediately, on the half shell.

JAPANESE-STYLE GRILLED OYSTERS

Put on each open grilled oyster:

1/4 teaspoon wasabi paste

1/4 teaspoon Chinese plum sauce

1/2 teaspoon toasted sesame oil, heated

1/4 teaspoon very finely chopped green onion, as garnish after the oyster comes off the grill

MEXICAN-STYLE GRILLED OYSTERS

Put on each open grilled oyster:

1 small piece Dungeness, snow, or king crab meat, slightly smaller than the oyster

1 teaspoon Chipotle Butter (recipe follows)

2 very thin slices fresh kumquat, as garnish after oyster comes off the grill

1/4 teaspoon finely chopped fresh cilantro, as garnish after the oyster comes off the grill

CHIPOTLE BUTTER

1/2 cup (1 stick) salted butter, softened

1 tablespoon very finely chopped oil-packed sun-dried tomatoes

2 tablespoons chopped canned chipotle chile in adobo sauce

> Mix all the ingredients together with a fork in a small saucepan until well blended. Melt over medium heat, then reduce the heat to low until needed.

Skewered Chicken Livers with Fresh Lime and Cilantro

This is an unusual combination, but one that works exceedingly well, especially as an appetizer. For a dish so simple, the flavors are surprisingly complex and pleasing: The piquant lime juice beautifully complements the richness of the chicken livers, and the cilantro adds a fresh "green" flavor all its own. Because the livers cook up so quickly, you can grill them easily before the main course.

1 pound chicken livers

4 bamboo skewers, soaked in water for 30 minutes and drained

Vegetable oil

Kosher salt and freshly ground black pepper to taste

1/2 cup coarsely chopped fresh cilantro

1 lime, quartered

1. Preheat the grill with all the burners on high for 10 minutes and the lid down.

2. While the grill is preheating, rinse the chicken livers in cold water and dry well with paper towels. Thread or weave about 5 livers onto each skewer. Rub them with a little vegetable oil, then dust lightly with salt and pepper.

3. Once the grill is hot, turn all the burners to low. Place the skewered chicken livers on the grill, close the lid, and cook until still just a little pink in the middle, 7 to 9 minutes, turning them once.

4. Serve the livers hot off the grill with the cilantro sprinkled over the top and the lime wedges on the side, ready for a good squeeze.

SERVES 4 TO 6

Rumaki

This blast from the past was a standard hors d'oeuvre at cocktail parties circa 1960. A generation later, these chicken livers still taste good, especially hot off the grill. Far from snickering at such a passé canapé, your guests may embark on a vivid trip down memory lane.

18 strips bacon

1/2 pound chicken livers, rinsed, patted dry, and cut into 1-inch cubes

About 1/4 cup soy or teriyaki sauce

One 8-ounce can whole water chestnuts, rinsed and drained

6 to 12 bamboo skewers, soaked in water for 30 minutes and drained

1. Preheat the grill with all the burners on high for 10 minutes and the lid down.

2. While the grill is preheating, cut the bacon strips in half and cook them in a large skillet over medium heat until about half-cooked; don't let them get crisp at all—you just want them to render some of their fat and to get limp. Drain the bacon well on paper towels.

3. In a small bowl, combine the chicken livers with just enough soy sauce to cover and let sit for 5 minutes. Pair one chicken liver cube and one water chestnut, wrapping the two with a piece of the partially cooked bacon. String as many as you can onto the bamboo skewers.

4. Once the grill is hot, turn off the center burner and turn the others to medium. Place the skewers over the center burner, close the lid, and cook until the bacon is nicely browned, 18 to 25 minutes, turning the skewers several times. Serve hot off the grill.

SERVES 4 TO 6

Red Wings

These spicy chicken wings are just the thing for a pregame appetizer or for when folks drop by for a beer or glass of wine. They're tasty, messy, and easy to prepare. Encased as they are in their fatty skin, chicken wings really benefit from a long marination. For the best flavor, allow to marinate in the refrigerator for 24 hours, or at least overnight.

4 pounds chicken wings (about 20)

HOT RED MARINADE

1/4 cup vegetable oil

1/2 cup red wine vinegar

2 tablespoons paprika

1 tablespoon cayenne pepper

4 cloves garlic, pressed or minced

1 teaspoon freshly ground black pepper

1 teaspoon ground cumin

1 bay leaf

1 teaspoon kosher salt

1/2 cup ketchup

1. Cut the tips off the chicken wings and place the wings in a 1-gallon zippered-top plastic bag.

2. Put all the marinade ingredients in a blender and process until smooth, or whisk together in a bowl. Pour the marinade into the plastic bag, seal, and squish around to make sure all the wings are coated. Let marinate in the refrigerator overnight or up to 24 hours.

3. Preheat the grill with all the burners on high for 10 minutes and the lid down.

4. Leave the back burner on high; turn the other burners to low. Place the wings over the burners on low, close the lid, and cook, turning every 5 minutes, until completely cooked through, about 20 minutes.

NOTE The wings closest to the back burner may cook faster than the ones in front. If so, rotate the front wings to the back, and vice versa, until all are evenly browned.

SERVES 4 TO 6

Grilled Chicken "Sashimi"

The very idea of grilled chicken masquerading as sashimi might cause some purists alarm, but it sure is good! Chicken thighs tend to be the most flavorful part of the chicken and they stand up well to the intense flavor of pickled ginger. This makes a substantial addition to a party where only appetizers are being served; in fact, chicken "sashimi" would qualify as a "heavy puu-puu," as they say in Hawaii (*puu-puu* is Hawaiian for "appetizer").

8 boneless, skinless chicken thighs

6 to 8 tablespoons pickled ginger slices (look in the Asian section of your supermarket)

16 toothpicks

1 tablespoon toasted sesame oil

1 tablespoon ground cumin

1 tablespoon kosher salt

DRIZZLING SAUCE

2 tablespoons seasoned rice vinegar

1 tablespoon Thai sweet chili sauce

1 tablespoon hoisin sauce

$1^1/2$ teaspoons toasted sesame oil

OPTIONAL GARNISHES

Wasabi paste

Carrots, cut into matchsticks

Daikon (Japanese radish), cut into matchsticks

1. Lay the chicken thighs open, cut side up, on a platter. Place 6 to 8 slices of the pickled ginger on one end of each thigh. Roll up the thigh and fasten with a couple of toothpicks. Pour the sesame oil over the thighs and roll to coat evenly.

2. In a small bowl, mix together the cumin and salt. Sprinkle liberally over the thighs, top and bottom.

3. Preheat the grill with all the burners on high for 10 minutes and the lid down.

4. Turn off the front two burners, leaving the back burner on high. Place the thighs over the off burners, close to but not over the lit burner. Close the lid, and grill the thighs until cooked through, for a total of about 24 minutes, 12 minutes per side.

5. When cool enough to handle, cut the chicken thighs jelly-roll fashion into $1/2$-inch-thick slices.

6. In a small bowl, whisk together the sauce ingredients and drizzle over the chicken slices. Garnish with the wasabi paste, carrots, and daikon if desired, and serve.

SERVES 4 TO 6

Fresh Ginger-Garlic Chicken Satay

My trusty, dog-eared copy of *The New Food Lover's Companion* by Sharon Tyler Herbst (Barron's, 2001) defines a satay as "an Indonesian favorite consisting of small marinated cubes of meat, fish or poultry threaded on skewers and grilled or broiled." Over the years, I've come to favor strips rather than cubes of meat, and I've all but abandoned the peanut dipping sauce that usually accompanies satays.

1 pound boneless, skinless chicken breast, cut into 3/8-inch-thick slices

FRESH GINGER-GARLIC MARINADE

1/4 cup sake

1/4 cup soy sauce

1/4 cup chopped green onions

1 tablespoon finely chopped fresh ginger

2 to 3 cloves garlic, to your taste, finely chopped or pressed

6 to 8 wooden skewers, soaked in water for 30 minutes and drained

1. Place the chicken strips in a quart-size zippered-top plastic bag.

2. Combine the marinade ingredients in a measuring cup, pour into the plastic bag, seal, and squish around to coat all the strips. Let marinate in the refrigerator for at least 2 hours and preferably overnight.

3. Preheat the grill with all the burners on high for 10 minutes and the lid down.

4. Thread the meat onto the skewers, accordion style.

5. Turn all the burners to a little lower than medium heat, place the skewers on the grill, and cook, with the lid up, for a total of 10 minutes, 5 minutes per side. You may want to have a thin-bladed spatula on hand when it comes time to flip the satays. Use it upside down, sliding the blade gently under the meat to loosen it from the grill. Serve them hot or at room temperature.

SERVES 4 TO 6

Hot Peanut-Sesame Beef Satay

This satay is so good and flavorful on its own that it needs no embellishment.

1 pound beef (top round, sirloin, flank, or other steak), cut into $3/8$-inch-thick slices

HOT PEANUT-SESAME MARINADE

$1/2$ cup soy sauce

$1/4$ cup creamy peanut butter

1 tablespoon toasted sesame oil

1 tablespoon hot pepper sauce of your choice

6 to 8 wooden skewers, soaked in water for 30 minutes and drained

1. Place the beef strips in a quart-size zippered-top plastic bag.

2. Combine the marinade ingredients in a measuring cup, pour into the plastic bag, seal, and squish all around to coat the strips. Let marinate in the refrigerator for at least 2 hours and preferably overnight.

3. Preheat the grill with the burners on high for 10 minutes and the lid down.

4. Thread the meat onto the skewers, accordion style.

5. Turn all the burners to a little lower than medium heat, place the skewers on the grill, and cook, with the lid up, for a total of 10 minutes, 5 minutes per side. You may want to have a thin-bladed spatula on hand when it comes time to flip the satays. Use it upside down, sliding the blade gently under the meat to loosen it from the grill. Serve hot or at room temperature.

SERVES 4 TO 6

Hoisin-Chili Pork Satay

Marinate this overnight if you have the time. These skewers grill up in a hurry.

1 pound boneless pork chops, cut into about 3/8-inch-thick strips

HOISIN-CHILI MARINADE

1/4 cup soy sauce

1/4 cup hoisin sauce

1/4 cup Thai sweet chili sauce

1 tablespoon vegetable oil

6 to 8 wooden skewers, soaked in water for 30 minutes and drained

1. Place the pork strips in a quart-size zippered-top plastic bag.

2. Combine the marinade ingredients in a measuring cup, pour into the plastic bag, seal, and squish all around to coat the pork strips. Let marinate in the refrigerator for at least 2 hours and preferably overnight.

3. Preheat the grill with the burners on high for 10 minutes and the lid down.

4. Thread the meat onto the skewers, accordion style.

5. Turn all the burners to a little lower than medium heat, place the skewers on the grill, and cook, with the lid up, for a total of 10 minutes, 5 minutes per side. You may want to have a thin-bladed spatula on hand when it comes time to flip the satays. Use it upside down, sliding the blade gently under the meat to loosen it from the grill. Serve hot or at room temperature.

SERVES 4 TO 6

Spicy Asian Lamb Chops

Serving small lamb chops as an appetizer has increased in popularity in recent years. They're a welcome, substantial treat, especially at cocktail parties where you may feel like if you don't get something real to eat soon, you may fall over. The best way to get appetizer-size lamb chops is to cut your own from a rack of lamb. Butchers usually cut lamb chops for use as an entrée too thick for easy, stand-up eating.

1 rack tiny rib lamb chops (about 2 pounds), top half of the bones fully frenched (meat and so forth removed so each chop comes with its own convenient "handle")

SPICY ASIAN MARINADE

1/2 cup Thai sweet chili sauce

1/2 cup soy sauce

2 tablespoons toasted sesame oil

1/3 cup finely chopped fresh mint

1. Slice the rack into individual chops (or ask the butcher to do it for you). Place them in a 1-gallon zippered-top plastic bag.

2. Combine the marinade ingredients in a large measuring cup, pour into the plastic bag, seal, and squish around to make sure the chops are coated. Let marinate in the refrigerator for 2 to 4 hours.

3. Preheat the grill with all the burners on high for 10 minutes and the lid down.

4. Turn all the burners to medium. Remove the chops from the marinade; reserve the leftover marinade. Place the chops on the grill and cook, with the lid up, for a total of 3 to 4 minutes, 1 1/2 to 2 minutes per side for medium-rare. Place the grilled chops on a platter and loosely tent with aluminum foil.

5. Pour the reserved marinade into a small saucepan and bring to a boil for 2 minutes. Pour the hot marinade into a small bowl and serve as a dipping sauce for the chops.

SERVES 4 TO 6

Lamb Riblets with Garlic and Rosemary

There isn't much meat on lamb riblets, from a rack of lamb, but what there is sure is good. This simple marinade adds to their succulence. Just be sure to make a lot of them, as they tend to disappear in an instant. Serve with plenty of napkins!

1^1/2 pounds lamb riblets

ROSEMARY-GARLIC MARINADE

^{1}/3 cup olive oil

^{1}/4 cup dry white wine

6 cloves garlic, peeled

2 teaspoons freshly ground black pepper

2 teaspoons dried rosemary, crumbled

^{1}/4 teaspoon cayenne pepper

1 teaspoon kosher salt

1. Place the riblets in a 1-gallon zippered-top plastic bag.

2. Combine the marinade ingredients in a blender and blend on low until smooth. Pour it into the plastic bag, seal, and squish around to make sure the riblets are coated. Let marinate in the refrigerator overnight.

3. Preheat the grill with all the burners on high for 10 minutes and the lid down.

4. Leave the back burner on high; turn the others to low. Place the riblets over the burners on low and grill, with the lid up, for a total of 20 minutes, turning every 5 minutes or so. Aside from their flavor, the best part of these morsels is their crunchiness, so try to stack them on their narrow sides to brown.

5. Transfer to a platter and loosely tent with aluminum foil for 10 minutes, then serve.

SERVES 2 TO 4

3

Fish and Shellfish

Fish has become so popular with Americans that it is now possible to buy an excellent assortment of fresh fish in almost every part of the country. Preparing fish on a gas grill is one of the easiest and best ways to cook this healthful and delicious food. ✳ The first rule in grilling fish and shellfish is to buy only the freshest available. How can you tell what's fresh? Whole fish should have shiny skin and bright eyes with clear, black—not cloudy—pupils. It should smell fresh, not fishy. Fillets and steaks should look moist, with no discoloration toward the edges. The shells of clams and oysters should be shut tight. Scallops should be pale, creamy white, with a fresh briny scent. No matter what type of fish or shellfish you choose, if it's truly fresh, you're already more than halfway to a wonderful meal.

Keep the fish refrigerated until about 30 minutes before grilling. It should be near room temperature when it goes on the grill. If the fish is to be marinated for longer than 30 minutes, begin marinating it in the refrigerator. Take it out of the refrigerator—but not out of the marinade—about 30 minutes before grilling.

Because fish cooks so quickly, it is easy to overcook it. Nothing ruins a nice piece of fish like overcooking. Years ago, Canada's Department of Fisheries produced a small pamphlet on cooking fish that has since become a classic. In it, they suggest determining the cooking time for any fish (using any cooking method) by simply measuring the fish at its thickest part and then cooking it for 10 minutes per inch of thickness. A 1-inch-thick steak (or fillet, or whatever) would take 10 minutes to cook; 5 minutes per side. If you're scrupulous about following this timing method, you'll please everyone—even those who say American home cooks always overcook fish.

People on the cutting edge of cuisine may say that this method is too generalized (and results in cooking times that are too long), but it's a very reliable starting point until you've had a chance to determine your personal preferences and the nuances of your own gas grill. Because there are so many different models and types of grills out there, it is best to rely on your own good sense for judging doneness and to use the times given in each recipe as a rough guideline.

Fish is considered done when its flesh just begins to flake when probed with a fork. Another way to determine doneness is to peek and see if the flesh is uniformly opaque. Translucent flesh is generally undercooked, though some people prefer it that way—especially with fresh tuna. A large piece of fish or thick steak can be tested for doneness with an instant-read thermometer. Look for a minimum temperature of 140°F.

When it comes to grilling shellfish, remember that the meat is at its peak the instant it has turned opaque all the way through. Follow the times given in each recipe as a guideline, but use your judgment. The fastest way to ruin any shellfish is to over-cook it.

Sometimes fish will stick to the grill; there are several ways to avoid the problem. First, always preheat the grill as instructed in the recipes. Once the grill is hot, use your wire brush to clean it. Fish is less likely to stick to a clean, hot grill. Also, make sure to oil the fish, per the instructions in each recipe, just before you put it on the grill. Some cooks like to brush the grill surface lightly with oil before preheating. Since it's harder to clean

Brazilian Mixed Grill
Fish Soup 50

Barbecued Catfish
Sandwiches 52

Grape Leaf–Wrapped
Dover Sole 53

Halibut with
Lemon-Caper Butter 54

Halibut with Wilted
Escarole and Light
Lemon Sauce 56

Vietnamese-Style
Lettuce-Wrapped Marlin 57

Red Snapper
à la Veracruz 59

Whole Snapper
with Spicy Ginger
Dipping Sauce 60

Salmon Fillets with
Black Beans and
Red Pepper Puree 62

Salmon Steaks with
Cucumber-Dill Sauce 64

Spicy Salmon Skewers
with Udon Noodles and
Fresh Cilantro Sauce 65

Grilled Whole Salmon 67

Sea Bass with
Lemon Beurre Blanc 68

Chilean Sea Bass with
Minted Pea Sauce 70

Shark Steaks with
Chili-Lime Butter 71

Swordfish Steaks with
Sauce Niçoise 72

Swordfish with Black
and White Sesame Crust 74

Swordfish Brochettes
with Lemon and
Garlic Marinade 75

Piquant Swordfish
Brochettes 76

Tunisian Tilapia with Pita 77

Whole "Camp-Style"
Trout 79

Grilled Tuna with
Homemade Tartar Sauce 80

Seared Tuna Steaks
with Mango Salsa 81

Tuna Steaks with
Green Olive Tapenade 83

Grilled Tuna with
Tuscan White Beans 84

Seared Fresh Tuna
Salad with Lemon-
Ginger Dressing 86

Salade Niçoise with
Grilled Tuna 87

Fresh Tuna Fish
Sandwiches 89

Grilled Fish Sandwiches 90

Fish Tacos 92

Lebanese-Style
Salt-Grilled Whole Fish 94

Grilled Lobster Tails 96

Scallop and Salmon
Brochettes 97

Skewered Scallops
with Bay Leaves 98

Skewered Sake Scallops 99

Creamed Grilled Scallops
on Sourdough Toast 100

Grilled Shrimp
à la Scampi 102

Bacon-Wrapped
Spicy Barbecued Shrimp 103

Blue Thai Prawns
with Green Curry
Dipping Sauce 104

the grill rack than a grill basket, I use a hinged wire grill basket, which I coat with non-stick cooking spray.

If the fish's skin is intact (which will help it retain its shape), put it on the grill skin side first. Plan on turning fish only once—halfway through the total cooking time.

Generally speaking, fish should be served hot off the grill—within seconds, if possible. So have all the accompaniments ready to go before putting the fish on the grill. Heated plates help keep the fish piping hot; slip the plates into a 250°F oven about 15 minutes before serving, along with a platter to catch the fish immediately after grilling.

Brazilian Mixed Grill Fish Soup

This is a delicious, full-strength combination of flavors and textures. Add more fresh jalapeño pepper if you want a spicier broth. Err on the side of slightly under-cooking the fish and shellfish, as it will continue to cook in the hot broth.

BROTH

One 13.5-ounce can unsweetened coconut milk

One 14-ounce can vegetable broth

1 cup milk

Juice of 1^1/$_2$ limes

^{1}/$_4$ cup finely chopped red onion

1 ear fresh corn, kernels cut from the cob

2 small russet potatoes, peeled and cut into bite-size cubes

^{1}/$_2$ red bell pepper, seeded and diced

^{1}/$_2$ jalapeño, seeded and diced

2 tablespoons chopped green onions (green part only)

2 teaspoons kosher salt

FISH

1/2 pound sea scallops

1/2 pound shark steak, cut into 1-inch cubes

1/2 pound medium-size shrimp, peeled, with tails left intact

1 tablespoon vegetable oil

Ground white pepper to taste

Sweet paprika to taste

6 to 8 bamboo skewers, soaked in water for 30 minutes and drained

1/2 pound mussels, scrubbed and debearded, if necessary

1/4 cup chopped fresh cilantro for garnish (optional)

1. Combine the broth ingredients in a large saucepan and bring just to a boil. Remove from the heat.

2. Coat the scallops, shark cubes, and shrimp with the vegetable oil. Dust with white pepper and paprika. Skewer the scallops through their thin side with two parallel skewers; do the same with the shark cubes and shrimp to make turning on the grill easier. Reserve the mussels in the refrigerator until needed.

3. Preheat the grill with all the burners on high for 10 minutes and the lid down.

4. Turn all the burners to medium. Place the skewers on the grill and cook, with the lid up, for a total of 6 to 8 minutes, turning once midway through the cooking time.

5. While the fish is grilling, bring the broth back to a boil and add the mussels. Let boil for 1 minute, then reduce the heat to low.

6. Ladle the broth into individual bowls. Place equal amounts of the grilled scallops, shark, and shrimp in each bowl. Garnish with the chopped cilantro if desired and serve immediately.

SERVES 4 TO 6

Barbecued Catfish Sandwiches

Okay, okay: I couldn't resist. When I came up with this recipe, I was living right in the middle of what some folks consider the Barbecue Capital of the World—Kansas City, Missouri—and I just had to try this finned variation on the traditional pork or beef barbecue sandwich. And I'm here to tell you it's darn good. Serve with—you guessed it—French fries, and a lot of them. And how about some black-eyed peas? Ice-cold beer would be the beverage of choice here.

1¹/₂ pounds catfish fillets

3 tablespoons packaged barbecue dry rub

6 tablespoons cornbread mix

Nonstick cooking spray

EXTRAS

Inexpensive white sandwich bread

Dill pickle chips

Fresh Coleslaw with Light Lemon Dressing (page 353)

Bottled barbecue sauce of your choice

Hot pepper sauce of your choice

1.   Preheat the grill with all the burners on high for 10 minutes and the lid down.

2.   While the grill is preheating, rinse the catfish under cold running water; blot dry with several thicknesses of paper towels.

3.   Combine the dry rub and cornbread mix in a 1-gallon zippered-top plastic bag. Add the catfish, seal, and shake to evenly coat the fish. Lay the fillets out on a large platter or cookie sheet. Coat both sides of the fish with nonstick cooking spray.

4.   Reduce all the burners to medium, place the fillets on the grill, and cook, with the lid up, for a total of 5 to 6 minutes, 2¹/₂ to 3 minutes per side, until just cooked through. Remove from the grill.

5.   Once you've got the catfish off the grill, have everyone gather around and get busy making some sandwiches: Take a piece of white bread in your palm. On it lay one or two

pieces of the catfish. Top with dill pickle chips, a wad of coleslaw, and a little barbecue sauce or hot sauce, or both if you're feeling frisky. Fold the bread over and get ready to smile.

SERVES 4

Grape Leaf–Wrapped Dover Sole

Wrapping sole fillets in grape leaves not only adds wonderful, tangy flavor, but also makes this delicate fish much easier to cook on the grill (grape leaves pickled in brine are available in most gourmet markets and large supermarkets or can be ordered online at www.tavolo.com). The Moroccan-style pickled lemons can be easily made at home (page 363), but if you need them right away, they are available at many specialty food stores or can be ordered online at www.welcome-to-china.com. Serve these tasty bundles with Savory Rice (page 343) and Grilled Ratatouille (page 319).

3 or 4 wedges Preserved Moroccan Lemons (page 363)

$1^1/2$ pounds sole fillets

18 grape leaves, packed in brine

1 tablespoon olive oil

1 recipe Light Lemon Sauce (recipe follows)

1. Preheat the grill with all the burners on high for 10 minutes and the lid down.

2. Place one thin (about $^1/4$ x $1^1/2$ inches) slice of preserved lemon at the end of each sole fillet and roll up. Put the rolled fish fillet in the middle of a single grape leaf. Using overlapping folds, create a compact "bundle." Place the bundles on a platter and coat both sides with olive oil. Use a toothpick to secure the folded sides together.

3. Turn all the burners to medium. Place the bundles, folded side down, on the grill and cook, with the lid up, for a total of 6 to 8 minutes, turning once. Serve hot off the grill, drizzled with a little of the lemon sauce.

SERVES 4

LIGHT LEMON SAUCE

Early on in writing this cookbook, I was convinced that there must be a way of making a lemon-flavored white sauce that wouldn't add mountains of calories to a piece of cooked fish—basically a lowfat food. A couple of years ago, I discovered (by accident) that while nonfat cream cheese may be perfectly horrendous when spread on a toasted bagel, something quite wonderful happens to it when it is heated in a liquid. Surprisingly, it provides a rich, velvety quality very hard to distinguish from high-fat ingredients like butter and cream, and it became the basis of this sauce.

One 14.5-ounce can chicken broth

One 8-ounce package nonfat cream cheese (Neufchâtel)

$1/2$ teaspoon pure lemon extract (do not use imitation)

$1/4$ teaspoon ground white pepper

$1/4$ teaspoon kosher salt

1 teaspoon dry mustard

Bring the broth to a boil in a medium-size saucepan, then add the cream cheese and allow to melt over medium heat, stirring with a wire whisk. Add the lemon extract, white pepper, salt, and mustard. Continue to whisk over medium-high heat until the sauce thickens slightly, 3 to 5 minutes. Remove from the heat until ready to serve. Reheat just before serving.

MAKES A LITTLE MORE THAN 1 CUP

Halibut with Lemon-Caper Butter

Fresh halibut is one of the finest fish there is for grilling: delicate, sweet, and moist. Unfortunately, the process of freezing and thawing halibut robs it of most of its moisture and delicacy, so stick to the fresh form if at all possible.

LEMON-CAPER BUTTER

1/2 cup (1 stick) butter

Juice of 1 lemon

1 teaspoon minced lemon zest

3 tablespoons capers, drained

4 halibut steaks or fillets (1 1/2 to 2 pounds total), about 1 inch thick

Vegetable oil

Sweet paprika to taste

Ground white pepper to taste

Minced fresh parsley and lemon slices for garnish (optional)

1. Melt the butter in a small saucepan. Add the remaining lemon-caper butter ingredients, mix well, and set aside to cool completely.

2. Preheat the grill with all the burners on high for 10 minutes and the lid down.

3. While the grill is preheating, rinse the halibut in cold water and blot dry with paper towels. Rub a little vegetable oil into both sides of each steak or fillet, then dust with paprika and white pepper. Coat a hinged wire grill basket with nonstick cooking spray and place the halibut inside.

4. Once the grill is hot, turn all the burners to medium-high, place the halibut on the grill, and cook, with the lid down, until it just begins to flake when probed with a fork, 5 to 6 minutes per side, turning once.

5. To serve, whip the cooled lemon-caper butter with a fork. Place a couple of tablespoons of the butter on top of each piece of fish. Garnish with a sprinkling of parsley and a slice or two of lemon if desired.

SERVES 4

TURNING TIP

TO AVOID UNDUE PROBLEMS WHEN TURNING FISH ON THE GRILL, ALWAYS PLACE IT PERPENDICULAR TO THE GRILL BARS.

Halibut with Wilted Escarole and Light Lemon Sauce

This combination of fish, greens, and sauce is a variation of the justly famous halibut à la Florentine—halibut served over a bed of spinach topped with Mornay sauce and run under the broiler. This version is lighter and more intensely flavored. If throwing a whole head of escarole on the grill seems strange to you, I urge you to give it a try: It's wonderful!

1 1/2 pounds halibut, preferably steaks (if steaks are large, they can be split in half after cooking; one half per person), at least 1 inch thick

1 tablespoon vegetable oil

Ground white pepper to taste

Sweet paprika to taste

1 head escarole

3 to 4 tablespoons sherry vinegar, to your taste

Kosher salt to taste

1 recipe Light Lemon Sauce (page 54)

1. Preheat the grill with all the burners on high for 10 minutes and the lid down.

2. Coat the halibut steaks with the vegetable oil; dust with white pepper and paprika.

3. Once the grill is hot, turn all the burners to medium-high, place the halibut on the grill, and cook, with the lid down, until it just begins to flake when probed with a fork, 5 to 6 minutes per side, turning once. Remove from the grill. Transfer the halibut to a platter and loosely tent with aluminum foil.

4. Turn all the burners to low. Wash the head of escarole briefly in cold running water. Do not dry; the extra water will help keep the outer leaves from burning. Place the escarole, stem end up, in the middle of the grill. Close the lid and cook until just wilted, about 8 minutes total, turning once after about 4 minutes.

5. Remove the escarole from the grill, remove the core, and chop coarsely. (*Note:* If any of the ends of the escarole leaves are burned, simply scrape them off with the edge of a

sharp butcher knife before chopping.) Place the chopped escarole in a bowl and toss with the sherry vinegar and salt to taste. Serve hot or at room temperature.

6. Warm the lemon sauce to just below the boiling point.

7. At serving time, place a halibut steak on top of bed of wilted escarole and top with the sauce. Serve immediately.

SERVES 4

Vietnamese-Style Lettuce-Wrapped Marlin

I can just about guarantee that if you make this recipe once, you'll make it again. Its high, fresh flavors invite a repeat performance—especially during the warm-weather months. Marinate the marlin strips, then skewer, grill, and roll them up in lettuce leaves with perfumed sticky rice, bean sprouts, shredded carrots, sriracha sauce, lime juice, and fresh cilantro.

1^1/$_2$ pounds marlin, cut into ^{3}/$_4$-inch strips (substitute tuna or swordfish if marlin is not available)

ORANGE-TOMATO MARINADE

2 tablespoons fresh orange juice

1 tablespoon tomato paste

1 teaspoon ground cumin

1 teaspoon kosher salt

^{1}/$_2$ teaspoon red pepper flakes

4 cloves garlic, pressed

PERFUMED STICKY RICE

2 cups short-grain rice

1 1/2 cups water

1 teaspoon kosher salt

1 teaspoon sugar

1 tablespoon rice vinegar

6 to 8 bamboo skewers soaked in water for 30 minutes and drained

8 large lettuce leaves (iceberg works best)

EXTRAS

Bean sprouts

Shredded carrots

Sriracha sauce ("red rooster" sauce)

Lime wedges

Chopped fresh cilantro

1. Place the marlin strips in a 1-gallon zippered-top plastic bag.

2. Combine all the marinade ingredients in a small bowl and mix well. Pour in the bag, seal, and squish around to coat the strips evenly with the marinade. Let marinate in the refrigerator for 1 to 2 hours.

3. Place the rice in a strainer and rinse under cold running water, shaking the strainer while rinsing until the water runs clear. Bring the 1 1/2 cups water, salt, and sugar to a boil over high heat in a medium-size saucepan. Add the rice, allow the water to return to a boil, then immediately reduce the heat to low, cover the pan, and cook for 17 minutes. Remove from the heat, leave the pan covered for 10 minutes, then open and sprinkle the rice vinegar over the rice. Fluff lightly with a fork. Admire the perfume. Keep covered until needed.

4. Preheat the grill with all the burners on high for 10 minutes and the lid down.

5. Thread the marlin strips, accordion style, onto the skewers.

6. Turn all the burners to medium, place the skewered marlin on the grill, and cook, with the lid up, for a total of 5 to 6 minutes, 2 1/2 to 3 minutes per side.

7. Put the skewered marlin, lettuce leaves, rice, and extras in separate bowls and allow people to build their own "lettuce wraps."

SERVES 4

Red Snapper à la Veracruz

This authentic recipe comes from friends who have spent a great deal of time in Mexico, traveling and sampling the cuisine from each region. This is how they serve red snapper in Veracruz.

VERACRUZ SAUCE

2 tablespoons vegetable oil

1 large onion, chopped

3 garlic cloves, pressed

8 plum tomatoes, peeled, seeded, and chopped

15 to 20 pitted green olives, cut in half

Juice of $1/2$ lemon

4 to 6 tablespoons chopped canned jalapeños, to your taste

1 teaspoon kosher salt

$1/2$ teaspoon sugar

$1/4$ teaspoon ground cinnamon

$1/4$ teaspoon ground cloves

3 pounds red snapper fillets

Light vegetable oil, such as canola

Sweet paprika to taste

Ground white pepper to taste

Chopped fresh cilantro and lemon wedges for garnish (optional)

1. Heat the oil in a medium-size saucepan over medium heat. Add the onion and garlic and cook, stirring, until softened and transparent but not browned, about 4 minutes. Add the remaining sauce ingredients and simmer, uncovered, for 5 to 10 minutes. Remove from the heat and cover until you are ready to serve the fish.

2. Preheat the grill with all the burners on high for 10 minutes and the lid down.

3. While the grill is preheating, coat the red snapper fillets lightly with oil, then dust with paprika and white pepper. Coat a hinged wire grill basket with nonstick cooking spray and place the fish inside.

4. Once the grill is hot, turn off the center burner and turn the others to medium. Position the snapper over the center burner, close the lid, and cook until it just begins to flake when probed with a fork, 6 to 10 minutes total for $1/2$- to 1-inch-thick fillets, turning them once.

5. While the fish cooks, reheat the Veracruz sauce.

6. To serve, arrange the fish fillets on a heated serving platter and top with the sauce. Garnish with cilantro and lemon wedges if desired.

SERVES 6

Whole Snapper with
Spicy Ginger Dipping Sauce

Grilled whole fish are very impressive served hot off the fire. In this recipe, fresh small red snappers (about 2 pounds each) are first marinated in the clean, spicy flavors favored in Japanese cuisine, then grilled. The leftover marinade is brought to a boil and served as a dipping sauce. The dish is excellent served with steamed rice and steamed or sautéed bok choy (Chinese cabbage), dressed with a little rice vinegar and toasted sesame seeds.

SPICY GINGER DIPPING SAUCE

3/4 cup sake

1/4 cup light vegetable oil, such as canola

1/4 cup soy sauce

1/4 cup peeled and grated fresh ginger

Juice of 1 lemon

2 large cloves garlic, pressed

1 teaspoon red pepper flakes

2 whole red snappers (about 2 pounds each), dressed

Chopped fresh cilantro for garnish (optional)

1. Combine all the marinade ingredients in a shallow, nonreactive container large enough to hold the fish, and mix well.

2. Wash the snappers in cold water and blot dry with paper towels. Using a sharp knife, cut diagonal slashes in both sides of the fish, as deep as the rib cage, but not through it or the backbone; this allows the marinade to penetrate the fish. Add the fish to the marinade, coating them on both sides, cover, and let marinate in the refrigerator for 1 to 2 hours, turning them several times.

3. Preheat the grill with all the burners on high for 10 minutes with the lid down.

4. While the grill is preheating, remove the snappers from the marinade. Pour the marinade into a small saucepan. Coat a hinged wire grill basket with nonstick cooking spray and place the fish inside.

5. Once the grill is hot, turn off the center burner and turn the others to medium. Place the snappers over the center burner, close the lid, and cook until the flesh is uniformly white and registers at least 140°F with an instant-read thermometer, 20 to 25 minutes total, turning them once.

6. While the fish cooks, bring the leftover marinade to a boil for 2 minutes; reduce the heat to low, cover, and hold until ready to serve.

7. To serve, arrange the fish on a heated serving platter. Serve each person a portion of the fish and offer the bowl of heated marinade as a dipping sauce (chopsticks come in handy for this). Garnish the snapper with cilantro if desired.

SERVES 6

Salmon Fillets with Black Beans and Red Pepper Puree

The distinctive flavor of salmon stands up well to assertive foods, as witnessed in this recipe. Although the combination of salmon, black beans, and red peppers may sound a little questionable, wait until you try it! This is best served with a simple side dish, such as steamed white rice.

BEANS

One 15-ounce can black beans, drained and rinsed

1 cup chicken or vegetable broth

$1/2$ cup minced onion

1 large clove garlic, pressed

2 teaspoons chili powder

2 teaspoons ground cumin

1 teaspoon kosher salt

RED PEPPER PUREE

4 to 6 red bell peppers, roasted (page 303) peeled, seeded, and cut into strips, or $3/4$ cup sliced roasted red peppers from a jar

2 tablespoons extra-virgin olive oil

1 teaspoon kosher salt

4 salmon fillets (each $1/3$ to $1/2$ pound)

Vegetable oil

Sweet paprika to taste

Ground white pepper to taste

$1/2$ cup sour cream or crème fraîche

Fresh cilantro leaves and lime wedges for garnish

1. Combine the bean ingredients in a small saucepan, bring to a boil, reduce the heat to medium-low, and simmer, covered, for 30 minutes, stirring occasionally. Allow the mixture to cool. Puree half the bean mixture in a blender or food processor; return it to the pan with the remaining beans and mix well. Adjust the seasonings to your taste. Keep the beans warm until serving time, adding a little more broth if the mixture becomes too thick (it should be thin enough to spoon onto a plate, but not runny).

2. To make the red pepper puree, place the peppers, olive oil, and salt in a blender or food processor and process until smooth. Transfer to a bowl and set aside until serving time.

3. Preheat the grill with all the burners on high for 10 minutes and the lid down.

4. While the grill is preheating, rinse the salmon fillets under cold running water and blot dry with paper towels. Rub a little vegetable oil on both sides and dust with paprika and white pepper. Coat a hinged wire grill basket with nonstick cooking spray and place the fillets inside.

5. Once the grill is hot, turn off the center burner and turn the others to medium. Place the salmon over the center burner, close the lid, and cook until it just begins to flake when probed with a fork, about 5 minutes per side, turning once.

6. To serve, divide the black bean mixture among 4 warm plates. Top each plate with a salmon fillet. Carefully spoon some red pepper puree over each fillet, then a little sour cream. Garnish with cilantro and a couple of lime wedges.

SERVES 4

Salmon Steaks with Cucumber-Dill Sauce

Salmon combined with the flavors of cucumbers and dill is a classic in the world of good eating. This dish is excellent served with Skewered Herbed Potatoes (page 307) and a green vegetable.

4 salmon steaks, about 1 inch thick

Vegetable oil

Sweet paprika to taste

Ground white pepper to taste

CUCUMBER-DILL SAUCE

3/4 cup peeled, seeded, and minced cucumber

1/2 cup sour cream

1/4 cup (1/2 stick) butter, softened

2 teaspoons dillweed or 1 tablespoon chopped fresh dill

1 teaspoon kosher salt

1. Preheat the grill with all the burners on high for 10 minutes and the lid down.

2. While the grill is preheating, rinse the salmon steaks under cold running water and blot dry with paper towels. Rub a little vegetable oil on both sides and dust with paprika and white pepper. Coat a hinged wire grill basket with nonstick cooking spray and place the salmon steaks inside.

3. In a medium-size bowl, combine the cucumber sauce ingredients and mix well with a fork. Keep at room temperature until the fish is ready. (If you make the sauce ahead of time, refrigerate it until about 30 minutes before serving time.)

4. Once the grill is hot, turn all the burners to medium-high. Place the salmon on the grill, close the lid, and cook until it just begins to flake when probed with a fork and measures at least 140°F with an instant-read thermometer, 5 to 6 minutes per side, turning them once.

5. To serve, dish out each salmon steak with a couple of tablespoons of the cucumber-dill sauce on top.

SERVES 4

HOW MUCH IS ENOUGH?

A HALF POUND OF BONELESS FISH IS CONSIDERED A GOOD SERVING SIZE FOR ONE PERSON.

Spicy Salmon Skewers with Udon Noodles and Fresh Cilantro Sauce

Although this recipe takes multiple liberties with several Asian cuisines, the end result, with its rich, complex flavors, is very appealing. The cilantro sauce is patterned after pesto, substituting cilantro, peanuts, and peanut oil for the basil, pine nuts, and olive oil. Udon noodles are relatively thick, sturdy Japanese wheat noodles (sometimes a combination of wheat and brown rice flour), which stand up well to the flavors of the cilantro sauce. Because of the intensity of the marinade, the strips of salmon need only spend about 30 to 40 minutes in the marinade. This is best served with ice-cold Thai or Japanese beer.

$1^1/2$ pounds salmon fillet, skin removed (ask your fishmonger to do this for you if you'd rather not tackle it at home)

SPICY TOASTED SESAME MARINADE

3 tablespoons light vegetable oil

3 tablespoons toasted sesame oil

3 tablespoons tamari or other soy sauce

1 tablespoon sriracha sauce ("red rooster" sauce)

FRESH CILANTRO SAUCE

2 to 3 cups packed fresh cilantro leaves (about 1 large bunch), coarsely chopped

$1/3$ cup unsalted dry-roasted peanuts

2 cloves garlic, peeled

Juice of $1/2$ lime

2 teaspoons mirin

1 teaspoon kosher salt

1 teaspoon sriracha sauce ("red rooster" sauce)

$1/2$ cup peanut oil

One 8-ounce package udon noodles

6 to 8 bamboo skewers, soaked in water for 30 minutes and drained

Chopped fresh cilantro

Lime wedges

1. Cut the salmon into strips about $3/4$ inch wide and 3 or 4 inches long and place them in a 1-gallon zippered-top plastic bag.

2. In small bowl, combine the marinade ingredients. Pour it into the plastic bag, seal, and squish around to coat the salmon with the marinade. Let marinate in the refrigerator for 2 to 4 hours.

3. To make the cilantro sauce, combine everything except the peanut oil in a food processor or blender and process until finely chopped. With the motor running, drizzle the peanut oil through the feed tube until the sauce has a pourable consistency. Transfer to a bowl, cover, and refrigerate until needed.

4. Preheat the grill with all the burners on high for 10 minutes and the lid down.

5. While grill is preheating, cook the udon noodles in boiling water according to package directions. Drain the noodles, return them to the pan, and toss with the cilantro sauce. Cover the pan and reheat briefly just before serving with the salmon.

6. Thread the salmon onto the skewers, accordion style.

7. Turn all the burners to medium. Place the salmon skewers on the grill and cook, with the lid up, just until cooked through, 6 to 8 minutes, turning once midway. Remove from the grill, place on a platter, and loosely tent with aluminum foil.

8. Divide the dressed udon noodles evenly between 4 plates. Lay a skewer of salmon on top of the noodles and garnish with chopped cilantro and a wedge or two of lime.

SERVES 4

Grilled Whole Salmon

Grilling a whole salmon is not for the faint of heart. To do it properly, you need your wits about you—and another person to help play "stereo" spatulas when it's time to turn the fish. That said, a whole salmon is one of the most impressive items to come off any grill. Serve with either Lemon Beurre Blanc (page 69) or Cucumber-Dill Sauce (page 64).

1 whole salmon (5 to 6 pounds), dressed, with head and tail left on

1 or 2 lemons, thinly sliced

1 medium-size onion, thinly sliced

3 or 4 celery tops, with leaves

Sprigs fresh dill (dillweed will do, if necessary)

Vegetable oil

Lemon wedges for garnish

1. Preheat the grill with all the burners on high for 10 minutes and the lid down.

2. While the grill is preheating, rinse the salmon well under cold running water and blot dry with paper towels. Layer the lemon and onion slices, celery tops, and dill evenly in the cavity of the fish. Sew the cavity shut with a large needle and white cotton thread, using the most rudimentary of stitches. If a needle and thread are not available, thread a couple of presoaked bamboo skewers across the opening to keep the stuffing from falling out. Rub some vegetable oil lightly on both sides of the fish.

3. Once the grill is hot, turn off the center burner and turn the others to medium. Place the salmon over the center burner, close the lid, and cook until an instant-read thermometer inserted into the flesh reads 140°F, 40 to 60 minutes. Turn once halfway through the cooking process: This is when two sets of hands and two spatulas come in handy. Position the two spatulas under the salmon and roll it over gently.

4. When the fish is done, transfer it to a warm serving platter and garnish with lemon wedges. To serve, use a very sharp, heavy knife to remove the head and tail, then cut straight through the body of the fish crosswise, making individual salmon steaks.

SERVES 10 TO 12

Sea Bass with Lemon Beurre Blanc

Sea bass is a first-rate fish for grilling. Delicate in flavor and texture, it is beautifully complemented by the tangy richness of a beurre blanc. The literal translation of *beurre blanc* is "white butter." Once you learn how to make beurre blanc, you'll return to it again and again when you need something special to transform a good dish into a great one. It's best to make the beurre blanc before you grill the fish. To hold the sauce in the interim, you'll need a thermos bottle large enough to contain about 1 1/2 cups of the sauce. *Note:* You can modify the beurre blanc very easily by adding 2 to 3 tablespoons of your favorite minced herb (such as basil, tarragon, or chervil) to the shallot-and-vinegar mixture.

LEMON BEURRE BLANC

3 to 4 shallots, minced, or $1/4$ cup minced green onions (white part only)

$1/4$ cup white wine vinegar

$1/4$ cup white wine or, for a more complex flavor, dry vermouth

Juice of $1/2$ lemon

$1/2$ teaspoon grated lemon zest

1 cup (2 sticks) unsalted butter, cut into about 10 pats

4 sea bass fillets, $1/3$ to $1/2$ pound each

Vegetable oil

Ground white pepper to taste

Lemon wedges and chopped fresh parsley for garnish (optional)

1. To make the beurre blanc, combine the shallots, vinegar, wine, and lemon juice and zest in a small saucepan, bring to a boil, and let continue to boil rapidly until only 2 tablespoons of liquid remain. Watch carefully and stir or swirl the mixture more or less constantly. Reduce the heat to medium-low and begin adding the butter, one pat at a time, whisking constantly. Allow each pat of butter to dissolve almost completely before adding the next. By the time the last pat of butter has been added, the sauce should be thick and creamy. Pour the sauce into a preheated thermos bottle to hold until serving time.

2. Preheat the grill with all the burners on high for 10 minutes and the lid down.

3. While the grill is preheating, rinse the sea bass fillets under cold running water and blot dry with paper towels. Rub a little vegetable oil on both sides of each fillet, then dust with white pepper. Coat a hinged wire grill basket with nonstick cooking spray and place the fillets inside.

4. Once the grill is hot, turn all the burners to medium-high. Place the sea bass on the grill and cook, with the lid down, until it just begins to flake when probed with a fork, 4 to 5 minutes per side, turning them once.

5. To serve, pour a few tablespoons of the beurre blanc over each fillet and garnish with lemon wedges and a little parsley if desired.

SERVES 4

Chilean Sea Bass with Minted Pea Sauce

I'd come across references to a pea sauce for a couple of years, but never turned up a recipe for it. Writers and reviewers were unanimous in their praise for this unusual idea for a sauce, and it certainly sounded good to me, especially combined with the sweet, delicate flavor of Chilean sea bass. So several experiments later, here's a delicious, novel sauce, just right for a spring dinner.

MINTED PEA SAUCE

1 cup frozen baby peas (*petits pois*)

1/2 cup dry white wine

1 clove garlic, pressed

1/2 teaspoon sugar

1/4 teaspoon kosher salt

2 teaspoons chopped fresh mint

1 teaspoon fresh lemon juice

1 1/2 pounds Chilean sea bass fillets, skin removed (ask your fishmonger to do this for you), about 1 inch thick

1 tablespoon vegetable oil

Ground white pepper to taste

Sweet paprika to taste

1. Combine the peas, wine, garlic, sugar, and salt in a small saucepan and let simmer over medium heat for 4 minutes. Allow to cool slightly, then transfer to a blender. Add the mint and lemon juice and blend until smooth. Pour back into the saucepan and set aside until needed.

2. Preheat the grill with all the burners on high for 10 minutes and the lid down.

3. Coat the sea bass with the vegetable oil; dust both sides with white pepper and paprika.

4. Turn all the burners to medium. Place the sea bass on the grill, close the lid, and cook until it just begins to flake when probed with a fork, 6 to 10 minutes total, depending on the thickness of the sea bass, turning once about midway.

5. While the sea bass is cooking, reheat the pea sauce over medium heat; keep it below the boiling point.

6. Top the sea bass with the pea sauce and serve.

SERVES 4

Shark Steaks with Chili-Lime Butter

As frightening as sharks may be in the briny deep, you definitely shouldn't shy away from them in the fish market. Your local fishmonger may sell both small sharks (as steaks) and large ones (in slices). All have a firm texture and a flavor similar to that of swordfish. Excellent side dishes to serve with this recipe include black beans and steamed rice, with a spicy, fresh salsa for the top of the fish.

CHILI-LIME BUTTER

1/4 cup (1/2 stick) butter

3 tablespoons fresh lime juice

2 teaspoons chili powder

1 teaspoon grated lime zest

Kosher salt and freshly ground black pepper to taste

4 shark steaks, about 1 inch thick

Vegetable oil

Ground white pepper to taste

Lime wedges and chopped fresh cilantro for garnish (optional)

1. Melt the butter in a small saucepan. Remove from the heat and let it cool partially. Add the remaining chili-lime butter ingredients and mix well. Keep warm to use as a sauce at serving time or let it cool completely to use as a topping for the grilled shark.

2. Preheat the grill with all the burners on high for 10 minutes and the lid down.

3. While the grill is preheating, rinse the shark under cold running water and blot dry with paper towels. Rub a little vegetable oil on both sides and dust with white pepper. Coat a hinged wire grill basket with nonstick cooking spray and place the shark inside.

4. Once the grill is hot, turn all the burners to medium-high. Place the shark on the grill and cook, with the lid down, until the flesh is opaque, 5 to 6 minutes per side, turning them once.

5. To serve, pour or spoon a few tablespoons of the chili-lime butter over each piece of shark. Garnish with lime wedges and a little cilantro if desired.

SERVES 4

THE BEST FISH FOR THE GRILL

THESE ARE THE EASIEST FISH TO HANDLE ON THE GRILL:
SALMON ✳ SHARK ✳ SWORDFISH ✳
TROUT ✳ TUNA

Swordfish Steaks with Sauce Niçoise

With its firm, almost meatlike texture, swordfish is one of the easiest fish to cook on the grill—not to mention one of the tastiest. Swordfish has a distinctive flavor that stands up well to strong-flavored sauces and marinades. In this Mediterranean-style recipe, the sauce niçoise is redolent with the aromas of garlic, lemon, and anchovy.

SAUCE NIÇOISE

1/2 cup (1 stick) butter

Juice of 1 lemon

2 cloves garlic, pressed

4 anchovy fillets, or more to your taste, rinsed

2 tablespoons minced fresh parsley

1 teaspoon freshly ground black pepper

4 swordfish steaks (about 2 pounds), about 1 inch thick

Vegetable oil

Sweet paprika to taste

Ground white pepper to taste

Minced fresh parsley and lemon slices for garnish (optional)

1.   Melt the butter in a small saucepan. Add the remaining sauce ingredients, using a fork or spoon to mash the anchovy into unrecognizable bits. (Even people who say they hate anchovies will like this sauce, as long as they can't see the anchovies.) Remove from the heat and let it cool completely.

2.   Preheat the grill with all the burners on high for 10 minutes and the lid down.

3.   While the grill is preheating, rinse the swordfish steaks under cold running water and blot dry with paper towels. Rub a little vegetable oil on both sides and dust with paprika and white pepper. Coat a hinged wire grill basket with nonstick cooking spray and place the swordfish inside.

4.   Once the grill is hot, turn all the burners to medium. Place the swordfish on the grill and cook, with the lid down, until the flesh is completely opaque and measures at least 140°F with an instant-read thermometer, 5 to 6 minutes per side, turning it once.

5.   To serve, whip the sauce with a fork and place a few tablespoons of it on top of each piece of fish. Garnish with a sprinkling of parsley and a slice or two of lemon if desired.

SERVES 4

Swordfish with Black and White Sesame Crust

Aside from being delicious, this recipe makes a beautiful and unusual presentation. Black sesame seeds are available at most Asian food markets; if you can't find them locally, they, along with the pickled ginger suggested as a condiment, can be ordered online at www.localflavor.com. Tamari is a high grade of soy sauce with a smoother, richer flavor—substitute regular soy sauce if you cannot find it. Serve with Coconut-Cilantro Basmati Rice (page 344) for an outstanding meal.

2 tablespoons white sesame seeds

2 tablespoons black sesame seeds

1 1/2 to 2 pounds swordfish steaks, 1 to 1 1/2 inches thick

Olive oil spray

Pickled ginger (optional)

Tamari or regular soy sauce (optional)

1. Preheat the grill with all the burners on high for 10 minutes and the lid down.

2. Mix the black and white sesame seeds together. Spread in an even layer on a dinner plate. Place the steaks on top of the seeds, one at a time, and press down gently. The seeds will naturally stick to the fish. Coat both sides of each steak completely. Just before grilling, coat both sides of the steaks with an olive oil cooking spray.

3. With all the burners still on high, place the swordfish steaks on the grill and cook, with the lid up, until still a little pink in the middle, a total of 8 to 10 minutes, turning once after 5 minutes. If the steaks are thinner than 1 inch, reduce the cooking time proportionately.

4. Serve hot off the grill, garnished with pickled ginger and a small cup of tamari sauce for dunking if desired.

SERVES 4

Swordfish Brochettes with Lemon and Garlic Marinade

The firm texture of swordfish makes it ideal for cooking on skewers. Serve these meaty nuggets with steamed rice and a steamed green vegetable for a healthy, satisfying meal.

LEMON AND GARLIC MARINADE

2/3 cup dry white wine

Juice of 2 lemons

3 tablespoons extra-virgin olive oil

2 tablespoons minced onion

2 cloves garlic, pressed

1/4 teaspoon kosher salt

Freshly ground black pepper to taste

1 1/2 to 2 pounds swordfish steaks, rinsed under cold running water, patted dry, and cut into 1 1/4-inch cubes

12 bamboo skewers, soaked in water for 30 minutes and drained

1. Combine the marinade ingredients in a 1-gallon zippered-top plastic bag. Add the swordfish cubes, making sure the marinade covers them all, seal, and let marinate in the refrigerator for 45 to 60 minutes.

2. Preheat the grill with all the burners on high for 10 minutes and the lid down.

3. While the grill is preheating, thread the cubes of swordfish onto the skewers, with the sides just touching. Coat a hinged wire grill basket with nonstick cooking spray and place the brochettes inside.

4. Once the grill is hot, turn all the burners to medium. Place the skewered swordfish on the grill and cook, with the lid down, until the flesh is uniformly opaque, 5 to 6 minutes per side, turning them once. Place the brochettes on a warm serving platter and serve at once.

SERVES 4

Piquant Swordfish Brochettes

The fresh-tasting marinade that flavors the swordfish in this recipe is complemented by a garnish of sliced black olives and chopped parsley.

LEMON AND WHITE WINE MARINADE

2/3 cup dry white wine

Juice of 2 lemons

3 tablespoons extra-virgin olive oil

1 tablespoon soy sauce

1/2 teaspoon dried oregano, crumbled

Freshly ground black pepper to taste

1 1/2 to 2 pounds swordfish steaks, rinsed under cold running water, patted dry, and cut into 1 1/4-inch cubes

12 bamboo skewers, soaked in water for 30 minutes and drained

Sliced black olives and minced fresh parsley for garnish

1. Combine the marinade ingredients in a 1-gallon zippered-top plastic bag. Add the swordfish cubes, making sure the marinade covers them all, seal, and let marinate in the refrigerator for 45 to 60 minutes.

2. Preheat the grill with all the burners on high for 10 minutes and the lid down.

3. While the grill is preheating, thread the cubes of swordfish onto the skewers, with the sides just touching. Coat a hinged wire grill basket with nonstick cooking spray and place the brochettes inside.

4. Once the grill is hot, turn all the burners to medium. Place the skewered swordfish on the grill and cook, with the lid down, until the flesh is uniformly opaque, 5 to 6 minutes per side, turning once.

5. Place the swordfish brochettes on a warm serving platter, garnish with the olives and parsley, and serve.

DON'T MARINATE TOO LONG!

IF YOUR MARINADE CONTAINS AN ACID COMPONENT, SUCH AS CITRUS JUICE OR VINEGAR, LIMIT THE TIME YOU MARINATE FISH TO UNDER 30 MINUTES; ANY LONGER AND THE ACID WILL BREAK DOWN THE TEXTURE OF THE FLESH, MAKING IT TOO SOFT.

SERVES 4

Tunisian Tilapia with Pita

Tilapia in Tunis? It's not as far-fetched as you might think: Although it's increasingly farm raised in this country, tilapia is actually native to parts of Africa and the Middle East. Called St. Peter's fish there, tilapia was, during biblical times, common in the Sea of Galilee. If the apostles caught fish, this would have been the one they caught. When you want a casual, pick-it-up-in-your-hands-and-eat-it dinner—but you want a good meal—give this a try. Unusual and very tasty, these filled pita sandwiches—with the wonderful garlic-infused yogurt, diced cucumbers, tomatoes, and fresh mint—are excellent paired with Tabbouleh (page 350) and maybe a Mediterranean-style salad of crisp greens, feta cheese crumbles, black olives, and a simple vinaigrette. Truth be known, the pita sandwiches are a meal in themselves.

GARLIC-YOGURT SAUCE

1 cup plain yogurt (nonfat is okay)

3 to 4 cloves garlic, to your taste, minced or pressed

CORIANDER-CARAWAY RUB

1 tablespoon ground coriander

1 teaspoon ground caraway seeds

1/4 teaspoon garlic powder

1/4 teaspoon cayenne pepper

1/4 teaspoon curry powder

1/4 teaspoon kosher salt

1 1/2 pounds tilapia fillets

1 tablespoon vegetable oil

6 to 8 bamboo skewers, soaked in water for 30 minutes and drained

EXTRAS

4 to 6 pita breads

1 medium-size cucumber, peeled, seeded, and cut into small chunks

Chopped fresh tomatoes

Chopped fresh mint

Hot pepper sauce (preferably harissa)

1. Combine the yogurt and garlic in a small bowl. Keep in the refrigerator until needed.

2. Combine the dry rub ingredients in a small bowl.

3. Slice the tilapia into strips about $3/4$ inch wide and 3 or 4 inches long. Place them in a medium-size bowl and lightly coat with the vegetable oil.

4. Put one third of the rub in a plastic bag. Put half of the tilapia slices in the bag; top with another third of the dry rub. Place the remaining tilapia into the bag; sprinkle the last of the dry rub over the top. Twist the top of the bag closed and shake vigorously to coat the fish evenly with the rub.

5. Preheat the grill with all the burners on high for 10 minutes and the lid down.

6. Thread the tilapia slices, accordion style, onto the skewers.

7. Wrap the pita breads in aluminum foil and put them into a 250°F oven or on the edge of the grill to warm.

8. With all the burners still on high, place the tilapia skewers on the grill and cook, with the lid up, until cooked through, 2 to 3 minutes per side.

9. When done, remove the tilapia from the grill. Cut the top quarter from the warm pitas, using scissors or a sharp knife. Fill each pita sandwich with the following ingredients, in any order you choose: grilled tilapia, garlic yogurt sauce, cucumbers, tomatoes, mint, and hot sauce.

SERVES 4

Whole "Camp-Style" Trout

Now that fresh farm-raised trout are so readily available in markets across the country, you needn't go camping to obtain and eat these delicacies. Even so, we all should continue to experience the wonderful aroma and flavor of trout wrapped in bacon and cooked over an open fire, whether in the wild or in our own backyards. Count on 1 trout per person.

4 whole trout, 10 to 12 inches long, dressed

4 sprigs fresh thyme or 1 teaspoon dried thyme

4 strips bacon, partially cooked until limp, to render some of the fat (don't let them get crispy)

Lemon wedges for garnish

1. Preheat the grill with all the burners on high for 10 minutes and the lid down.

2. While the grill is preheating, rinse the trout well under cold running water and blot dry with paper towels. Place 1 sprig thyme in the cavity of each fish. Wrap each trout around the middle with a strip of partially cooked bacon; hold the bacon in place with toothpicks if necessary. Coat a hinged wire grill basket with nonstick cooking spray and place the trout inside.

3. Once the grill is hot, turn off the center burner and turn the other burners to medium. Place the trout over the center burner, close the lid, and cook until the flesh is opaque in the center, and it just begins to flake when probed with a fork, about 7 minutes per side, turning once.

4. Transfer the trout to a warm serving platter; discard the bacon. Garnish the fish with lemon wedges and serve.

SERVES 4

Grilled Tuna with Homemade Tartar Sauce

If you're a little reluctant to cook fish on the grill, this recipe will win you over. Tuna, with its dense, firm texture, is probably the easiest of all fish to grill to perfection. Serve this dish with steamed rice or baked potatoes.

TARTAR SAUCE

$1/2$ cup mayonnaise

3 tablespoons Dijon mustard

3 tablespoons extra-virgin olive oil

1 tablespoon white wine vinegar or white cider vinegar

2 tablespoons minced green onion (white part only)

$1/4$ cup minced sweet or dill pickles

4 tuna steaks (about 2 pounds), about 1 inch thick

Vegetable oil

Sweet paprika to taste

Ground white pepper to taste

Lemon wedges and chopped fresh parsley for garnish (optional)

1. Combine the tartar sauce ingredients in a small bowl and mix well. Refrigerate until serving time.

2. Preheat the grill with all the burners on high for 10 minutes and the lid down.

3. While the grill is preheating, rinse the tuna steaks under cold running water and blot dry with paper towels. Rub a little vegetable oil on both sides and dust with paprika and white pepper. Coat a hinged wire grill basket with nonstick cooking spray and place the tuna inside.

4. Once the grill is hot, turn all the burners to medium-high. Place the tuna on the grill and cook, with the lid down, until only slightly translucent in the center, 5 to 6 minutes per side, turning once.

5. To serve, spoon a few tablespoons of the tartar sauce over each piece of tuna. Garnish with lemon wedges and a little parsley if desired.

SERVES 4

Seared Tuna Steaks with Mango Salsa

Although this recipe calls for simply searing the tuna, leaving the interior quite "rare," feel free to cook the fish longer if you prefer it that way. The sprightly flavors of the mango salsa are an excellent match for the rich flavor of the tuna. Serve with steamed rice and sautéed Chinese cabbage splashed with a little rice vinegar.

MANGO SALSA

2 ripe mangoes, peeled and cut off the pit into small cubes

$1/2$ cup minced red onion

$1/4$ cup minced fresh cilantro

2 tablespoons chopped canned jalapeños

2 tablespoons fresh lime juice

4 tuna steaks (about 2 pounds), about 1 inch thick

2 tablespoons vegetable oil

2 tablespoons mixed freshly ground black, green, red, and white pepper

1 lime, cut into 4 wedges, for garnish

1. In a medium-size bowl, combine the salsa ingredients and mix well. Let sit at room temperature for at least 30 minutes, stirring it occasionally.

2. Preheat the grill with all the burners on high for 10 minutes and the lid down.

3. While the grill is preheating, rinse the tuna steaks under cold running water and blot dry with paper towels. Place the tuna in a shallow dish and completely coat both sides of each piece with vegetable oil. Sprinkle each with the pepper mixture, pressing it lightly into the tuna to help it adhere.

4. With all the burners still on high, place the tuna steaks on the grill and cook, with the lid down, 2 to 3 minutes per side, turning them once. This short cooking time will leave the interior of the fish "rare." For more well-done tuna, grill over medium-high heat for 5 minutes per side, turning once.

5. Serve the fish with the mango salsa on the side and a wedge of lime.

SERVES 4

DON'T FORGET TO RINSE

NO MATTER HOW MUCH YOU TRUST YOUR FISH-MONGER, ALWAYS WASH FRESH FISH IN COLD WATER ONCE YOU GET IT HOME FROM THE STORE.

Tuna Steaks with Green Olive Tapenade

The distinctive flavor of grilled tuna is nicely complemented by the equally distinctive flavor of the olive tapenade. Serve this hot off the grill; if there are any leftovers, they'll make a wonderful tuna salad or salade niçoise. This is delicious served with Orzo with Basil (page 350).

4 tuna steaks (2 to 2^1/$_2$ pounds), 1 to 1^1/$_2$ inches thick

1 tablespoon olive oil

Ground white pepper to taste

Sweet paprika to taste

GREEN OLIVE TAPENADE

^{1}/$_2$ cup green olive tapenade (store-bought is fine)

^{1}/$_4$ cup dry vermouth

Juice of ^{1}/$_2$ lemon

2 cloves garlic, pressed

1. Rinse the tuna steaks under cold running water and blot dry with paper towels. Coat them with the olive oil on both sides; dust with white pepper and paprika.

2. Preheat the grill with all the burners on high for 10 minutes and the lid down.

3. While the grill is preheating, in a small saucepan over medium heat combine the sauce ingredients. Bring to a boil, and remove from the heat.

4. With the burners still on high, place the tuna steaks on the grill and cook, with the lid up, to your desired degree of doneness, 3 to 5 minutes per side.

5. Remove from the grill and top with the warm sauce. Serve immediately.

SERVES 4

Grilled Tuna with Tuscan White Beans

This highly unlikely combination makes for a delicious warm-weather meal. All that's needed as an accompaniment is a loaf of crusty Italian bread and some chilled white wine. *Bellissimo!*

BEANS

3 tablespoons olive oil

1 medium-size onion, minced

Two 15-ounce cans small white beans, drained and rinsed

2 cups chicken or vegetable broth

2 to 3 large cloves garlic, to your taste, pressed

2 bay leaves

2 teaspoons kosher salt

2 teaspoons freshly ground black pepper

FRESH BASIL DRESSING

$1^1/2$ cups extra-virgin olive oil

$1/2$ cup red wine vinegar

$1/2$ cup fresh basil leaves

$1/4$ cup water

2 cloves garlic, pressed

2 tablespoons Dijon mustard

2 teaspoons freshly ground black pepper

1 teaspoon kosher salt

4 tuna steaks (about 2 pounds), about 1 inch thick

Vegetable oil

Ground white pepper to taste

2 medium-size ripe red tomatoes, cut into wedges

2 lemons, cut into wedges

2 to 3 tablespoons chopped fresh parsley, to your taste

2 to 3 tablespoons chopped fresh basil, to your taste

1. To make the beans, warm the oil in a large saucepan over medium heat. Add the onion and cook, stirring, until softened, about 3 minutes. Add the beans, broth, garlic, and seasonings, bring to a boil, reduce the heat to medium-low, and simmer, uncovered, for 30 minutes, stirring occasionally. Remove from the heat and allow to cool to room temperature. Taste the beans, adjust the seasonings, and hold at room temperature until serving time.

2. Combine the dressing ingredients in a blender. Blend well and hold at room temperature until serving time.

3. Preheat the grill with all the burners on high for 10 minutes and the lid down.

4. While the grill is preheating, rinse the tuna under cold running water and blot dry with paper towels. Rub a little vegetable oil on both sides and dust with white pepper. Coat a hinged wire grill basket with nonstick cooking spray and place the tuna inside.

5. Once the grill is hot, turn the burners to medium-high. Place the tuna on the grill and cook, with the lid down, until only slightly translucent in the center, about 5 minutes per side, turning it once.

6. To serve, use a slotted spoon to place the white beans on a large serving platter. Break up the grilled tuna into chunks $1^1/2$ to 2 inches in diameter. Pour the dressing over the tuna, spilling some dressing onto the beans. (You may have more dressing than you need, but in this case it's better to have too much than too little—especially if there are any leftovers.) Garnish the platter with the tomato and lemon wedges, sprinkle the parsley and basil all over, and serve.

SERVES 4 TO 6

Seared Fresh Tuna Salad with Lemon-Ginger Dressing

When fresh tuna is seared on the outside but still pink on the inside, it approximates the taste and texture of Japanese sashimi. This salad, which is an ideal luncheon dish, is at once light and pungent.

LEMON-GINGER DRESSING

2/3 cup light vegetable oil, such as canola

1/3 cup rice vinegar

1 tablespoon soy sauce

1 tablespoon peeled and grated fresh ginger

Juice of 1/2 lemon

1 clove garlic, pressed

4 tuna steaks (about 2 pounds total), about 1 inch thick

Vegetable oil

Ground white pepper to taste

8 to 12 cups mixed salad greens

Green onions, sliced in half lengthwise, then cut crosswise into 2-inch pieces, for garnish

1. Combine the dressing ingredients in a blender and blend well. Set aside at room temperature.

2. Preheat the grill with all the burners on high for 10 minutes and the lid down.

3. While the grill is preheating, rinse the tuna steaks under cold running water and blot dry with paper towels. Rub a little vegetable oil on both sides and dust with white pepper. Coat a hinged wire grill basket with nonstick cooking spray and place the tuna inside.

4. Divide the salad greens among 4 to 6 plates and set aside.

5. With the burners still on high, place the steaks on the grill and cook, with the lid down, for 2 to 3 minutes per side, turning them once. This short cooking time will leave

the interior of the fish "rare." For more well-done tuna, grill the steaks over medium-high heat for about 5 minutes per side, turning once.

6. To serve, break up the tuna into chunks that are $1^1/_2$ to 2 inches in diameter. Place equal portions of the tuna on top of the greens on each plate. Drizzle some of the dressing over each plate and garnish with green onions. Pass additional dressing at the table.

SERVES 4 TO 6

Salade Niçoise with Grilled Tuna

This salad from the Riviera is hearty enough to serve as a main course. Replacing the customary canned tuna with grilled fresh tuna dramatically improves upon this traditional recipe. You can grill the tuna ahead of time and refrigerate it until you are ready to assemble the salad.

NIÇOISE VINAIGRETTE

$3/_4$ cup extra-virgin olive oil

$1/_4$ cup red wine vinegar

2 tablespoons minced fresh parsley

1 tablespoon minced green onion (white part only)

$1/_2$ teaspoon Dijon mustard

$1/_8$ teaspoon kosher salt

Freshly ground black pepper to taste

4 tuna steaks (1^1/2 to 2 pounds total), about 1 inch thick

Olive oil

Freshly ground black pepper to taste

8 medium-size new potatoes, scrubbed well

1^1/2 pounds green beans, ends and strings removed

About 6 cups lettuce greens

2 large ripe tomatoes, cut into wedges

2 hard-boiled eggs, peeled and quartered

^{1}/2 cup black olives (preferably the small niçoise variety), drained

1^1/2 tablespoons capers, drained

12 anchovy fillets (optional), rinsed

1.   Combine the vinaigrette ingredients in a small nonreactive bowl and whisk together well. Refrigerate until serving time.

2.   Preheat the grill with all the burners on high for 10 minutes and the lid down.

3.   While the grill is preheating, rinse the tuna steaks under cold running water and blot dry with paper towels. Brush on both sides with olive oil and sprinkle with pepper.

4.   Once the grill is hot, turn all the burners to medium-high. Place the tuna on the grill and cook, with the lid down, to your desired degree of doneness, 5 to 6 minutes per side, turning once. Transfer to a plate, let cool, cover with plastic wrap, and refrigerate until serving time.

5.   Cook the potatoes in boiling salted water to cover, until the tip of a sharp knife easily penetrates to the middle, about 15 minutes. Drain and immediately plunge the potatoes into ice water to stop the cooking process. Drain the potatoes again, then cut them into ^{1}/4-inch-thick slices. Pour enough of the vinaigrette over the potatoes to coat them lightly. Refrigerate until serving time.

6.   Cook the green beans in boiling salted water to cover until just tender, about 5 minutes. Drain and immediately plunge the beans into ice water to stop the cooking. Drain again and refrigerate until serving time.

7.   To assemble the salad, arrange the lettuce greens in an even layer on a large platter. Mound the potatoes, green beans, tomato wedges, and egg quarters evenly around the platter. Break up the grilled tuna into good-size chunks and pile them in the center. Scatter the olives and capers all over the salad, and garnish with the anchovy fillets if desired. Pour the remaining dressing over everything, and let the guests help themselves.

SERVES 4 GENEROUSLY

Fresh Tuna Fish Sandwiches

This may appear to be a common tuna sandwich: tuna fish, mayonnaise, mustard, lettuce, and bread. But all the ingredients have been cranked up a notch or two, transforming a simple meal into an uncommon delight.

$1/2$ cup mayonnaise

$1/4$ cup Dijon mustard

$1^1/2$ to 2 pounds tuna steaks, rinsed under cold running water, patted dry, and cut into $1^1/4$-inch cubes

12 bamboo skewers, soaked in water for 30 minutes and drained

Vegetable oil

Sweet paprika to taste

Good-quality crusty Italian or French bread, cut into $3/4$-inch-thick slices

Softened butter

Romaine lettuce leaves

Lemon wedges for garnish (optional)

1. Combine the mayonnaise and mustard in a small bowl and mix well. Refrigerate until needed.

2. Preheat the grill with all the burners on high for 10 minutes and the lid down.

3. While the grill is preheating, thread the tuna cubes onto the skewers, brush with vegetable oil, and sprinkle with paprika.

4. Once the grill is hot, turn all the burners to medium-high. Place the skewered tuna on the grill and cook, with the lid down, until only slightly translucent in the center, about 5 minutes per side, turning once.

5. When the tuna is 3 or 4 minutes away from being done, brush each slice of bread on both sides with softened butter. Toast on the grill for a minute or two on each side.

6. To assemble the sandwiches, put a lettuce leaf on each slice of toasted bread, pile the cubes of tuna on top of half the slices, add a dollop or two of the mustard sauce to the tuna, and cover with the remaining bread. Garnish the sandwiches with lemon wedges if desired.

SERVES 4 GENEROUSLY

Grilled Fish Sandwiches

This recipe may sound fairly plebeian, but these fish sandwiches were a big hit around here, with young and old alike. Somewhat surprisingly, grilling the breaded fish fillets results in a nice, crusty exterior and a steamy, moist interior. Don't forget to toast the buns on the grill—it's an important component in the success of this dish. In terms of accoutrements, there are two ways to go with these sandwiches: 1) shredded lettuce and Homemade Tartar Sauce or 2) coleslaw and spicy Caribe Sauce, along with a little fresh lime juice. The choice is yours. These sandwiches are great with French fries or the ever popular Tater-Tots.

One 19-ounce box frozen breaded fish fillets

Vegetable oil

1 bag good-quality hamburger buns

Softened butter or margarine

Tartar Sauce (page 80) or Caribe Sauce (recipe follows)

Shredded lettuce or Fresh Coleslaw with Light Lemon Dressing (page 353)

Lime wedges (optional)

1. Let the fillets thaw for 20 to 30 minutes before you put them on the grill.

2. Preheat the grill with all the burners on high for 10 minutes and the lid down.

3. Turn all the burners to medium. Brush or spray the fillets with vegetable oil, place on the grill, and cook, with the lid up, for 6 and 8 minutes, turning once halfway through the cooking time.

4. Brush the buns lightly with butter or margarine. After turning the fish, place the buns at the edges of the fire to toast lightly. Spread the top and bottom buns with tartar or Caribe sauce. Place one or two fish fillets on the bun and top with shredded lettuce or coleslaw. If you opt for the spicier version, don't forget to squeeze lime juice on the fillet.

SERVES 6 TO 8

CARIBE SAUCE

This spicy mayonnaise is a notch or two hotter than other "cocktail" sauces usually served with fish. It's a great complement to the flavors of the fish and the coleslaw.

2/3 cup mayonnaise (you can use a light version if desired)

1 tablespoon sriracha sauce or other hot pepper sauce (more if you like spicier sauce)

1 tablespoon ketchup

1 teaspoon chili powder

Juice of 1 lemon

Combine all the ingredients in a small bowl and whisk to blend well. Store in a glass jar, tightly covered. Keeps indefinitely in the refrigerator.

MAKES ABOUT 1 CUP

Fish Tacos

The very idea of tacos filled with fish may at first seem startling, but after your first bite, you'll understand.

APPLE-CABBAGE COLESLAW

4 cups cored and finely shredded cabbage

1 large apple (any variety), peeled, cored, and finely shredded

1 medium-size onion, minced

$1/2$ cup mayonnaise

2 tablespoons fresh lemon juice

1 teaspoon ground cumin

Salt and freshly ground black pepper to taste

LEMON-LIME MARINADE

$1/4$ cup light vegetable oil, such as canola

Juice of 2 limes

Juice of 1 lemon

2 teaspoons crushed fresh oregano or 1 teaspoon dried oregano

1 teaspoon ground cumin

1 teaspoon kosher salt

1 teaspoon freshly ground black pepper

2 pounds mild white fish fillets, such as red snapper, cut into 1-inch-wide strips

12 bamboo skewers, soaked in water for 30 minutes and drained

8 soft corn tortillas

1 or 2 ripe avocados, peeled, pitted, and sliced

2 medium-size ripe tomatoes, cut into thin wedges

Chopped fresh cilantro

Lime wedges

Salsa of your choice

1. Combine the coleslaw ingredients in a large bowl and mix well. Refrigerate until serving time.

2. Combine the marinade ingredients in a large nonreactive container and mix well. Add the fish strips, making sure they're completely covered, and set aside at room temperature for 20 to 30 minutes. (Don't leave the fish in the marinade any longer, or the citrus juices will "cook" the fish.)

3. Preheat the grill with all the burners on high for 10 minutes and the lid down.

4. While the grill is preheating, weave or thread the fish strips onto the skewers. Coat a hinged wire grill basket with nonstick cooking spray and place the skewered fish inside.

5. Once the grill is hot, turn off the center burner and turn the others to medium. Place the skewered fish over the center burner, close the lid, and cook until the fish is opaque all the way through, 8 to 10 minutes total, turning them once. While the fish cooks, wrap the tortillas in aluminum foil and place on the grill next to the fish. They will be soft and warm by the time the fish is done.

6. To serve, place a couple of pieces of fish in each warm tortilla, along with some avocado slices, tomato wedges, and a little coleslaw. Top with some cilantro, a squeeze of lime, and a little of your favorite salsa and enjoy!

SERVES 4

HEATING TORTILLAS

YOU CAN HEAT INDIVIDUAL TORTILLAS DIRECTLY ON THE GRILL, WITH OR WITHOUT A LITTLE OIL. IF YOU'RE HEATING A LARGE QUANTITY OF TORTILLAS, WRAP THEM TIGHTLY IN A COUPLE OF LAYERS OF ALUMINUM FOIL AND PLACE THE PACKET AWAY FROM DIRECT HEAT ON THE GRILL.

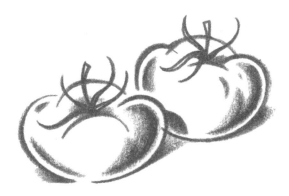

Lebanese-Style Salt-Grilled Whole Fish

I had my doubts about this recipe, told to me by my friend and world-traveler Sally Uhllman. And even though you're not supposed to serve an untried recipe to guests, that's exactly what I did one warm summer night in my backyard. Luckily, it was a hit with everyone around the table and, in all truthfulness, it may be my favorite recipe in this entire book. Don't let anyone tell you that there's no difference between bone-in and boneless fish: The bones really do add succulence and flavor to the end product.

CUCUMBER-YOGURT SAUCE

1 small cucumber, peeled, seeded, and finely chopped

1 large clove garlic, minced or pressed

2 tablespoons finely chopped red onion

2 tablespoons finely chopped fresh mint

1 1/2 cups plain yogurt

Juice of 1/2 of lemon

1/4 teaspoon kosher salt

Freshly ground black pepper to taste

1 whole fish (3 to 4 pounds), such as red snapper or striped bass, gutted and scaled (ask your fishmonger to do this for you), head and tail left on

3 pounds kosher salt

4 large egg whites

1 to 2 lemons, cut into 1/4-inch-thick slices

4 bay leaves

EXTRAS

Pita breads (at least 4)

2 cups diced fresh tomatoes

$^1/2$ cup chopped fresh mint

1. Combine the yogurt sauce ingredients in a medium-size bowl. Place in the refrigerator until ready to use.

2. Rinse the fish under cold running water; pat dry (including the cavity) with paper towels.

3. In a large bowl, thoroughly combine the salt and egg whites.

4. Preheat the grill with all the burners on high for 10 minutes and the lid down.

5. Insert lemon slices and bay leaves in the fish's cavity. On a large platter or a rimmed baking sheet, pat into place a $^1/2$-inch-thick layer of the salt-and-egg mixture, slightly larger than the fish. Put the fish on top of the salt layer; pour the remaining salt mixture over the fish and pat into place, completely sealing the fish in salt.

6. With all the burners still on high, place the salt-encrusted fish on the grill, close the lid, and cook for a total of 14 minutes, 7 minutes per side.

7. Turn all the burners off. Wrap the pitas in aluminum foil and place on the grill to warm slightly.

8. Remove the fish from the grill, then crack, remove, and discard the salt layer from the fish. Wipe the fish gently with a towel to remove any remaining salt. Transfer the fish to a serving platter. Give everyone a pita and instruct them to take a few pieces of fish (including some of the skin) and put them in the pita, along with some of the yogurt sauce, chopped tomatoes, and mint. Absolutely delicious!

SERVES 4

Grilled Lobster Tails

Those in the know say that the true flavor of lobster is achieved not by boiling or steaming but by grilling. The trick, as with all shellfish, is not to overcook it! You'll know the lobster is done the minute (the second, actually) the meat turns opaque white and the shell glows bright red. With lobster's distinctive taste, the only flavors most people want to add are a little melted butter and a squeeze or two of fresh lemon juice. If you're a fan of spicy foods, however, you may want to eschew the melted butter, as they do throughout most of the Caribbean, and try a little fresh lime juice and as much of your favorite bottled hot sauce as you like (any hot sauce made from habanero peppers is great with lobster).

4 lobster tails, each about $1/2$ pound

$1/2$ cup (1 stick) salted butter, melted and divided equally between 2 bowls

2 lemons or 2 to 4 limes, cut into wedges

Hot sauce of your choice

1. Preheat the grill with all the burners on high for 10 minutes and the lid down.

2. While the grill is preheating, wash the lobster tails under cold running water and pat dry with paper towels. Using a sharp knife or a pair of kitchen shears, cut down the middle of the hard top shell, then bend the tail backward to partially crack the back shell; this will prevent the tails from curling while on the grill. Brush the lobster meat with some melted butter from one of the bowls, reserving the other bowl for dipping at the table.

3. Once the grill is hot, turn off the center burner and turn the others to medium. Place the lobster tails over the center burner, close the lid, and cook for 10 to 12 minutes total, turning them once. Remove the lobster tails from the grill as soon as the meat has turned opaque white and the shell is bright red.

4. Serve the lobster immediately with the butter reserved for dipping, the lemon or lime wedges, and hot sauce.

SERVES 4

Scallop and Salmon Brochettes

This dish is not only one of the most beautiful things you can serve from the grill, but one of the most delicious. Accompany the brochettes with one of the small pastas (such as *semi de melone*, or melon-seed pasta, which looks almost like rice when cooked), boiled in chicken broth and dressed with minced fresh parsley, a little olive oil, and some grated Parmesan cheese, along with Cherry Tomatoes en Brochette (page 315).

LEMON-WINE MARINADE

3/4 cup dry white wine

1/3 cup light vegetable oil, such as canola

1 tablespoon minced shallot or green onion (white part only)

1 tablespoon chopped fresh parsley

1 clove garlic, pressed

Juice of 1/2 lemon

1/4 teaspoon kosher salt

3/4 pound sea scallops

One 3/4-pound salmon fillet, rinsed, patted dry, and cut into 1 1/4-inch cubes

12 bamboo skewers, soaked in water for 30 minutes and drained

2 teaspoons cornstarch

1 tablespoon soy sauce

1. Combine the marinade ingredients in a 1-gallon zippered-top plastic bag and mix well.

2. Rinse the scallops under cold running water. Submerge the scallops and salmon in the marinade, seal, and let marinate in the refrigerator for 1 hour or a little longer.

3. Preheat the grill with all the burners on high for 10 minutes and the lid down.

4. While the grill is preheating, drain the marinade, reserving it. Thread the scallops through their thin side and the salmon cubes alternately onto two parallel skewers (this will keep them from spinning when you turn the skewers on the grill).

5. Combine the cornstarch and soy sauce in a small bowl. Pour the reserved marinade into a small saucepan, stir in the cornstarch mixture, and bring to a boil for 2 minutes. Remove from the heat and allow to cool.

6. Once the grill is hot, turn off the center burner and turn the others to medium. Place the brochettes over the center burner, close the lid, and cook until opaque all the way through, 8 to 10 minutes total, turning the skewers once.

7. While the brochettes cook, reheat the marinade.

8. To serve, transfer the skewers to a warm platter and pass the sauce on the side.

SERVES 4

Skewered Scallops with Bay Leaves

Sweet and fine-textured, sea scallops are a true delicacy. As with any other shell-fish, however, it is important not to overcook scallops: they go from tender to tough in seconds. The inspiration behind this pairing of scallops and bay leaves originally came from Julia Child.

$1^1/2$ pounds sea scallops

12 bamboo skewers, soaked in water for 30 minutes and drained

About 18 bay leaves (cut in half if large)

$1/4$ cup ($1/2$ stick) butter, melted

2 or 3 lemons, cut into wedges, for garnish

1. Preheat the grill with all the burners on high for 10 minutes and the lid down.

2. While the grill is preheating, rinse the scallops under cold running water and blot as dry as you can. Thread them through their thin side onto two parallel skewers, with the scallops' sides touching, placing a bay leaf between every second or third one. Brush the skewers liberally with the melted butter.

3. Once the grill is hot, turn all the burners to medium-high. Place the skewered scallops on the grill and cook, with the lid down, for 2 to 3 minutes total, turning once. Remove the scallops from the grill as soon as they turn opaque white. Serve immediately with the lemon wedges.

SERVES 4

HOW TIGHTLY DO YOU LOAD YOUR SKEWERS?
FOOD PACKED TIGHTLY ON SKEWERS WILL TAKE LONGER TO COOK THAN FOOD PACKED LOOSELY.

Skewered Sake Scallops

Scallops simply refuse to put up with much fuss in the preparation department. If the sauce is too rich or the cooking time too long, the whole reason for serving scallops is lost. Here's a very simple recipe, just right for when the count around the table doesn't exceed four and you want to serve something special. Accompany the scallops with steamed white rice and sautéed Chinese cabbage doused with a little rice vinegar.

SAKE MARINADE/DIPPING SAUCE

2/3 cup sake

2 tablespoons light vegetable oil, such as canola

Juice of 1/2 lemon

1 tablespoon peeled and grated fresh ginger

1 clove garlic, pressed

1/4 teaspoon kosher salt

1 1/2 pounds sea scallops

12 bamboo skewers, soaked in water for 30 minutes and drained

Vegetable oil

1 tablespoon soy sauce

1. Combine the marinade ingredients in a 1-gallon zippered-top plastic bag.

2. Rinse the scallops under cold running water and blot as dry as you can. Submerge them in the marinade, seal, and let marinate in the refrigerator for 45 to 60 minutes.

3. Preheat the grill with all the burners on high for 10 minutes and the lid down.

4. While the grill is preheating, drain the marinade, reserving it. Thread the scallops through their thin side onto two parallel skewers, with the scallops' sides touching. Brush lightly with vegetable oil.

5. Pour the marinade into a small saucepan, add the soy sauce, and bring to a boil for 2 minutes. Remove from the heat and let cool.

6. Once the grill is hot, turn all the burners to medium-high. Place the skewered scallops on the grill and cook, with the lid down, for 2 to 3 minutes total, turning once. Remove the scallops from the grill as soon as they turn opaque white.

7. To serve, place the scallops on a warm platter and pass the dipping sauce separately.

SERVES 4

Creamed Grilled Scallops on Sourdough Toast

This is a special dish with a great contrast of flavors and textures, and is best enjoyed served hot off the grill. Be careful not to overcook the scallops; they can go from tender and delectable to rubbery in a matter of a couple of minutes.

WHITE SAUCE

$1^1/4$ cups milk

2 tablespoons butter

2 tablespoons all-purpose flour

$1/2$ teaspoon dry mustard

$^1/_4$ teaspoon grated lemon rind

$^1/_4$ teaspoon kosher salt

$^1/_4$ teaspoon ground white pepper

2 dashes of Tabasco sauce

1 large oval slice crusty French or Italian bread, 1 inch thick, per person, crusts cut off

2 to 3 tablespoons butter, melted

$1^1/_2$ pounds sea scallops

1 tablespoon olive oil

6 to 8 bamboo skewers, soaked in water for 30 minutes and drained

Finely chopped fresh parsley for garnish

1. Bring the milk to a simmer in a small saucepan over medium heat. In a medium-size heavy saucepan, melt the butter over low heat. Stir in the flour and cook, stirring, over medium-low heat until no longer pasty. Slowly whisk in the warm milk and bring to a simmer over low heat, whisking to prevent lumps, until thickened, 8 to 10 minutes. Add the dry mustard, grated lemon rind, salt, white pepper, and Tabasco sauce and continue to whisk for a couple more minutes. Remove from the heat.

2. Brush both sides of the bread lightly with the melted butter. Set aside.

3. Preheat the grill with all the burners on high for 10 minutes and the lid down.

4. While the grill is preheating, coat the scallops with the olive oil. Thread the scallops through their thin side onto two parallel skewers; this will keep them from spinning on the skewers when you turn them.

5. Keep the back burner on high; turn the other burners to medium. Place the scallops over the burners on medium and cook, with the lid up, for a total of 2 to 3 minutes, turning once. Do not overcook.

6. Heat the white sauce again, almost to the boiling point. Add a little more milk if the sauce is too thick.

7. Toast the slices of buttered bread directly over the medium burner, 30 to 60 seconds per side. Put a slice of toast on each plate. Place scallops on top of the toast and top with white sauce. Garnish with chopped parsley and serve immediately.

SERVES 4

Grilled Shrimp à la Scampi

Shrimp, lemon, butter, and garlic is a famous lineup. While the stovetop version is fairly rich, grilled shrimp "scampi style" is far less fattening but no less flavorful. Serve this dish with pasta tossed with a little olive oil, chopped fresh parsley, red pepper flakes, and grated Parmesan cheese.

SCAMPI MARINADE

1/2 cup extra-virgin olive oil

1/2 cup dry white wine

Juice of 1 lemon

3 to 4 large cloves garlic, to your taste, pressed

2 tablespoons minced fresh parsley

2 pounds large shrimp, shelled, deveined, and rinsed under cold running water

2 dozen bamboo skewers, soaked in water for 30 minutes and drained

1. Combine the marinade ingredients in a 1-gallon zippered-top plastic bag. Add the shrimp, making sure they are submerged, seal, and let marinate in the refrigerator for about an hour.

2. Preheat the grill with all the burners on high for 10 minutes and the lid down.

3. While the grill is preheating, thread the shrimp one at a time onto two parallel skewers, to keep them from spinning around when you turn them on the grill.

4. When the grill is hot, turn all the burners to medium-high. Place the skewered shrimp on the grill and cook, with the lid down for 3 to 4 minutes total, turning once. Do not overcook; they are done just as soon as they turn opaque throughout. Serve immediately.

SERVES 4

Bacon-Wrapped Spicy Barbecued Shrimp

This recipe has quite an assortment of flavors: shrimp stuffed with a sliver of fresh jalapeño, wrapped in bacon, and basted with barbecue sauce. It's great for a midsummer outdoor meal, served with steamed rice, a platter full of sliced ripe tomatoes, and plenty of ice-cold beer.

2 pounds large shrimp, shelled, deveined, rinsed under cold running water, and blotted dry

15 fresh jalapeños, seeded and quartered lengthwise

15 strips bacon, cut in half and partially cooked until limp to render some of the fat (don't let them get crispy)

12 bamboo skewers, soaked in water for 30 minutes and drained

Bottled tomato-based barbecue sauce of your choice

1. Cut a slit lengthwise about halfway through the back of each shrimp. Insert a jalapeño quarter into the opening. Wrap each chile-stuffed shrimp with a piece of bacon, then thread the shrimp onto two parallel skewers, to keep them from spinning when you turn them on the grill. Coat the nuggets liberally with barbecue sauce.

2. Preheat the grill with all the burners on high for 10 minutes and the lid down.

3. Once the grill is hot, turn off the center burner and turn the other burners to medium. Place the shrimp skewers over the center burner, close the lid, and cook for 4 to 5 minutes total, turning once and basting them with additional barbecue sauce if desired. Do not overcook: they are done just as soon as they turn opaque throughout. Serve immediately.

SERVES 4

Blue Thai Prawns with Green Curry Dipping Sauce

These freshwater prawns have recently started showing up at my local market. They are a nice medium size and have a fresh flavor. Remove the legs but not the body shell and tail, as they will help keep the prawns moist and intact on the grill. If you can't find prawns, regular shrimp are just fine. Serve these with the dipping sauce and Coconut Cilantro-Basmati Rice (page 344) for a very tasty meal.

1^1/$_2$ pounds blue Thai prawns or any medium-size shrimp

12 to 16 bamboo skewers, soaked in water for 30 minutes and drained

GREEN CURRY DIPPING SAUCE

One 14-ounce can unsweetened coconut milk

2 teaspoons fish sauce (look in the Asian section of the supermarket)

2 teaspoons brown sugar

2 tablespoons green Thai curry paste (look in the Asian section of the supermarket)

1.   Rinse the prawns under cold running water. Remove the legs, but not the body shell or tail. Thread the prawns onto two parallel bamboo skewers, to keep them from flipping around when you turn them.

2.   Preheat the grill with all the burners on high for 10 minutes and the lid down.

3.   While the grill heats, pour coconut milk into a medium-size saucepan and bring to a boil. Reduce the heat to medium-low, stir in the fish sauce, brown sugar, and curry paste and whisk until well blended. You can use this hot or at room temperature.

4.   With all the burners still on high, place the skewers on the grill and cook, with the lid up, just until opaque all the way through, 7 to 8 minutes total, turning once. Do not overcook.

5.   Remove the shell before dipping into the sauce.

SERVES 4

4

Poultry and Game Birds

Today's "factory-farmed" poultry bear little resemblance to the barnyard fowl of yesterday, which were raised on what they could grub in the yard, supplemented with grains. And game birds, once the exclusive quarry of the hunters, are now just another frozen food you can pick up at almost any supermarket. But what our modern birds lack in flavor, they compensate for in low cost and ready availability. And on the bright side, their blandness benefits from any number of seasonings and marinades. ✳ Anyone who has ever eaten a piece of charred "barbecued" chicken that was still red at the bone knows that grilling chicken can be tricky. Not so with the gas grill.

Bone-in poultry is ideal for cooking with indirect heat, something that a gas grill accommodates very well. After preheating the grill on high heat, simply reduce the heat to medium on one side and turn the other burners off. Place the bird over the burner that is off, close the lid, and let the grill do its work. With indirect heat, there are no worries about flare-ups and unevenly cooked meat. If you place presoaked wood chips wrapped in a perforated aluminum foil packet over the burner that is on, you will get plenty of barbecue flavor.

BETTER WITH THE SKIN ON

WHEN GRILLING ANY TYPE OF BIRD, THE SKIN KEEPS THE JUICES IN AND PREVENTS THE MEAT FROM DRYING OUT. AFTER THE MEAT IS DONE, GUESTS CAN REMOVE THE SKIN THEMSELVES IF THEY WISH.

Whole Roast Chicken
with Lemon and Garlic   111

Whole Roast Chicken
Provençal   112

Beer Can Chicken   113

Brined Spring Chicken   115

Flattened Chicken
Dijonaise   116

Flattened Whole
Chicken Boursin   117

Chicken Mediterranean   118

Chicken Chimichurri   119

Jamaican Jerked
Chicken   120

Old-Fashioned
Barbecued Chicken   121

Tandoori Chicken   122

Southwestern Chicken   124

Chicken in
Zinfandel Marinade
with Grilled Onions
and Mushrooms   125

Grilled Curried Chicken   126

Chicken in Fresh Herb
Marinade   127

Pesto Chicken Breasts   129

Chicken Breasts
Marsala   130

Chicken Breasts
with Thai Lemongrass
Marinade   131

Chicken Breasts with
Chèvre and Yellow
Pepper Puree   132

Chickalone   133

Boneless Chicken Breasts
with Fresh Herb Butter   135

Grilled Chicken Fajitas   136

Skewered Chicken
Teriyaki   137

Grilled Chinese-Style
Chicken Salad   138

Thunder Thighs   140

Spicy Apple-Lime
Chicken Thighs   141

Hot and Spicy Chinese
Chicken Wings   142

Chicken Burgers   143

Whole Roast Turkey   144

Flattened Turkey
with Sausage   145

Mexican Fiesta Turkey   146

Teriyaki Turkey Breast   148

Turkey Tonnato   148

Beau Monde
Turkey Breast   151

Prosciutto-Wrapped
Turkey Brochettes with
Marsala Sauce   152

Ginger-Garlic Turkey
Brochettes   153

Cumin Turkey Breast
Tenders in Pita   154

Sage Turkey Burgers   156

Herbed Mustard
Cornish Game Hens   157

Sweet Chinese
Cornish Game Hens   158

Quartered Duckling
with Fig and Green
Olive Sauce   159

Peking Duck Breasts   160

Duck Breasts with
Tuscan Rub   162

Pancetta-Wrapped
Grilled Quail   163

Grilled Pheasant   164

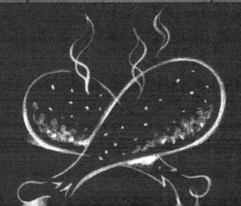

Flattening the Bird for Even Cooking

You'll get very good results with whole birds if you flatten them before grilling. By doing so, you create a piece of meat of uniform thickness that will cook more evenly. If you are going to marinate the bird, flatten it before putting it into the marinade. Here's how it's done.

1. Place the bird on a cutting board, breast side up. With a heavy chef's knife, cleaver, or pair of poultry shears, cut through the ribs on one side, as close to the backbone as possible. Make a second cut on the other side of the backbone, again as close to the backbone as possible. Remove the backbone completely.

2. Turn the bird breast side down and spread the rib cage apart. If you make a notch in the end of the breastbone near the wishbone, it will be easier to spread the rib cage.

3. Turn the bird over and flatten it with the heel of your hand. Expect some of the rib bones to break.

4. Make a slit in the bird's skin near the edge of each breast and tuck in the legs. Fold the wing tips under the wings.

The bird is now ready for marinating or cooking.

Marinating

Chicken, which is plain tasting, benefits a great deal from marinating, especially the skinless, boneless breasts. Remember to combine marinade ingredients in a nonreactive bowl or baking dish, such as one made of glass, stainless steel, or ceramic. A zippered-top plastic bag also works very well. Unless a recipe specifies a very brief period of marinating (less than 20 minutes), refrigerate the poultry in the marinade, taking it out of the refrigerator about 20 minutes before grilling.

Judging Doneness

Poultry should be cooked to medium, the point at which the juices near the joints run clear, instead of pink, after you insert the tip of a sharp knife into the thickest part of the meat or near the joint between the leg and the thigh. On an instant-read meat thermometer, the internal temperature should read between 170° and 185°F. A whole bird will continue to cook after it is removed from the heat, so it is generally safe to take an unstuffed bird off the grill when the internal temperature of the breast reaches 170°F or the thickest part of the thigh measures 180°F. Cover it with aluminum foil, then wait 10 minutes before carving a whole bird, to allow it to finish cooking and to let the flesh reabsorb its juices.

Choosing the Right Bird for the Job

CHICKEN

In general, the best chickens for the grill are the youngest. And if you can find them, always favor a free-range chicken over a factory-raised bird: its superior flavor is worth the extra cost and shopping effort. Approximately $2^1/2$ to 3 pounds of dressed (bone-in) chicken will feed 4 people.

The youngest chickens are called spring chickens or *poussins*. They are about 35 days old and weigh from 1 to $1^1/2$ pounds. They are excellent for the grill, especially when flattened. Broiler-fryers are young chickens, at least 45 days old, and weigh $2^1/2$ to 5 pounds. They are also superb for the grill.

Beyond fryers are young roasters and stewing and baking hens, all of which need long, slow, moist cooking or stewing to tenderize their tough flesh. They are not generally recommended for grilling.

TURKEY

When shopping for a turkey, look for a bird that is broad and plump rather than tall and scrawny. As a general rule, hens are always favored over toms, and the hen's skin should be pearly white rather than bluish. Count on about 1 pound of whole, dressed turkey per person, which means that a 16-pound turkey will feed 16 people.

If the turkey comes with a thermometer in the breast, don't rely on it for grilling. Use your own meat thermometer, inserting it into the thickest part of the turkey thigh, where it meets the body. The turkey will be done when the thermometer registers 180° to 185°F. In a whole or half turkey breast, the internal temperature should reach 170°F.

ROCK CORNISH GAME HENS

Rock Cornish game hens are a cross between Cornish gamecocks and White Rock hens. They are generally available only frozen and weigh between 1 and $1^1/2$ pounds. One game hen will feed one big eater, or two with more modest appetites.

Rock Cornish game hens are easiest to grill if they have been flattened first (see page 108), then marinated. Cornish game hens should be cooked to 170°F, at which point the juices run clear (instead of pink) when you insert the tip of a sharp knife into the thickest part of the thigh. If you're using a meat thermometer, that part of the thigh—where it joins the body—is also where you should insert the thermometer.

DUCK, QUAIL, AND PHEASANT

Unless you count some hunters in your circle of friends, you'll most likely find these game birds only in a supermarket freezer. All three are excellent cooked on the grill.

In general, these three game birds have richer, darker flesh than chicken: Quail is the mildest and goose is the richest. Though most people prefer their poultry cooked well done, there is a current trend to cook both quail and duck (especially the breast meat) only to the point where the meat is still translucent all the way to the bone.

POULTRY SAFETY

WHEN IT COMES TO POULTRY, ESPECIALLY THAWING IT AND CLEANING UP AFTER PREPPING IT, A CLICHÉ SAYS IT BEST: BETTER SAFE THAN SORRY. SALMONELLA BACTERIA ARE KILLED AT 140°F, SO THE REAL HEALTH RISKS COME NOT WITH A BIRD COOKED TO 170°F, BUT AT THE BEGINNING STAGES OF PREPARING POULTRY.

SLOW DEFROSTING IN THE REFRIGERATOR IS THE PREFERRED METHOD WITH ANY FROZEN POULTRY. A FROZEN CHICKEN MAY TAKE 2 TO 3 DAYS TO DEFROST; A TURKEY UP TO 3 TO 4 DAYS. ALL POULTRY SHOULD BE THOROUGHLY DEFROSTED BEFORE COOKING—MAKE SURE THAT THERE ARE NO ICE CRYSTALS IN THE CAVITY AND NO FROZEN AREAS IN THE BREAST MEAT.

THOROUGHLY RINSE BOTH DEFROSTED AND FRESH POULTRY IN WATER BEFORE COOKING. AFTER CUTTING OR DEBONING, WASH ALL UTENSILS, INCLUDING THE CUTTING BOARD AND KITCHEN TOWELS, IN HOT, SOAPY WATER.

DO NOT LEAVE UNCOOKED POULTRY—IN MARINADE OR NOT—OUT OF THE REFRIGERATOR FOR LONGER THAN 30 MINUTES BEFORE COOKING.

MARINADES USED FOR RAW POULTRY SHOULD NEVER BE REUSED, BECAUSE BLOOD FROM THE RAW MEAT WILL HAVE LEACHED INTO THE MARINADE, POSING A RISK OF SALMONELLA POISONING. BEFORE USING THE MARINADE AS A BASTING SAUCE, BRING IT TO A BOIL FOR 2 MINUTES TO KILL OFF ANY BACTERIA.

Whole Roast Chicken with Lemon and Garlic

Some recipes follow the inverse rule of cooking: The simpler the recipe, the more flavorful the results. Take this recipe, for example: It's simplicity itself and yet the outcome is uniquely delicious. Once you try this method of roasting a chicken, you'll probably make it a staple in your culinary repertoire.

One 3- to 4-pound chicken

1 lemon

12 cloves garlic, peeled

Extra-virgin olive oil

Kosher salt and freshly ground black pepper to taste

Chopped fresh parsley and lemon wedges for garnish (optional)

1. Wash the chicken inside and out under cold running water, removing the excess fat, gizzards, heart, liver, and so on. Pat the bird dry with paper towels. Using a skewer or a knitting needle, pierce the lemon several times all around and insert it into the cavity of the chicken. Arrange the garlic cloves around the lemon in the cavity. Force the wings of the chicken under the back to hold them in place. Using a piece of cotton string, tie the legs together tightly, gathering up the tail of the bird in between the two legs as you tighten the string. Rub the outside of the chicken with olive oil and dust with salt and pepper.

2. Preheat the grill with all the burners on high for 10 minutes and the lid down.

3. Once the grill is hot, turn off the center burner and turn the other burners to medium. Place the chicken breast side up over the center burner, close the lid, and cook until the juices run clear at the thigh and an instant-read meat thermometer registers 170°F when inserted into the breast, 55 to 75 minutes.

4. When the bird is done, transfer it to a serving platter, loosely tent with aluminum foil, and let sit for 10 minutes before carving. Garnish each plate of sliced chicken with parsley and lemon wedges if desired, and serve.

SERVES 4 TO 6

Whole Roast Chicken Provençal

A perfectly roasted chicken—skin brown and crisp on the outside, meat tender and moist on the inside—is one of the simplest and best meals ever devised. Though a whole chicken can be somewhat difficult to handle on the grill, a whole chicken that has been flattened is decidedly not. Flattening a chicken, or any poultry, from a quail to a turkey, is easy. If you don't feel up to it yourself, ask your butcher to do it for you. This country meal is delicious served with White Onion Kebabs with Rosemary and Balsamic Vinegar (page 300) and grilled potatoes.

One 3- to 4-pound chicken

PROVENÇAL MARINADE

3/4 cup dry white wine

1/2 cup extra-virgin olive oil

1 tablespoon dried herbes de Provence (available at most large supermarkets and specialty food shops)

Juice of 1 lemon

1 teaspoon kosher salt

1 teaspoon freshly ground black pepper

Chopped fresh parsley and lemon wedges for garnish (optional)

1. Flatten the chicken according to the directions on page 108, or ask your butcher to do it for you. Wash the bird under cold running water and pat dry with paper towels.

2. Combine the marinade ingredients in a 1-gallon zippered-top plastic bag. Place the chicken in the marinade, turning to coat well, seal, and let marinate in the refrigerator for at least 4 to 6 hours or overnight if desired.

3. Preheat the grill with all the burners on high for 10 minutes and the lid down.

4. While the grill is preheating, drain the marinade into a small saucepan. Bring to a boil for 2 minutes, remove from the heat, and set aside for basting.

5. Once the grill is hot, turn off the center burner and turn the other burners to medium. Place the chicken, breast side up, over the center burner, close the lid, and cook until the juices run clear at the thigh and an instant-read meat thermometer registers 170°F when inserted into the breast, 55 to 75 minutes. Turn the bird every 15 minutes, basting with the boiled marinade.

6. Transfer to a serving platter, loosely tent with aluminum foil, and let it rest for 10 minutes before carving. Garnish each plate of sliced chicken with parsley and lemon wedges if desired, and serve.

SERVES 4 TO 6

Beer Can Chicken

Almost like an urban myth, the idea of beer can chicken swept around the country a couple of years ago. An admittedly strange concept, it does indeed work, producing a very moist, flavorful whole chicken. I had my doubts about whether or not the procedure could be accomplished on a gas grill, but was pleasantly surprised at how easily and well it worked.

One 4- to 5-pound chicken

1/4 cup dry rub, store-bought variety of your choice or homemade version (recipe follows)

One 12-ounce can beer

1. Rinse the chicken inside and out under cold running water. Remove the giblets and excess fat from the body cavity. Blot as dry as you can with paper towels. Dust liberally inside and out with the dry rub.

2. Preheat the grill with all the burners on high for 10 minutes and the lid down.

3. Open the can of beer and pour off about 1/2 cup. Make additional holes in the top of the can using a beer-can opener. Holding the chicken upright (legs down), insert the beer can into the chicken's cavity.

4. Leave the back burner on high; turn the other burners to low. Position the chicken over the burners on low, with the back of the chicken facing the burner on high. The combination of the can and the chicken's legs acts like a tripod; carefully arranging the legs will result in a stable position for the chicken. Close the lid. With an instant-read thermometer, check the temperature of the chicken after about 50 minutes, inserting it into the thickest part of the breast, without touching a bone. The chicken will be done when the juices run clear when it is pierced at the thigh with the tip of a sharp knife and the internal temperature is 170°F in the breast and 180°F in the thickest part of the thigh.

5. Remove the chicken from the grill; carefully remove and discard the beer can. Transfer to a platter and loosely tent with aluminum foil for 10 minutes, then carve into pieces and serve immediately.

SERVES 4

SPICY BARBECUE DRY RUB

Adjust the ingredient amounts or add or subtract ingredients as you wish. For instance, if you cannot abide spicy food, reduce or eliminate the cayenne.

4 tablespoons paprika

2 tablespoons chili powder

2 tablespoons ground cumin

2 tablespoons dark brown sugar

2 tablespoons kosher salt

1 tablespoon ground oregano

1 tablespoon granulated sugar

1 tablespoon ground black pepper

1 tablespoon ground white pepper

2 teaspoons cayenne pepper

Mix all ingredients in small bowl.

MAKES ABOUT 1 CUP

Brined Spring Chicken

The term *spring chicken* isn't used much anymore. Essentially a baby chicken, weighing in at 1½ to 2 pounds, you may encounter it marketed as *pollito* or by the French term, *poussin*. Whatever you call them, they're tender and delicious, especially when grilled. You can safely count on one bird feeding two people. The easiest way to grill them is to cut out the backbone and rib cage and flatten them with the heel of your hand (or ask your butcher to do it for you). Brining adds an extra dimension of flavor and firms the flesh slightly—just don't overdo it or you'll overwhelm the delicate flavor of the chicken.

BRINE

6 cups water

³/4 cup kosher salt

³/4 cup sugar

1 baby chicken (1¹/2 to 2 pounds), butterflied as described above

2 tablespoons vegetable oil

1 tablespoons dried fines herbes or herbes de Provence

Freshly ground black pepper to taste

1. Combine the brine ingredients in a large bowl and stir until the salt and sugar dissolve. Add the flattened chicken, cover, and allow to brine in the refrigerator for 3 to 4 hours.

2. Preheat the grill with all the burners on high for 10 minutes and the lid down.

3. Remove the chicken from the brine; do not rinse. Pat dry with paper towels. Coat both sides of the chicken with the vegetable oil; dust with the herbs and pepper.

4. Turn off the center burner and turn the other burners to medium. Place the chicken, breast side up, over the center burner, close the lid, and grill just until cooked through, a total of 20 to 25 minutes, turning once midway. Transfer to a platter and loosely tent with aluminum foil for at least 10 minutes before serving.

SERVES 2

Flattened Chicken Dijonaise

Small, young chickens (around 2 to 2 1/2 pounds) are perfect for this dish. Flattened chickens are not only easier to handle on the grill than unflattened ones, but are also harder to under- or overcook than those cut into pieces. With the bones and skin intact, the end result is a more succulent, flavorful bird. Serve with Skewered Herbed Potatoes (page 307) and Grilled Pesto Tomatoes (page 314).

2 small chickens (each 2 to 2 1/2 pounds)

DIJONAISE MARINADE

1/2 cup dry white wine or dry vermouth

1/3 cup extra-virgin olive oil

Juice of 1 lemon

2 to 3 cloves garlic, to your taste, minced

3 tablespoons Dijon mustard

2 teaspoons freshly ground black pepper

1. Flatten the chickens according to the directions on page 108, or ask your butcher to do it for you. Wash the birds under cold running water and pat them dry with paper towels.

2. In a large nonreactive container, combine the marinade ingredients. Place the chickens in the marinade, turning several times to coat thoroughly. Cover and let marinate in the refrigerator for at least 1 and up to 4 hours.

3. Preheat the grill with all the burners on high for 10 minutes and the lid down.

4. Once the grill is hot, turn off the center burner and turn the other burners to medium. Place the chickens, breast sides up, over the center burner, close the lid, and cook until the juices run clear when they are pierced at the thighs with the tip of a sharp knife and an instant-read meat thermometer inserted into the breasts registers 170°F, 35 to 45 minutes, turning them every 10 minutes or so.

5. Transfer to a carving board, loosely tent with aluminum foil, and let rest for 10 minutes. Use a sharp butcher knife or cleaver to cut each chicken along the breastbone into two equal halves.

SERVES 4

Flattened Whole Chicken Boursin

Boursin cheese made the scene about a decade ago and became quite popular. Then came the flood of artisanal cheeses from around the world, eclipsing Boursin's garlicky, flavorful appeal. Luckily, it's still widely available and does amazing things for your ordinary, store-bought chicken.

One 4- to 5-pound chicken

One 5.2-ounce round Boursin cheese

1 tablespoon olive oil

Kosher salt and freshly ground black pepper to taste

1. Rinse the chicken under cold running water and blot dry with paper towels. Using poultry shears, cut along the middle of both sides of the rib cage, along the entire length of the chicken. Discard the backbone and rib cage portions. Turn the chicken over and, using the heel of your hand, press hard on the breastbone of the chicken; you should hear a few cracks as the chicken "flattens." Loosen the skin over the top of the chicken and drumsticks using a sharp paring knife and your fingers, starting at the point where the chicken's neck used to be. Be careful not to cut or tear the skin.

2. Remove the Boursin from the refrigerator. Unwrap, place in a small bowl, and work the cheese with a fork until it's easy to spread. Carefully spoon the cheese under the skin of the chicken, pressing with your fingers to distribute it evenly over the chicken and drumsticks.

3. Preheat the grill with all the burners on high for 10 minutes and the lid down.

4. Coat the outside of the chicken with the olive oil. Dust liberally with salt and pepper.

5. Turn off the center burner and turn the other burners to medium. Place the chicken over the center burner, skin side up, close the lid, and cook until it is nicely browned and the legs move easily up and down, $1^{1}/4$ to $1^{1}/2$ hours, turning the chicken every 20 minutes or so.

6. Transfer to a platter and loosely tent with aluminum foil for 10 minutes, then cut the chicken into quarters and serve immediately.

SERVES 4

Chicken Mediterranean

Brining greatly improves the texture and flavor of any chicken. In this recipe, the brining process replaces marinating the chicken, and the Mediterranean dressing, applied after the chicken is grilled, adds the distinctive flavor.

BRINE

6 cups water

$3/4$ cup kosher salt

$3/4$ cup sugar

One 3- to 4-pound chicken, cut into serving pieces

MEDITERRANEAN DRESSING

$1/4$ cup fresh lemon juice

2 tablespoons red wine vinegar

2 cloves garlic, pressed

1 tablespoon chopped fresh dill

1 tablespoon chopped fresh mint

1 teaspoon red pepper flakes

$1/2$ teaspoon kosher salt

$1/3$ cup extra-virgin olive oil

$1/2$ cup crumbled feta cheese

2 to 3 tablespoons vegetable oil

1. Combine the brine ingredients in a large bowl, stirring until the salt and sugar dissolve. Add the chicken to the brine and let sit in the refrigerator for 3 to 4 hours.

2. Meanwhile, whisk together the lemon juice, vinegar, garlic, dill, mint, red pepper, and salt. While whisking, slowly drizzle in the olive oil. Stir in the feta. Refrigerate until needed.

3. Preheat the grill with all the burners on high for 10 minutes and the lid down.

4. Remove the chicken from brine; do not rinse. Pat dry with paper towels. Coat both sides of the chicken with the vegetable oil.

5. Once the grill is hot, turn off the center burner and turn the other burners to medium. Place the chicken over the center burner, close the lid, and cook until the juices run clear and the internal temperature registers 180°F in the thickest part of the thighs and 170°F in the breasts when tested with an instant-read thermometer, 30 to 50 minutes, turning every 10 minutes. The drumsticks and thighs will take 40 to 50 minutes and the breast and wing pieces will take 30 to 40 minutes.

6. Transfer to a platter, loosely tent with aluminum foil, and let rest at least 10 minutes. Then pour the Mediterranean dressing over the chicken and serve immediately.

SERVES 4

Chicken Chimichurri

You can quickly transform simple grilled chicken into an exotic flavor vacation with this marinade based on the Argentine chimichurri sauce. If there's anyone in your house who can't abide the flavor of cilantro, substitute an equal amount of fresh basil.

One 3^1/2- to 4-pound chicken, cut into serving pieces

CHIMICHURRI MARINADE

^{1}/2 cup red wine vinegar

^{1}/2 cup ketchup

^{1}/4 cup vegetable oil

1^1/2 tablespoons hot paprika

1 teaspoon ground cumin

1 teaspoon cayenne pepper

1 teaspoon kosher salt

1 teaspoon freshly ground black pepper

2 bay leaves

^{1}/4 cup fresh cilantro, finely chopped

4 cloves garlic, minced or pressed

1. Rinse the chicken under cold running water and place in a 1-gallon zippered-top plastic bag.

2. Combine the marinade ingredients in a measuring cup. Pour the marinade into the bag, seal, and squish around until the chicken is coated. Let marinate in the refrigerator for 2 to 4 hours.

3. Preheat the grill with all the burners on high for 10 minutes and the lid down.

4. Turn off the center burner and turn the other burners to medium. Place the chicken over the center burner, skin side up, close the lid, and cook until the juices run clear and the internal temperature registers 180°F in the thickest part of the thighs and 170°F in the breasts when tested with an instant-read thermometer, 30 to 50 minutes, turning every 10 minutes. The drumsticks and thighs will take 40 to 50 minutes and the breast and wing pieces will take 30 to 40 minutes.

5. Transfer to a platter and loosely tent with aluminum foil for 10 minutes before serving.

SERVES 4

Jamaican Jerked Chicken

Jamaican jerk is an intense seasoning: It's very spicy and usually very hot. It blends sweet spices, such as allspice and nutmeg, with fiery hot peppers. If your tastes run toward the exotic and you can stand the heat, this is a wonderful dish. Although you can find recipes for homemade Jamaican jerk seasoning, none quite compare to the marinades and rubs that are available in specialty food stores and through the mail. (One of my favorites is Walkerswood Jamaican Jerk Seasoning, from St. Ann, Jamaica, available from the gourmet foods department of (believe it or not) www.amazon.com.

One 3- to 4-pound chicken, cut into serving pieces
Bottled Jamaican jerk seasoning rub or marinade of your choice
Vegetable oil (optional)

1.   Wash the chicken parts under cold running water and pat dry with paper towels. If you are using a dry jerk seasoning, mix it with the vegetable oil in a small bowl, according to the label directions, to make a paste-like marinade. Otherwise, use the marinade straight from the bottle. Coat the chicken parts with the jerk seasoning paste or marinade, cover, and refrigerate for 1 to 3 hours.

2.   Preheat the grill with all the burners on high for 10 minutes and the lid down.

3.   Once the grill is hot, turn off the center burner and turn the other burners to medium. Place the chicken, skin side up, over the center burner, close the lid, and cook until the juices run clear and the internal temperature registers 180°F in the thickest part of the thighs and 170°F in the breasts when tested with an instant-read thermometer, 30 to 50 minutes, turning every 10 minutes. The drumsticks and thighs will take 40 to 50 minutes and the breast and wing pieces will take 30 to 40 minutes. Serve hot off the grill.

SERVES 4

DEFROSTING SAFELY

THE SAFEST WAY TO DEFROST ANY POULTRY IS TO ALLOW IT TO THAW SLOWLY AND COMPLETELY IN THE REFRIGERATOR.

Old-Fashioned Barbecued Chicken

Sometimes we need to forget what's currently fashionable and return to a favorite meal from way back when. For many people, grilled chicken with that wonderful, sticky, spicy, red barbecue sauce is one of those dishes. Served up with potato or macaroni salad and some sliced garden-fresh tomatoes—well, it's hard to beat. Even better, with a gas grill and the following instructions, you won't have to worry about burning the chicken the way your dad probably did.

One 3- to 4-pound chicken, cut into serving pieces
Bottled tomato-based barbecue sauce of your choice

1. Wash the chicken parts under cold running water and pat dry with paper towels. Pour a cup or so of the barbecue sauce into a nonreactive container, add the chicken, and turn to coat them well. Cover and refrigerate for 1 to 2 hours.

2. Preheat the grill with all the burners on high for 10 minutes and the lid down.

3. Once the grill is hot, turn off the center burner and turn the other burners to medium. Place the chicken, skin side up, over the center burner, close the lid, and cook until the juices run clear and the internal temperature registers 180°F in the thickest part of the thighs and 170°F in the breasts when tested with an instant-read thermometer, 30 to 50 minutes, turning every 10 minutes and basing with additional barbecue sauce, if desired. The drumsticks and thighs will take 40 to 50 minutes and the breast and wing pieces will take 30 to 40 minutes.

4. Serve the chicken hot off the grill, or let it cool, then refrigerate until needed. Remove from the refrigerator about 30 minutes before serving.

SERVES 4

Tandoori Chicken

The first time you make this traditional dish from India, you may wonder about the ingredients and doubt that the chicken will really turn out okay. Trust me, it will. A gas grill is particularly well suited to preparing perfectly cooked tandoori chicken, without many of the burning problems associated with charcoal grills. Serve the chicken with steamed rice and Grilled Whole Eggplant (page 288), doused with a little rice vinegar and your favorite chutney on the side.

One 3- to 4-pound chicken, cut into serving pieces and skin removed

TANDOORI MARINADE

2 cups plain yogurt

1/4 cup vegetable oil (preferably peanut oil)

2 tablespoons paprika

2 tablespoons peeled and grated fresh ginger

1 tablespoon turmeric

2 teaspoons ground cumin

1 teaspoon kosher salt

$1/8$ teaspoon cayenne pepper, or more to taste

2 large garlic cloves, pressed

Chopped fresh cilantro for garnish (optional)

1. Wash the chicken under cold running water and pat dry with paper towels. Using a sharp knife, make diagonal slices about $1/4$ inch deep across each piece, to help the marinade penetrate the meat.

2. Combine the marinade ingredients in a 1-gallon zippered-top plastic bag. Place the chicken in the marinade, turning to coat, seal, and let marinate in the refrigerator for 4 to 6 hours.

3. Preheat the grill with all the burners on high for 10 minutes and the lid down.

4. Once the grill is hot, turn the center burner off and turn the other burners to medium. Place the chicken over the center burner, close the lid, and cook until the juices run clear and the internal temperature registers 180°F in the thickest part of the thighs and 170°F in the breasts when tested with an instant-read thermometer, 30 to 50 minutes, turning every 10 minutes. The drumsticks and thighs will take 40 to 50 minutes and the breast and wing pieces will take 30 to 40 minutes. Watch closely, because the skinless meat will dry out if overcooked.

5. Transfer to a serving platter, garnish with cilantro if desired, and serve.

SERVES 4

DOUBLE-TIME DEFROSTING

NEED A QUICK DEFROST METHOD? SUBMERGE THE POULTRY IN A LARGE CONTAINER OF COLD WATER. ALLOW 30 MINUTES OF DEFROSTING TIME FOR EACH POUND, AND CHANGE THE WATER EVERY 30 MINUTES.

Southwestern Chicken

The flavors of the Southwest are authoritative and spicy; just right for chicken. Try combining this recipe with a side of Cowpoke Beans (page 357), steamed rice, and your favorite salsa.

One 3- to 4-pound chicken, cut into serving pieces

SOUTHWESTERN MARINADE

1/4 cup fresh lime juice

1/4 cup apple juice

1/4 cup vegetable oil

2 teaspoons chili powder (hot or mild)

2 cloves garlic, pressed

Chopped fresh cilantro for garnish (optional)

1. Wash the chicken under cold running water and pat dry with paper towels.

2. Combine the marinade ingredients in a 1-gallon zippered-top plastic bag. Place the chicken in the marinade, turning to coat well, seal, and let marinate in the refrigerator for 4 to 6 hours.

3. Preheat the grill with all the burners on high for 10 minutes and the lid down.

4. While the grill is preheating, drain the marinade into a small saucepan. Bring to a boil for 2 minutes, remove from the heat, and set aside for basting.

5. Once the grill is hot, turn off the center burner and the other burners to medium. Place the chicken, skin side up, over the center burner, close the lid, and cook until the juices run clear and the internal temperature registers 180°F in the thickest part of the thighs and 170°F in the breasts when tested with an instant-read thermometer, 30 to 50 minutes, turning every 10 minutes, and basting with the boiled marinade. The drumsticks and thighs will take 40 to 50 minutes and the breast and wing pieces will take 30 to 40 minutes.

6. Transfer to a serving platter, garnish with cilantro if desired, and serve.

SERVES 4

Chicken in Zinfandel Marinade with Grilled Onions and Mushrooms

This recipe for grilled marinated chicken was inspired by the famous French country dish *coq au vin*. The hearty flavors are great for fall and winter dining. Serve with buttered, parsleyed noodles or brown rice and Garlicky Grilled Tomatoes (page 313).

One 3- to 4-pound chicken, cut into serving pieces

ZINFANDEL MARINADE

3/4 cup Zinfandel wine

3 tablespoons extra-virgin olive oil

2 cloves garlic, pressed

1 tablespoon Dijon mustard

1/2 teaspoon dried thyme

1/4 teaspoon freshly ground black pepper

1 pound fresh mushrooms, wiped clean and stems trimmed

1 pound small white boiling onions, peeled

2 dozen bamboo skewers, soaked in water for 30 minutes and drained

Chopped fresh parsley for garnish (optional)

1. Wash the chicken under cold running water and pat dry with paper towels.

2. Combine the marinade ingredients in a 1-gallon zippered-top plastic bag. Add the chicken, mushrooms, and onions, turning to coat everything well, seal, and let marinate in the refrigerator for 2 to 3 hours or overnight.

3. Preheat the grill with all the burners on high for 10 minutes and the lid down.

4. While the grill is preheating, thread the mushrooms onto one set of skewers and the onions onto another.

5. Once the grill is hot, turn off the center burner and turn the other burners to medium. Place the chicken, skin side up, over the center burner; position the skewered mushrooms and onions next to it. Close the lid and cook, turning the skewers after 5 minutes. The mushrooms will be done in 8 to 12 minutes, the onions in 15 to 20 minutes. When the vegetables are done, remove them from the grill and keep warm. Continue to grill the chicken until the juices run clear and the internal temperature registers 180°F in the thickest part of the thighs and 170°F in the breasts when tested with an instant-read thermometer, 30 to 50 minutes, turning every 10 minutes.

6. Serve the chicken hot off the grill, along with the mushrooms and onions. Garnish each serving with a little parsley if desired.

SERVES 4

Grilled Curried Chicken

Using an intensely flavored dry rub, such as this curry combination, is a great way to flavor chicken in a hurry. The taste will be improved if you rub the chicken parts with the curry, then allow them to "marinate" in the refrigerator for a couple of hours before grilling.

One 3- to 4-pound chicken, cut into serving pieces

CURRY DRY RUB

3 tablespoons curry powder

1 teaspoon sweet paprika

1/2 teaspoon ground white pepper

1/4 teaspoon kosher salt

Chopped fresh cilantro for garnish (optional)

Chutney (optional)

1. Wash the chicken under cold running water and pat dry with paper towels.

2. Combine the dry rub ingredients in a large bowl. Add the chicken and cover with the rub. If time allows, refrigerate the coated chicken, covered with plastic wrap, for 1 to 2 hours.

3. Preheat the grill with all the burners on high for 10 minutes and the lid down.

4. Once the grill is hot, turn off the center burner and turn the other burners to medium. Place the chicken, skin side up, over the center burner, close the lid, and cook until the juices run clear and the internal temperature registers 180°F in the thickest part of the thighs and 170°F in the breasts when tested with an instant-read thermometer, 30 to 50 minutes, turning every 10 minutes. The drumsticks and thighs will take 40 to 50 minutes and the breast and wing pieces will take 30 to 40 minutes.

5. Transfer to a serving platter, then garnish with cilantro and pass a jar of chutney at the table if desired.

SERVES 4

Chicken in Fresh Herb Marinade

If you have an herb garden, this dish is for you. Anytime from late summer to early fall, when the plants are in their full glory, pluck a handful of this and a handful of that. Serve the chicken with Rosemary Potato Wedges (page 307) and Mixed Vegetable Brochettes (page 318).

One 3- to 4-pound chicken, cut into serving pieces

FRESH HERB MARINADE

2/3 cup dry white wine or dry vermouth, for a slightly stronger, more complex flavor

1/3 cup extra-virgin olive oil

Juice of 1 lemon

3 tablespoons chopped fresh basil

3 tablespoons chopped fresh parsley

1 teaspoon chopped fresh rosemary

1 teaspoon chopped fresh thyme

1 teaspoon freshly ground black pepper

Lemon wedges for garnish (optional)

1. Wash the chicken under cold running water and pat dry with paper towels.

2. Combine the marinade ingredients in a 1-gallon zippered-top plastic bag. Place the chicken in the marinade, turning to coat, seal, and let marinate in the refrigerator for 2 to 3 hours or overnight if desired.

3. Preheat the grill with all the burners on high for 10 minutes and the lid down.

4. While the grill is preheating, drain the marinade into a small saucepan. Bring to a boil for 2 minutes, remove from the heat, and set aside for basting.

5. Once the grill is hot, turn off the center burner and turn the other burners to medium. Place the chicken, skin side up, over the center burner, close the lid, and cook until the juices run clear and the internal temperature registers 180°F in the thickest part of the thighs and 170°F in the breasts when tested with an instant-read thermometer, 30 to 50 minutes, turning every 10 minutes and basting with the boiled marinade if desired. The drumsticks and thighs will take 40 to 50 minutes and the breast and wing pieces will take 30 to 40 minutes.

6. Transfer to a serving platter, garnish with lemon wedges if desired, and serve.

SERVES 4

Pesto Chicken Breasts

Pesto, that legendary Italian concoction of basil, garlic, and pine nuts, imparts a wonderful pungent flavor to chicken, especially when it is spread under the skin of the chicken breasts. Excellent ready-made pesto is available in your grocer's refrigerator case, or you can make your own.

4 bone-in, skin-on chicken breast halves

1 recipe Pesto (see page 314)

Extra-virgin olive oil

Freshly ground black pepper to taste

1.   Preheat the grill with all the burners on high for 10 minutes and the lid down.

2.   While the grill is preheating, wash the chicken under cold running water and pat dry with paper towels. Lift the skin from one end of a breast; using your fingers, separate the skin from the breast meat, but do not remove it. Spread a tablespoon or so of the pesto in an even layer between the skin and the meat. Repeat with the remaining breasts and pesto. Rub the surface of the chicken with olive oil and sprinkle with pepper.

3.   Once the grill is hot, turn off the center burner and turn the other burners to medium. Place the chicken, skin side up, over the center burner, close the lid, and cook until opaque all the way through but still juicy, 25 to 35 minutes, turning the pieces every 15 minutes. Serve hot off the grill.

SERVES 4

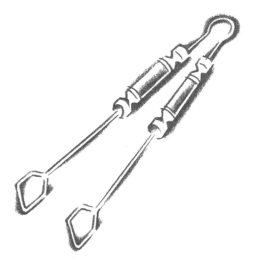

Chicken Breasts Marsala

Marsala, a fortified wine from Sicily, may be somewhat out of favor these days, but its intense, semisweet flavor adds a unique dimension to this dish. For the best quality, look for wine labeled *Superiore*.

Although these chicken breasts serve only four people, adaptations of this and other chicken breast recipes are ideal for large buffet gatherings. Because chicken breasts are uniform in size and thickness, they all cook in about the same length of time.

4 bone-in, skin-on chicken breast halves

MARSALA MARINADE

3/4 cup Marsala wine

3 tablespoons extra-virgin olive oil

1/4 teaspoon kosher salt

1/4 teaspoon freshly ground black pepper

4 Swiss cheese slices

Chopped fresh parsley for garnish (optional)

1. Wash the chicken under cold running water and pat dry with paper towels.

2. Combine the marinade ingredients in a 1-gallon zippered-top plastic bag. Add the chicken, turning to coat, seal, and let marinate in the refrigerator for 2 to 3 hours.

3. Preheat the grill with all the burners on high for 10 minutes and the lid down.

4. Once the grill is hot, turn off the center burner and turn the other burners to medium. Place the chicken, skin side up, over the center burner, close the lid, and cook until opaque all the way through but still juicy, 25 to 35 minutes, turning every 15 minutes.

5. About 10 minutes before the end of the cooking time, turn the breasts skin side up and top each one with a slice of Swiss cheese (folded in half, if necessary). Allow the cheese to melt and bubble slightly.

6. Serve the chicken hot off the grill, garnished with parsley if desired.

SERVES 4

Chicken Breasts with Thai Lemongrass Marinade

The bright, complex flavors of Thai cooking rely on, among other things, a combination of sweet and sour flavors. This marinade is a classic example and gives chicken breasts a big boost in the flavor department. Adjust the amount of fresh jalapeños up or down, depending on your tolerance of "heat." If you have trouble finding the lemongrass, fish sauce, and Thai sweet chili sauce in the Asian section of your supermarket, check at an Asian grocery, if there is one near you.

4 to 6 skin-on boneless chicken breast halves

THAI LEMONGRASS MARINADE

1/2 cup Thai sweet chili sauce

1/2 cup beer

1/2 cup chopped fresh cilantro

1/4 cup fresh lime juice

1/4 cup fish sauce

3 cloves garlic, pressed or sliced

2 jalapeños, seeded and thinly sliced

3 stalks fresh lemongrass, bottom third only, thinly sliced

1 shallot, thinly sliced

1 tablespoon peeled and chopped fresh ginger

1/2 teaspoon freshly ground black pepper

1. Rinse the chicken under cold running water, blot dry with paper towels, and place in a 1-gallon zippered-top plastic bag.

2. Combine the marinade ingredients in a large measuring cup, pour into the bag, seal, and squish around until the chicken is coated. Let marinate in the refrigerator for 2 to 3 hours.

3. Preheat the grill with all the burners on high for 10 minutes and the lid down.

4. When the grill is hot, turn all the burners to medium. Place the chicken on the grill, skin side up, and close the lid. Cook until opaque all the way through but still juicy, 8 to 12 minutes total, turning midway. Let rest on a platter for 10 minutes, tented with aluminum foil, before serving.

SERVES 2 TO 3

Chicken Breasts with Chèvre and Yellow Pepper Puree

This is another easy-to-prepare dish that falls into the "fancy" category. The flavors are so special and fresh that diners can't help sitting up and taking notice. I've pureed a few peppers in my time, but never just yellow ones. I was completely surprised by their unique, delicious flavor. If you have any sauce left over, it's great on pasta!

YELLOW PEPPER PUREE

3 large yellow bell peppers

2 tablespoon olive oil

1 tablespoon sherry vinegar

6 large fresh basil leaves

1/4 teaspoon kosher salt

4 skin-on boneless chicken breast halves (about 2 pounds), rinsed and patted dry

1 tablespoon olive oil

Kosher salt and freshly ground black pepper to taste

1 log plain chèvre cheese (about 8 ounces)

1. Preheat the grill with all the burners on high for 10 minutes and the lid down.

2. Rinse the peppers under cold running water. With all the burners on high, place the whole peppers on the grill, close the lid, and cook about 20 minutes, turning the peppers every 5 minutes or so. The goal is to completely char the outside of the peppers on all sides. Once charred, place the peppers in a double grocery sack and tightly curl the top. Allow peppers to steam in the sack for 10 minutes. Remove the peppers from the sack. Using a sharp paring knife, remove the stems, seeds, and skins from the peppers.

3. In a blender, combine the roasted peppers, olive oil, vinegar, basil, and salt and blend on low until smooth. Pour into a bowl and set aside.

4. Coat the chicken with the oil; dust with salt and pepper.

5. Turn all the burners to medium. Place the chicken on the grill, skin side up, close the lid, and cook until opaque all the way through but still juicy, 8 to 12 minutes total, turning once midway through.

6. Cut the chèvre into $3/8$-inch-thick rounds.

7. Let the chicken rest on a platter for 10 minutes, tented with aluminum foil, before carving into $3/8$-inch-thick slices. On a serving platter, interleave the slices of chicken with the slices of chèvre. Top with the yellow pepper puree and serve immediately.

SERVES 4

Chickalone

Did you hear the one about the chicken that got turned into an abalone? No, it's no joke: My friend Marsha Maher—one of the best cooks I've ever encountered—let me in on the ultra-secret procedure, gleaned, she seemed to remember, from some magazine in the 1950s. You simply pound boneless, skinless chicken breasts to a more-or-less even thickness, then marinate them in bottled clam juice—nothing more, nothing less—overnight in the refrigerator. Abracadabra: abalone! Well, not exactly, but it's darn close, and the clam juice does something magical to the texture of the chicken. Seeing is deceiving; tasting is believing.

4 boneless, skinless chicken breast halves (about 1 pound)

One 8-ounce bottle clam juice

1 tablespoon vegetable oil

Ground white pepper to taste

Sweet paprika to taste

EXTRAS

Finely chopped fresh parsley

Lemon wedges (optional)

Tartar sauce (optional)

1. Rinse the chicken under cold running water and pat dry with paper towels. Place the breasts between two sheets of waxed paper and pound, using the flat side of a cleaver, until they are of a more or less even thickness.

2. Pour the clam juice into a 1-quart zippered-top plastic bag. Add the chicken, seal, squish around to coat them, and let marinate in the refrigerator overnight or up to 24 hours.

3. Preheat the grill with all the burners on high for 10 minutes and the lid down.

4. Remove the chicken from the marinade and pat dry with paper towels. Coat the chicken evenly with the vegetable oil and dust lightly with the white pepper and paprika.

5. When the grill is hot, turn all the burners to medium. Place the chicken on the grill, close the lid, and cook until opaque all the way through but still juicy, 8 to 10 minutes total, turning once midway.

6. Serve garnished with chopped parsley, with lemon wedges and tartar sauce on the side if desired.

SERVES 4

KEEP IT CLEAN

AFTER CUTTING UP RAW POULTRY, ALWAYS CLEAN YOUR UTENSILS, CUTTING BOARDS, AND WORK SURFACES WITH HOT, SOAPY WATER. DOUSE YOUR WOODEN CUTTING AND CARVING BOARDS WITH A LITTLE CHLORINE BLEACH EVERY COUPLE OF WEEKS TO KEEP THEM CLEAN AND FREE FROM HARMFUL BACTERIA.

Boneless Chicken Breasts with Fresh Herb Butter

With the recent interest in lighter cooking, boneless, skinless chicken breasts fit right in. They cook up in a flash on the grill and are easy to combine with other low-calorie, low-fat side dishes, such as steamed white rice and steamed vegetables. Of course, the fresh herb butter in this recipe contributes some fat, but you don't need to use much to add a lot of flavor.

FRESH HERB BUTTER

1/2 cup minced mixed fresh basil, parsley, and chives

1/4 cup (1/2 stick) butter, at room temperature

1 tablespoon fresh lemon juice

4 boneless, skinless chicken breast halves

Vegetable oil

Kosher salt and freshly ground black pepper to taste

1. Combine the flavored butter ingredients in a small bowl and mix well with a fork. Let stand at room temperature for 1 hour.

2. Wash the chicken under cold running water and pat dry with paper towels. Rub each one with vegetable oil and sprinkle on both sides with salt and pepper.

3. Preheat the grill with all the burners on high for 10 minutes and the lid down.

4. Once the grill is hot, turn off the center burner and turn the other burners to medium. Place the chicken over the center burner, close the lid, and cook until opaque all the way through but still juicy, 8 to 10 minutes total, turning once.

5. Transfer to a serving platter, spoon a dollop of fresh herb butter on top of each breast, and serve.

SERVES 4

DON'T STICK TO THE GRILL

PREHEATING THE GRILL BEFORE YOU BEGIN COOKING HELPS ENSURE THAT FOOD WON'T STICK TO IT.

Grilled Chicken Fajitas

Not that long ago, fajitas were fairly exotic fare. Today, after being popularized by so many restaurants, fajitas have found their way into many a home cook's repertoire—and for good reason: They're delicious, they're relatively low in fat, and everyone, including kids, seems to love them.

6 boneless, skinless chicken breast halves

FAJITA MARINADE

1/2 cup vegetable oil

1/2 cup beer

Juice of 2 limes

2 cloves garlic, pressed

1/4 cup chopped onion

1 tablespoon chili powder

2 teaspoons ground cumin

1 teaspoon dried oregano, crumbled

1 teaspoon kosher salt

1 teaspoon freshly ground black pepper

6 soft flour tortillas

3 green bell peppers

Tomato slices

Diced red onion

Avocado slices (optional)

Chopped fresh cilantro

Salsa of your choice

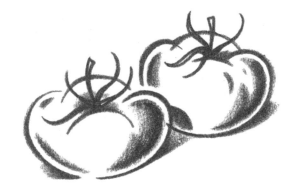

1. Wash the chicken under cold running water and pat dry with paper towels.

2. Combine the marinade ingredients in a 1-gallon zippered-top plastic bag. Add the chicken, turning to coat, seal, and let marinate in the refrigerator for 2 to 4 hours.

3. Preheat the grill with all the burners on high for 10 minutes and the lid down.

4. While the grill is preheating, drain the marinade into a small saucepan. Bring to a boil for 2 minutes, remove from the heat, and set aside for basting.

5. Once the grill is hot, turn off the center burner and turn the other burners to medium. Place the chicken over the center burner. Wrap the tortillas in aluminum foil and put them on the grill next to the chicken, along with the whole bell peppers. Close the lid and cook the chicken until opaque all the way through but still juicy, 8 to 10 minutes, turning and basting once with the boiled marinade, if desired. Grill the bell peppers, turning to cook on all sides, until nicely softened.

6. To serve, cut the chicken into thin slices and place on the warm tortillas. Remove the stems and seeds from the peppers and cut into thin strips. Top the chicken with the pepper strips, tomato slices, onion, avocado slices, cilantro, and your favorite salsa or hot sauce.

SERVES 6

Skewered Chicken Teriyaki

Chicken teriyaki is an old standby. Whether you soak the chicken in the marinade given here or in one of the excellent bottled teriyaki sauces available today, nothing tastes like good old chicken on a stick.

TERIYAKI MARINADE

1/2 cup soy sauce

1/3 cup dry sherry

1/4 cup firmly packed brown sugar

1/4 cup rice vinegar

1/4 cup vegetable oil

2 cloves garlic, pressed

1 tablespoon ground ginger

6 boneless, skinless chicken breast halves

2 dozen bamboo skewers, soaked in water for 30 minutes and drained

1. Combine the marinade ingredients in a small saucepan and heat just to the boiling point. Remove from the heat and let cool to room temperature. Transfer the marinade to a 1-gallon zippered-top plastic bag.

2. Wash the chicken under cold running water and pat dry with paper towels. Cut each one lengthwise into $1/2$-inch-thick strips. Place the strips in the marinade, turning to coat, seal, and let marinate in the refrigerator for 1 to 2 hours.

3. Preheat the grill with all the burners on high for 10 minutes and the lid down.

4. While the grill is preheating, thread the chicken strips onto the skewers so that they stay relatively flat.

5. Once the grill is hot, turn all the burners to medium. Place the skewered chicken on the grill, close the lid, and cook until just cooked through, 8 to 10 minutes, turning the skewers once. Serve hot off the grill.

SERVES 6

Grilled Chinese-Style Chicken Salad

This is a great summertime dish, especially when it's so hot you simply don't want to cook inside. This could be considered a rustic version of a more traditional Chinese chicken salad and has great appeal for young and old alike.

4 boneless, skinless chicken breast halves

CHINESE-STYLE MARINADE

1 tablespoon toasted sesame oil

1 tablespoon soy sauce

1 tablespoon hoisin sauce

1 tablespoon sake

SALAD

$1/2$ pound fresh Chinese egg noodles; if not available, angel hair pasta or fettuccine will do

$1/2$ pound snow peas, stringed and thinly sliced lengthwise

1 tablespoon toasted sesame oil

1 bunch green onions, thinly sliced

$1/2$ cup chopped fresh cilantro

1 jalapeño, seeded and finely minced

$1/2$ pound fresh bean sprouts

4 cups cored and thinly sliced Napa cabbage

PEANUT-LIME DRESSING

$1/2$ cup seasoned rice vinegar

$1/4$ cup soy sauce

$1/4$ cup creamy peanut butter (do not use old-fashioned style or freshly ground)

Juice of 1 fresh lime

2 tablespoons toasted sesame oil

2 tablespoons Thai sweet chili sauce

1. Rinse the chicken under cold running water and blot dry with paper towels. Place in a 1-gallon zippered-top plastic bag.

2. Combine the marinade ingredients in a small bowl, pour into the bag, seal, and squish around until the chicken is coated. Let marinate in the refrigerator for 1 to 2 hours.

3. Preheat the grill with all the burners on high for 10 minutes and the lid down.

4. When the grill is hot, turn all the burners to medium. Place the chicken on the grill, close the lid, and cook until opaque all the way through but still juicy, 8 to 10 minutes total, turning once about midway through. Transfer to a platter and loosely tent with aluminum foil.

5. Cook the Chinese egg noodles in large pot of boiling salted water until just tender but still firm. Add the snow peas and cook for another minute, just until crisp tender. Drain, then rinse under cold running water to cool, and drain well again. Transfer to a large bowl. Add the sesame oil; toss to blend. Cut the chicken into chunks and add to the bowl along with the green onions, cilantro, jalapeño, bean sprouts, and cabbage.

6. Combine the dressing ingredients in a blender or food processor and process until smooth. Pour over the salad and mix with your hands to blend well. Mound the salad in a large bowl and serve immediately.

SERVES 8

Thunder Thighs

I don't know about you, but in my book, thighs are the best morsels on a chicken. This is a very simple recipe, but one that could easily give the ubiquitous buffalo wings a run for their money. The secret is the sriracha sauce, a very pungent Vietnamese concoction of chiles and garlic. It's now made in this country and widely available. Because the thighs are skin-on, you'll want to use the indirect heating method to prevent flare-ups.

8 to 10 skin-on bone-in chicken thighs

SRIRACHA MARINADE

1/2 cup soy sauce

1/2 cup sriracha sauce ("red rooster" sauce)

1 teaspoon toasted sesame oil

3 to 4 cloves garlic, to your taste, finely minced or pressed

1. Rinse the thighs under cold running water and place in a 1-gallon zippered-top plastic bag.

2. Combine the marinade ingredients in a measuring cup, pour in the bag, seal, and squish around to coat the thighs evenly. Let marinate in the refrigerator for 1 to 3 hours.

3. Preheat the grill with all the burners on high for 10 minutes and the lid down.

4. When the grill is hot, turn off the center burner and turn the other burners to medium. Place the chicken thighs over the center burner, close the lid, and cook until the juices run clear when pierced with a sharp knife, about 40 minutes total, turning every 10 minutes. Transfer to a platter and loosely tent with aluminum foil for 10 minutes before serving.

SERVES 4

Spicy Apple-Lime Chicken Thighs

Among poultry lovers, chicken thighs have a bit of a cult following. Aficionados praise the thigh's succulence and meatiness, declaring it "the only part of the chicken really worth eating." Luckily for these folks, chicken thighs now come in their own packages. In this recipe, the thigh's flavorful meat is complemented by a complex and spicy marinade.

3 to 4 pounds skin-on bone-in chicken thighs

SPICY APPLE-LIME MARINADE

$1/3$ cup fresh lime juice

$1/3$ cup apple juice

3 tablespoons vegetable oil

2 cloves garlic, pressed

2 teaspoons chili powder

1 teaspoon hot pepper sauce

1. Wash the chicken under cold running water and pat dry with paper towels.

2. Combine the marinade ingredients in a 1-gallon zippered-top plastic bag. Add the chicken, turning to coat, seal, and let marinate in the refrigerator for 2 to 3 hours or overnight if desired.

3. Preheat the grill with all the burners on high for 10 minutes and the lid down.

4. While the grill is preheating, drain the marinade into a small saucepan. Bring to a boil for 2 minutes, remove from the heat, and set aside for basting.

5. When the grill is hot, turn off the center burner and turn the other burners to medium. Place the chicken, skin side up, over the center burner, close the lid, and cook until the juices run clear when pierced with a sharp knife, about 40 minutes total, turning every 15 minutes and basting with the boiled marinade if desired. Serve hot off the grill.

SERVES 4 TO 6

Hot and Spicy
Chinese Chicken Wings

In Hawaii, hors d'oeuvres are known as puu-puus. There are puu-puus, and there are "heavy puu-puus." A heavy puu-puu is any food substantial enough to qualify as a main dish. These wings fit in the heavy puu-puu category, and they are wonderful served with steamed rice.

2 to 2^1/2 pounds chicken wings

HOT AND SPICY CHINESE MARINADE

^{1}/2 cup soy sauce

^{1}/4 cup hoisin sauce

^{1}/4 cup distilled white vinegar

^{1}/4 cup honey

^{1}/4 cup pineapple juice

2 cloves garlic, pressed

^{1}/4 teaspoon red pepper flakes

3 tablespoons peanut or vegetable oil

Sesame seeds and chopped fresh cilantro for garnish (optional)

1.   Wash the chicken under cold running water and pat dry with paper towels. With a sharp knife, trim off each wing tip right at the joint.

2.   Combine the marinade ingredients in a 1-gallon zippered-top plastic bag. Add the wings, turning to coat, seal, and let marinate in the refrigerator for 4 to 6 hours or overnight if desired.

3.   Preheat the grill with all the burners on high for 10 minutes and the lid down.

4.   While the grill is preheating, drain the marinade into a small saucepan. Bring to a boil for 2 minutes, remove from the heat, and set aside for basting.

5.   Once the grill is hot, turn off the center burner and turn the other burners to medium. Place the chicken over the center burner, close the lid, and cook until the skin

is crispy and brown, 30 to 35 minutes, turning once and basting with the boiled marinade if desired.

6. Transfer to a serving platter, garnish with sesame seeds and cilantro if desired, and serve.

SERVES 3 TO 4

BASTING SAFELY

IF YOU'RE GOING TO USE ANY LEFTOVER MARINADE FOR BASTING OR AS A SAUCE FOR GRILLED FOOD, BE SURE TO BOIL IT FOR 2 MINUTES TO KILL ANY POTENTIALLY HARMFUL BACTERIA FROM THE RAW POULTRY OR OTHER MEAT.

Chicken Burgers

Now that ground poultry is easy to find in most supermarkets, making chicken or turkey burgers at home is easy. For an added taste treat, be sure to toast the buns (lightly buttered first) on the grill while you cook the burgers.

1 pound ground chicken

$1/4$ cup heavy cream

1 teaspoon kosher salt

1 teaspoon ground white pepper

1 teaspoon seasoned salt

$1/4$ cup ($1/2$ stick) butter, melted and cooled slightly

4 hamburger buns

1. Preheat the grill with all the burners on high for 10 minutes and the lid down.

2. While the grill is preheating, combine the ground chicken, cream, salt, pepper, and seasoned salt well in a medium-size bowl. Because the ground chicken is very sticky, put a little of the melted butter on your hands, then shape the mixture into 4 patties, each about $1/2$ inch thick. Place the patties on a plate and brush on both sides with some of the melted butter. The patties can be covered and refrigerated up to 4 hours ahead of cooking time.

3. Once the grill is hot, turn all the burners to medium-high. Place the chicken patties on the grill, close the lid, and cook 15 to 18 minutes, turning them once, until cooked all the way through.

4. A few minutes before the patties are done, brush the insides of the buns with the remaining melted butter and toast them on the grill. Serve the patties in the toasted buns.

SERVES 4

Whole Roast Turkey

There's no need to take up room in the oven when you can use your gas grill to roast a whole turkey to perfection. For this recipe, you'll need a disposable aluminum roasting pan large enough to hold the turkey.

One 10- to 12-pound turkey

2 teaspoons poultry seasoning

Vegetable oil

Kosher salt and freshly ground black pepper to taste

1. Preheat the grill with all the burners on high for 10 minutes and the lid down.

2. While the grill is preheating, rinse the turkey inside and out under cold running water, removing the neck, giblets, and any excess fat from the cavity. Pat dry with paper towels. Dust the cavity of the turkey with the poultry seasoning. Rub the outside of the turkey with vegetable oil, then sprinkle with salt and pepper. Pull the skin over the breast cavity and fasten below (on the back) with a skewer. Force the ends of the wings under the back to hold them in position, then, using a piece of cotton string, tie the legs together, with the tail end securely in between.

3. Once the grill is hot, turn off the center burner and turn the other burners to medium. Place a roasting rack (if you have one) in the aluminum roasting pan and the turkey on the roasting rack. Position the turkey, breast side up, in the pan over the center burner, close the lid, and cook for 2 to 3 hours. About 30 minutes before the turkey is due to be done, remove the bird from the roasting pan, cut the string holding the legs together, and place the bird directly on the cooking grill, over the turned-off burner (this allows for more even browning). Grill for about 15 minutes per side. The turkey is done when an instant-read meat thermometer inserted in the thickest part of the breast registers 170°F. Save the drippings in the roasting pan for gravy.

4. Transfer to a carving board, loosely tent with aluminum foil, and let rest for 10 to 15 minutes.

5. To carve the turkey, start on one side. First cut the leg and thigh sections completely off, then do the same with the wings. Slice the breast meat thin, then cut the meat from the legs, thighs, and wings. Repeat on the other side. Serve immediately.

SERVES 10 TO 14

Flattened Turkey with Sausage

Flattening a turkey before you grill it is somewhat unusual, but it results in an incredibly moist and flavorful bird. Another uncommon technique, cooking the bird with sausage stuffed under its skin, actually improves the taste of both meats: The turkey picks up subtleties from the sausage and the sausage absorbs flavors from the turkey.

One 10- to 12-pound turkey

About 3 pounds bulk pork sausage

Vegetable oil

Kosher salt and freshly ground black pepper to taste

1. Flatten the turkey according to the directions on page 108, or ask your butcher to do it for you. Wash the bird under cold running water and pat dry with paper towels. Remove the lumps of fat from inside the rib cage. Using your fingers, lift up the turkey skin, starting at the neck end, and separate the skin from the meat as completely as possible without tearing the skin. Push the sausage under the skin, making an even layer about $1/2$ inch thick over the breast, thighs, and legs, if possible, using as much sausage as you can. Smooth out the sausage layer by patting the turkey skin all over. Rub the turkey with vegetable oil and sprinkle with salt and pepper.

2. Preheat the grill with all the burners on high for 10 minutes and the lid down.

3. Once the grill is hot, turn off the center burner and turn the other burners to medium. Place the turkey, skin side up, over the center burner, close the lid, and cook until an instant-read meat thermometer inserted into the thickest part of the breast registers 170°F, turning it several times.

4. Transfer to a carving board, tent loosely with aluminum foil, and let rest for 10 to 15 minutes.

5. To carve the turkey, start on one side. First cut the leg and thigh sections completely off, then do the same with the wings. Slice the breast meat thin, then cut the meat from the legs, thighs, and wings. Repeat on the other side. Serve immediately.

SERVES 12 TO 16

Mexican Fiesta Turkey

The idea for butterflying a turkey, soaking it in a Mexican-style marinade, and grilling it originated in *Sunset* magazine some years back. The recipe has gone through a few permutations since that time and has become a favorite of all who have tried it. This is wonderful party food: tasty, inexpensive, and festive.

One 10- to 12-pound turkey

FRUITY MEXICAN MARINADE

3/4 cup vegetable oil

3/4 cup pineapple juice

1/2 cup fresh lime juice

2 teaspoons chili powder (hot or mild)

2 teaspoons dried oregano, crumbled

1 teaspoon kosher salt

Lime wedges and chopped fresh cilantro for garnish (optional)

1. Flatten the turkey according to the directions on page 108, or ask your butcher to do it for you. Wash the turkey under cold running water and pat dry with paper towels. Remove the lumps of fat from inside the rib cage.

2. Combine the marinade ingredients in a 2-gallon zippered-top plastic bag. Place the turkey in the bag, seal it, and turn the bag a few times to coat the turkey with the marinade. Let marinate in the refrigerator for 4 to 6 hours or preferably overnight.

3. Preheat the grill with all the burners on high for 10 minutes and the lid down.

4. Once the grill is hot, turn off the center burner and turn the other burners to medium. Place the turkey over the center burner, close the lid, and cook until an instant-read meat thermometer stuck into the thickest part of the breast registers 170°F, 1 1/2 to 2 hours, turning it several times.

5. Transfer to a carving board, tent loosely with aluminum foil, and let rest for 10 to 15 minutes.

6. To carve the turkey, start on one side. First cut the leg and thigh sections completely off, then do the same with the wings. Slice the breast meat thin, then cut the meat from the legs, thighs, and wings. Repeat on the other side. Garnish with lime wedges and cilantro if desired, and serve immediately.

SERVES 10 TO 14

Teriyaki Turkey Breast

Although you can use a boneless turkey breast for this recipe (which will shorten the cooking time slightly), a bone-in breast will turn out more flavorful and succulent. Feel free to substitute your favorite bottled teriyaki sauce for the recipe given here.

1 whole bone-in turkey breast (5 to 8 pounds)
1 recipe Teriyaki Marinade (page 137)

1. Wash the turkey under cold running water and pat dry with paper towels. Place in the marinade, turning to coat, cover, and let marinate in the refrigerator for 2 to 3 hours or overnight if desired.

2. Preheat the grill with all the burners on high for 10 minutes and the lid down.

3. Once the grill is hot, turn off the center burner and turn the other burners to medium. Place the turkey over the center burner, close the lid, and cook until an instant-read meat thermometer inserted in the thickest part of the breast reads 170°F, $1^1/2$ to 2 hours, depending on the size of the breast. Turn the turkey several times during the cooking process.

4. Transfer to a carving board, tent loosely with aluminum foil, and let rest for 10 to 15 minutes before carving into thin slices. Serve warm or at room temperature.

SERVES 6 TO 8

Turkey Tonnato

One has to be an adventurous cook to try this dish because, let's face it, at first glance the ingredients for the *tonnato* sauce—a variation on a recipe developed by the late Michael Field—seem highly suspicious. Rest assured, however, that this is a tried-and-true recipe and a real crowd pleaser, as well. An adaptation of the legendary Italian *vitello tonnato* (made with veal instead of turkey), this dish is superb served with crusty garlic bread and a fresh green salad—just the thing for an alfresco luncheon or dinner. Because the topping contains raw egg, make sure to use the freshest eggs possible and don't let the dish sit out too long at room temperature to minimize the possibility of salmonella developing.

1 whole bone-in turkey breast (5 to 8 pounds)

Olive oil

TONNATO SAUCE

3/4 cup extra-virgin olive oil

1 large egg yolk

One 3-ounce can Italian olive oil–packed tuna or domestic oil-packed tuna, drained

3 to 4 anchovy fillets, to your taste, cut into small pieces

Juice of 1 lemon

1/8 teaspoon cayenne pepper

1/4 cup heavy cream

1/4 cup chicken broth

2 tablespoons capers, rinsed and drained

2 tablespoons minced fresh parsley

1 bunch green onions, thinly sliced

4 medium-size ripe tomatoes, cut into wedges

2 lemons, cut into wedges

2 hard-boiled eggs, peeled and cut into thin rounds

1/2 cup small black or green olives (such as niçoise), drained

1. Preheat the grill with all the burners on high for 10 minutes and the lid down.

2. While the grill is preheating, wash the turkey under cold running water, pat dry with paper towels, and rub olive oil all over it.

3. Once the grill is hot, turn off the center burner and turn the other burners to medium. Place the turkey over the center burner, close the lid, and cook until an instant-read meat thermometer inserted in the thickest part of the breast reads 170°F, 1 1/2 to 2

hours, depending on the size of the breast. Turn the turkey several times during the cooking process.

4. Transfer to a carving board and let cool slightly. When it is cool to the touch, remove all the bones, which will cut away easily, and skin the breast. Let the meat finish cooling, then wrap tightly in plastic wrap and refrigerate until needed.

5. To make the *tonnato* sauce, combine the olive oil, egg yolk, tuna fish, anchovies, lemon juice, and cayenne in a blender and pulse no longer than it takes to produce a smooth puree. Pour the puree into a bowl and stir in the cream. Add enough chicken broth to produce a sauce with the consistency of heavy cream. Finally, mix in the capers.

6. Remove the turkey breast from the refrigerator. Using a large, sharp knife, cut the breast into $1/4$-inch-thick slices.

7. Spread a thin layer of the *tonnato* sauce on a large serving platter. Arrange a single layer of the sliced turkey, slightly overlapping, on top of the sauce. Top with another thin layer of sauce. Continue alternating the turkey slices with the sauce until all the turkey has been coated. Immediately cover the platter tightly with plastic wrap and refrigerate for 2 to 3 hours or overnight.

8. About an hour before serving time, remove the platter from the refrigerator and let it come just to room temperature (if you serve the dish too cold, the flavors will be masked). On a fresh platter, gently fold each slice of turkey over itself, arranging the slices in an overlapping fashion. Top the meat with any sauce that remains on the original platter, garnish with the parsley, green onions, tomatoes, lemons, hard-cooked egg slices, and olives, and serve.

SERVES 8 TO 12

DON'T WALK AWAY. . . .

ONCE THE FOOD HAS GONE ON THE GRILL, IT'S A GOOD IDEA TO STICK AROUND AND WATCH IT COOK. AN UNATTENDED GRILL IS AN INVITATION TO AN OVERCOOKED DISH.

Beau Monde Turkey Breast

My friend Debbie remembered this dish from her youth. It's the essence of simplicity and is really good. She says the *beau monde* seasoning is also a winner on a pork roast. You can use either a bone-in or a boneless turkey breast, although the bone-in one will always be a little more succulent and flavorful. Even though you probably won't have any, the leftovers make wonderful sandwiches.

1/2 turkey breast, preferably skin on and bone in

One 3.5-ounce jar *beau monde* seasoning

1. Preheat the grill with all the burners on high for 10 minutes and the lid down.

2. Liberally coat the turkey breast on all sides with the seasoning—at least a couple of tablespoons.

3. Once the grill is hot, leave the back burner on high; turn the other burners to low. Place the turkey, skin side up, over the burners on low, and close the lid. Cook for about 12 minutes, then flip and cook until an instant-read meat thermometer inserted in the thickest part registers 170°F, another 8 to 10 minutes.

4. Transfer to a platter and loosely tent with aluminum foil for about 10 minutes before slicing. Serve hot or cold—it's great either way.

SERVES 3 TO 4

Prosciutto-Wrapped Turkey Brochettes with Marsala Sauce

This recipe is an adaptation of the renowned Italian veal scaloppine Marsala with prosciutto. The turkey is an excellent (and much less expensive) substitute for the veal, and cooking it on skewers cuts the preparation time way down. If you can't find dry Marsala wine, substitute a medium-dry sherry.

One 3- to 3^1/$_2$-pound boneless, skinless turkey breast half

^{1}/$_2$ pound very thinly sliced prosciutto

12 bamboo skewers, soaked in water for 30 minutes and drained

Extra-virgin olive oil

MARSALA SAUCE

^{1}/$_2$ cup Marsala wine (preferably one marked *Superiore*)

^{1}/$_2$ cup chicken broth

2 tablespoons butter, softened

1 tablespoon minced fresh parsley

1. Cut the turkey into 1^1/$_4$-inch cubes. Cut the prosciutto slices in half. Wrap each turkey cube with a half slice of prosciutto. When all the turkey has been wrapped, thread the nuggets onto the skewers. Rub the brochettes lightly with olive oil.

2. Preheat the grill with all the burners on high for 10 minutes and the lid down.

3. While the grill is preheating, combine the Marsala, broth, and butter in a small saucepan. Bring just to a boil, reduce the heat to low, and simmer, uncovered, for 10 minutes. Remove from the heat.

4. Once the grill is hot, turn all the burners to medium. Place the skewers on the grill and cook, with the lid closed, 15 to 18 minutes, turning once or twice, until cooked through.

5. Transfer to a warm serving platter. Reheat the Marsala sauce, adding the parsley at the last minute. Pour the hot sauce over the skewers and serve immediately.

SERVES 6

Ginger-Garlic Turkey Brochettes

The relatively bland flavor of turkey takes well to this delicious marinade. Serve the turkey with steamed rice and a steamed green vegetable.

One 3- to 3^1/$_2$-pound boneless, skinless turkey breast half

GINGER-GARLIC MARINADE

^{3}/$_4$ cup dry white wine

^{1}/$_4$ cup vegetable oil

3 garlic cloves, pressed

^{1}/$_2$ cup grated unpeeled fresh ginger

12 bamboo skewers, soaked in water for 30 minutes and drained

Chopped fresh parsley or cilantro for garnish (optional)

1. Cut the turkey into 1^1/$_4$-inch cubes.

2. In a 1-gallon zippered-top plastic bag, combine the wine, oil, and garlic. Gather the grated ginger in your hands and squeeze tightly over the bag, allowing the juice to run into the marinade. Discard the grated ginger. Mix well. Add the cubed turkey, seal, squishing the bag to coat the cubes well, and let marinate in the refrigerator for 2 to 3 hours.

3. Preheat the grill with all the burners on high for 10 minutes and the lid down.

4. While the grill is preheating, thread the turkey onto the skewers, with the sides of the cubes touching.

5. Once the grill is hot, turn all the burners to medium. Place the skewered turkey on the grill and cook, with the lid closed, for 15 to 18 minutes, turning the brochettes once or twice, until cooked through.

6. Transfer to a warm serving platter, garnish with parsley if desired, and serve.

SERVES 6

Cumin Turkey Breast Tenders in Pita

These inexpensive cuts of turkey grill up in a hurry and make a great filling for sandwiches or pita bread. If your horde is hungry, you can have this meal on the table in a matter of minutes.

SALT-AND-CUMIN DRY RUB

1 tablespoon kosher salt

1 tablespoon ground cumin

GARLIC CUCUMBER YOGURT

One 8-ounce carton plain yogurt

$1/4$ cup seeded and coarsely shredded unpeeled cucumber

2 cloves garlic, pressed

BRINE

3 cups water

$1/2$ cup kosher salt

$1/2$ cup sugar

2 pounds turkey breast tenders

1 tablespoon vegetable oil

EXTRAS

Pita breads

Crumbled feta cheese

Shredded iceberg lettuce

Ripe tomatoes, cut into chunks

1. Mix the salt and cumin together. Set aside.

2. Combine the yogurt sauce ingredients in a small bowl and keep in the refrigerator until ready to use.

3. Combine the brine ingredients in a large bowl and mix well until the salt and sugar have dissolved.

4. Rinse the turkey tenders under cold running water; add to the brine, and place in the refrigerator for 1 to 2 hours.

5. Remove the turkey tenders from the brine and blot dry with paper towels. Coat them with the vegetable oil, then dust liberally with the rub.

6. Preheat the grill with all the burners on high for 10 minutes and the lid down.

7. Once the grill is hot, leave the back burner on high; turn the other burners to low. Place the turkey tenders over the burners on low, close the lid, and cook 10 to 12 minutes total, turning once midway, until just cooked through.

8. Carve the tenders into large chunks. Serve on warm pita bread, along with the feta, lettuce, tomatoes, and yogurt sauce.

SERVES 4

Sage Turkey Burgers

Not long ago, if you asked your butcher for ground turkey meat, you would have gotten a puzzled look in response. These days, ground turkey meat is readily available in most supermarkets, making short work of this recipe. For the record, my tasters—young and old alike—chose turkey burgers as one of their favorite recipes in this book. Just be sure to toast the hamburger buns and add a slice of jellied cranberry sauce on top of each turkey burger. Good eating!

1 pound ground turkey

1/4 cup heavy cream

1 teaspoon crumbled dried sage

1 teaspoon kosher salt

1 teaspoon ground white pepper

1 teaspoon seasoned salt

1/4 cup (1/2 stick) butter, melted and cooled slightly

4 hamburger buns

1. Preheat the grill with all the burners on high for 10 minutes and the lid down.

2. While the grill is preheating, combine the ground turkey, cream, sage, salt, pepper, and seasoned salt together well in a medium-size bowl. Put a little melted butter on your hands, because the ground turkey is very sticky, and shape the mixture into 4 patties, each about 1/2 inch thick. Place the patties on a plate and rub them on both sides with some of the melted butter. If necessary, you can cover and refrigerate the patties for up to 4 hours before cooking them.

3. Once the grill is hot, turn all the burners to medium-high. Place the turkey patties on the grill and cook, with the lid closed, 15 to 18 minutes, turning once, until cooked through.

4. A few minutes before the patties are done, brush the buns with the remaining melted butter and toast them on the grill. Serve the patties in the toasted buns.

SERVES 4

Herbed Mustard Cornish Game Hens

These Cornish game hens are great hot off the grill, but they're even better served cold or at room temperature as picnic fare.

4 Cornish game hens (each 1 to 1^1/$_2$ pounds)

HERBED MUSTARD MARINADE

^{3}/$_4$ cup extra-virgin olive oil

^{1}/$_4$ cup dry white wine

2 tablespoons Dijon mustard

2 teaspoons dried thyme, crumbled

1^1/$_2$ teaspoons dried rosemary

3 to 4 cloves garlic, to your taste, pressed

^{1}/$_4$ teaspoon freshly ground black pepper

1. Wash the Cornish game hens inside and out under cold running water and pat dry with paper towels.

2. Combine the marinade ingredients in a large nonreactive container. Add the hens, turning to coat well, cover, and let marinate in the refrigerator for 2 to 3 hours or overnight if desired.

3. Preheat the grill with all the burners on high for 10 minutes and the lid down.

4. While the grill is preheating, drain the marinade into a small saucepan. Bring to a boil for 2 minutes, remove from the heat, and set aside for basting.

5. Once the grill is hot, turn off the center burner and turn the other burners to medium. Place the hens, breast side up, over the center burner, close the lid, and cook until the juices run clear when the thickest part of the meat is pierced with the tip of a sharp knife, about 1 hour, turning the birds every 15 or 20 minutes and basting with the boiled marinade. Serve hot off the grill or at room temperature.

SERVES 4 GENEROUSLY

Sweet Chinese Cornish Game Hens

Cornish game hens lend themselves well to a Chinese-style marinade. This dish is excellent served with steamed rice and stir-fried vegetables, such as asparagus or broccoli and garlic.

4 Cornish game hens (each 1 to 1^1/$_2$ pounds)

SWEET CHINESE MARINADE

^{1}/$_2$ cup soy sauce

^{1}/$_2$ cup medium-dry sherry

3 tablespoons toasted sesame oil

3 tablespoons firmly packed brown sugar

^{1}/$_2$ cup minced green onions

3 garlic cloves, pressed

2 tablespoons peeled and grated fresh ginger

^{1}/$_8$ teaspoon cayenne pepper

1. Wash the Cornish game hens inside and out under cold running water and pat dry with paper towels.

2. Combine the marinade ingredients in a large nonreactive container. Add the hens, turning to coat well, cover, and let marinate in the refrigerator for 2 to 3 hours or overnight if desired.

3. Preheat the grill with all the burners on high for 10 minutes and the lid down.

4. While the grill is preheating, drain the marinade into a small saucepan. Bring to a boil for 2 minutes, remove from the heat, and set aside for basting.

5. Once the grill is hot, turn off the center burner and turn the other burners to medium. Place the game hens over the center burner, close the lid, and cook until the juices run clear when the thickest part of the meat is pierced with the tip of a sharp knife, about 1 hour, turning the hens every 15 or 20 minutes and basting with the boiled marinade. Serve hot off the grill or at room temperature.

SERVES 4 GENEROUSLY

GRILLING FOR NOW AND LATER

FOR A TERRIFIC PICNIC DINNER, SERVE CORNISH GAME HENS COLD THE DAY AFTER THEY ARE GRILLED.

Quartered Duckling with Fig and Green Olive Sauce

The rich flavor of duck can stand up to a variety of assertive flavors and sauces. This recipe is no exception, but the fig and green olive combination is not only new (at least to my knowledge), it's also really delicious. Although this is an easy recipe, the results fall into the "fancy" category. Serve it to your most discerning diners and stand by for compliments to the chef.

FIG AND GREEN OLIVE SAUCE

$1/2$ cup fig preserves

1 cup tawny port

$1/2$ cup pitted green olives, drained and cut in half

$1/4$ teaspoon kosher salt

$1/2$ teaspoon freshly ground black pepper

One 4- to 5-pound duckling, quartered

1. Combine the sauce ingredients in a medium-size saucepan over medium heat and allow the sauce to just come to a boil. Remove from the heat and set aside.

2. Preheat the grill with all the burners on high for 10 minutes and the lid down.

3. Rinse the duckling quarters under cold running water and blot dry with paper towels.

4. Once the grill is hot, turn off the center burner and turn the other burners to medium. Place the duckling quarters over the center burner, skin side up, close the lid, and cook until an instant-read meat thermometer inserted into the thickest part of the thigh (don't let the thermometer touch a bone) registers 180°F, 30 to 40 minutes, turning every 10 minutes or so.

5. Transfer to a platter and loosely tent with aluminum foil for 5 to 10 minutes. Reheat the sauce. Place a duckling quarter on individual serving plates and top with the sauce. Serve immediately.

SERVES 4

Peking Duck Breasts

The traditional method of making Peking duck is a long and arduous one, best left (in my opinion) to professional restaurant chefs. This recipe takes its cues and flavors from the famous Peking specialty, but is far quicker and easier to make. The flour tortillas make an acceptable substitute for the traditional Chinese pancakes in which the duck breast slices, sauce, and green onions are rolled.

PEKING SAUCE

2 tablespoons hoisin sauce

2 tablespoons sake

1 tablespoon toasted sesame oil

1 tablespoon smooth peanut butter

2 duck breast halves (about 1 1/2 pounds)

1/2 teaspoon Chinese five-spice mixture

Kosher salt to taste

4 flour tortillas

2 to 3 green onions, sliced into thin vertical strips, for garnish

1. Preheat the grill with all the burners on high for 10 minutes and the lid down.

2. While the grill is preheating, combine the sauce ingredients in a small saucepan over medium heat and whisk until smooth and hot, 4 to 5 minutes. Remove from the heat.

3. Sprinkle the duck breasts with the five-spice mixture and salt on both sides.

4. Once the grill is hot, turn the back burner to medium and turn the other burners to low. Place the duck breasts, skin side down, over the burners on low, close the lid, and cook for 4 minutes. Turn the center burner off. Immediately flip the breasts and cook over the center burner, with the lid closed, for another 6 minutes for rare; add another 2 minutes or so for medium-rare. Transfer to a platter and loosely tent with aluminum foil for 5 to 10 minutes.

5. Place the tortillas on the still-warm grill (all the burners off) and grill, with the lid closed, just until warm and soft, about a minute or so per side.

6. Using a sharp butcher knife, carve the duck breasts into $3/8$-inch-thick slices. Put the slices on a platter, pour the warm sauce over them, and garnish with the green onion strips. Serve immediately with the warm tortillas.

SERVES 2

Duck Breasts
with Tuscan Rub

When you're in the mood for something different, this recipe may fit the bill. The rosemary and fennel are unusual accompaniments to duck, but nicely complement its richness. This is excellent served with Polenta (page 348).

4 large duck breast halves

TUSCAN RUB MARINADE

2 tablespoons olive oil

2 cloves garlic, pressed

1 teaspoon paprika

1 teaspoon freshly ground black pepper

1 teaspoon ground fennel

1/2 teaspoon dried rosemary, crumbled

1. Rinse the duck breasts under cold running water and pat dry with paper towels. Place them in a 1-gallon zippered-top plastic bag.

2. Combine the marinade ingredients in a small bowl, add to the bag, seal, and squish around until the duck is coated. Let marinate in the refrigerator for 3 to 4 hours.

3. Preheat the grill with all the burners on high for 10 minutes and the lid down.

4. Once the grill is hot, turn all the burners to medium. Place the duck breasts on the grill, fat side down, close the lid, and cook about 20 minutes total for medium-rare, turning every 4 to 5 minutes. Remove to a platter and loosely tent with aluminum foil for 5 minutes before slicing.

SERVES 4

Pancetta-Wrapped Grilled Quail

Quail are becoming available in more supermarkets across the country. If you like the taste of grilled poultry, you'll probably enjoy quail, especially as it is done here: wrapped in pancetta to add a little extra flavor and moisture.

8 to 12 quail

Olive oil

Fresh lemon juice

Crumbled dried thyme to taste

Kosher salt and freshly ground black pepper to taste

8 to 12 thin slices pancetta (1 slice per quail)

1.   Flatten the quail according to the directions on page 108, or ask your butcher to do it for you. Rinse the quail well under cold running water and pat dry with paper towels. Rub each quail with a little olive oil and lemon juice, then sprinkle with thyme, salt, and pepper. Wrap each quail with a slice of pancetta.

2.   Preheat the grill with all the burners on high for 10 minutes and the lid down.

3.   Once the grill is hot, turn off the center burner and turn the other burners to medium. Place the quail, breast side up, over the center burner, close the lid, and cook until the juices run clear when the thickest part of the meat is pierced with the tip of a sharp knife, about 6 minutes per side, turning once. Serve hot off the grill or at room temperature.

SERVES 4

Grilled Pheasant

Farm-raised pheasant is becoming more widely available all the time. It is an elegant and delicious bird, needing only salt and pepper to allow its unique flavor to show through. Serve this dish with Buttered Grilled Carrots (page 285) and Wild Rice Casserole (page 348).

One 2- to 3-pound pheasant

Vegetable oil

Kosher salt and freshly ground black pepper to taste

1. Flatten the pheasant according to the directions on page 108, or ask your butcher to do it for you. Rinse the pheasant under cold running water and pat dry with paper towels. Rub vegetable oil liberally all over the bird and season with salt and pepper.

2. Preheat the grill with all the burners on high for 10 minutes and the lid down.

3. Once the grill is hot, turn off the center burner and turn the other burners to medium. Place the pheasant, breast up, over the center burner, close the lid, and cook until the juices run clear when the thickest part of the meat is pierced with the tip of a sharp knife, 1 to 1^1/$_2$ hours, turning every 15 minutes.

4. Transfer to a carving board, loosely tent with aluminum foil, and let rest for 10 minutes before carving.

SERVES 4

5

Beef

Over the past few years, most Americans have reduced the amount of beef they eat on a regular basis. If you follow this generally health-ful trend, when you do eat beef, treat yourself to the very best you can afford. The best beef will be labeled *prime*, the meat will be deep red, and the fat will be creamy white. The best beef also should have marbling—thin streaks of creamy yellow fat running through the meat—which adds immea-surably to its flavor and succulence. *Choice* beef is next in quality and is usually fine for most grilling. *Select* is the least expensive grade. ✳ Many cuts of beef benefit from the tenderizing effects of marinating. Whether or not the meat is marinated, remove it from the refrigerator about 30 minutes before you are ready to grill, to bring the temperature of the meat closer to room temperature.

Judging Doneness

Remember that beef continues to cook after it is taken off the grill. You should remove beef from the grill, especially large cuts such as roasts, when its internal temperature registers 5 to 10 degrees shy of the desired temperature. Place the meat on a carving board, cover it loosely with an aluminum foil tent, and let it rest for 10 to 15 minutes before carving. The resting period not only allows the meat to reach the level of doneness you desire, but also gives the flavorful juices time to be reabsorbed into the meat, creating a more succulent dish.

Beef is considered rare at 140°F, medium at 160°F, and well done at 170°F.

Filet Mignon with Grilled
Marinated Mushrooms   168

Marinated Filet Mignon
Steaks with Hidden
Wasabi Jolt   170

Chateaubriand with
Green Peppercorn Sauce 172

Chateaubriand with
Honey Mustard Glaze   173

Beefsteak with
Salsa Verde   174

Steaks with
Roquefort Butter   175

Strip Steaks with
Grilled Potato Skins   176

Rib-Eye Steaks with
Chili Butter   178

Porterhouse Steak
for Two with
Cambozola Butter   179

T-Bone Picante   180

Whole Tenderloin of Beef
with Béarnaise Sauce   181

Standing Rib Roast
with Horseradish Sauce 182

Garlic-Studded
London Broil   184

London Broil with Black
Bean and Corn Salsa   185

London Broil with
Sherried Mushrooms   186

Teriyaki Beef with Green
Onions and Mushrooms 188

Indonesian-Style
Beef Satay   189

Chili-Rubbed Beef
Fajitas with Peppers
and Onions   190

Vietnamese-Style
Sliced Steak in
Lettuce Leaf Wraps   192

Hanger Steaks with
Caramelized Onions,
Mushrooms, Chèvre,
and Arugula   193

Flat Iron Steak with
Black, White, and
Green Peppercorns   194

Skirt Steak with
Tequila Marinade   195

Everybody's Favorite
Flank Steak   196

Red Rooster–Soy
Marinated Flank Steak   197

Spicy Flank Steak   198

Flank Steak Sandwiches
with Grilled Bell Peppers
and Onions   199

Tried-and-True
Marinated Beef Kebabs 201

Skewered
Beef Bourguignon   202

Chuck Wagon
Chuck Roast   203

Boneless Chuck Roast
with Bourbon and Coke 204

Sherry and Garlic
Marinated Chuck Roast 206

Chuck Roast with
Argentine Squirt Sauce   207

Real Tasty Beef Brisket   208

The Classic Burger   209

The Commissioner's
Best Beef Ribs   211

Sweet, Hot, and Sour
Basted Beef Ribs   212

Savory Short Ribs
of Beef   213

Grilled Liver Steaks   214

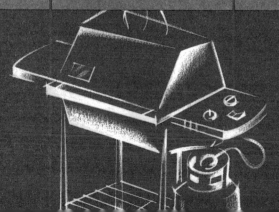

Filet Mignon with Grilled Marinated Mushrooms

If you're eating less red meat these days, you may find that when you have a craving for it, you want a really good steak. This is it. The classic pairing of filet mignon and mushrooms is even better when both are cooked on the grill. Excellent side dishes include Rosemary Potato Wedges (page 307) and Garlicky Grilled Tomatoes (page 313).

MARINATED MUSHROOMS

1/2 cup dry red wine

1/4 cup extra-virgin olive oil

Juice of 1/2 lemon

1 large clove garlic, pressed

2 teaspoons crushed fresh thyme leaves

1 teaspoon kosher salt

1/2 teaspoon cracked black peppercorns

1 pound fresh mushrooms, wiped clean and stems trimmed

4 filet mignon steaks, cut 1 to 1 1/2 inches thick

Olive oil

Cracked black peppercorns to taste

6 bamboo skewers, soaked in water for 30 minutes and drained

1. To make the marinated mushrooms, combine all the ingredients except the mushrooms in a 1-gallon zippered-top plastic bag and mix well. Toss the mushrooms in the marinade, seal, and refrigerate for 1 to 2 hours, squishing the bag a few times.

2. Brush the steaks with olive oil and sprinkle liberally with the cracked peppercorns.

3. Preheat the grill with all the burners on high for 10 minutes and the lid down.

4. While the grill is preheating, thread the mushrooms onto the skewers.

5. With all the burners still on high, place the steaks on the grill, close the lid, and sear one side, leaving them on the grill about 2 minutes for 1-inch-thick steaks and 4 minutes for 1^1/$_2$-inch steaks.

6. After searing the steaks, turn off the center burner and turn the other burners to medium. Turn the steaks (so the seared side is up), moving them so they are directly over the center burner, and place the skewered mushrooms next to them. Close the lid and finish cooking the steaks, turning them one more time. After searing, 1-inch-thick steaks will take 4 to 5 minutes to cook to rare, 5 to 7 minutes to cook to medium, and 7 to 9 minutes to cook to well done. Allow slightly more time for 1^1/$_2$-inch steaks. Depending on their size, the mushrooms will be tender in 8 to 12 minutes, so you may have to continue cooking them after the steaks are done; turn them every 4 minutes or so.

7. Serve the steaks hot off the grill, surrounded by the mushrooms.

SERVES 4

MAKING THE VERY BEST OF LEFTOVERS

WANT A GOOD SAUCE FOR LEFTOVER, COLD SLICED STEAK?
MIX TOGETHER EQUAL PARTS SOUR CREAM, MAYONNAISE, AND
PREPARED HORSERADISH WITH A LITTLE DIJON MUSTARD.

Marinated Filet Mignon Steaks with Hidden Wasabi Jolt

My friend Sean Behrens passed on the idea for this dish to me. Sean's folks owned the celebrated restaurant Folie Douce in Arcata, California, and this was one of the dishes that put the place on the map. It's a winner.

4 filet mignon steaks (about 1 1/2 pounds), cut at least 1 inch thick

GINGER AND GARLIC SAKE MARINADE

1/2 cup soy sauce

1/3 cup sake

2 tablespoons seasoned rice vinegar

2 tablespoons peeled and grated fresh ginger

2 to 3 cloves garlic, to your taste, pressed or finely chopped

1 teaspoon ground white pepper

1/2 teaspoon sesame oil

WASABI PASTE

1/4 cup wasabi powder

2 tablespoons water

GARNISH

2 tablespoons sesame seeds, toasted in a dry skillet over medium heat until light brown and fragrant

4 scallions, cut lengthwise into thin, 1-inch-long strips

1. Using a very sharp knife, cut a horizontal "pocket" in the side of each steak. The pocket should be as large as possible without cutting through to the other side.

2. Combine the marinade ingredients in a 1-gallon zippered-top plastic bag. Add the steaks, seal, and squish around to coat the steaks. Let marinate for 1 to 2 hours in the refrigerator, flipping the bag occasionally so all parts of the steaks are thoroughly submerged.

3. In a small bowl, combine the wasabi powder and water thoroughly with a fork. Using your hands, shape the paste into a roll; cut into 4 equal pieces. Flatten them slightly and insert one into the pocket of each filet mignon.

4. Preheat the grill with all the burners on high for 10 minutes and the lid down.

5. With all the burners still on high, place the steaks on the grill, close the lid, and cook 5 minutes per side, turning once midway through. This will produce medium-rare steaks; adjust the time to suit your desired degree of doneness.

6. Sprinkle each steak with the toasted sesame seeds and scallion strips, slice, and serve.

SERVES 4

TO MARINATE OR NOT TO MARINATE?

BEEFSTEAKS FALL INTO TWO CATEGORIES: THOSE THAT BENEFIT FROM MARINATING AND THOSE THAT DO NOT. TOUGHER CUTS SHOULD BE MARINATED FOR 2 TO 4 HOURS IN THE REFRIGERATOR. TWENTY TO 30 MINUTES BEFORE GRILLING, REMOVE THE MEAT FROM THE REFRIGERATOR TO ALLOW IT TO COME TO NEAR ROOM TEMPERATURE.

CUTS THAT BENEFIT FROM MARINATING:

CHUCK ROAST * EYE OF THE ROUND * FLANK STEAK * ROUND STEAK * SIRLOIN STEAK * SKIRT STEAK * TOP ROUND

CUTS THAT NEED NO MARINATING:

CLUB STEAK * FILET MIGNON * FLAT IRON STEAK * HANGAR STEAK * KANSAS CITY AND NEW YORK STRIP STEAK * LOIN * PORTERHOUSE STEAK * RIB EYE * SHELL STEAK * SIRLOIN STEAK (MAY ALSO BE MARINATED) * T-BONE STEAK * TENDERLOIN

Chateaubriand with Green Peppercorn Sauce

This recipe is a variation on the famous French steak *au poivre vert*. It's an impressive dish with assertive flavors, best served with simple side dishes such as baked potatoes and steamed broccoli or asparagus. If you're planning to serve a red wine, choose something "big," because this meal will stand up to the biggest red wine in town. *Note:* The name Chateaubriand is something of a misnomer. Originally, it referred to the very best filet steak, cut unusually thick—at least 2 inches. Nowadays, the term may refer to a variety of cuts of beef (most often the sirloin), the common denominator being the thickness of the cut.

One 3- to 4-pound Chateaubriand, about 2 inches thick

3 to 4 cloves garlic, to your taste, cut into about a dozen slivers total

Olive oil

Freshly ground black pepper

GREEN PEPPERCORN SAUCE

2 tablespoons butter

3 tablespoons chopped shallots or green onions (white part only)

1 cup beef broth

1/2 cup dry red wine

2 to 3 tablespoons green peppercorns (preferably brine packed), to your taste

1 tablespoon Dijon mustard

1. Using the tip of a sharp knife, make about 6 incisions on each side of the steak, deep enough to hold a sliver of garlic. Insert a sliver of garlic into each incision. Brush the steak with olive oil and dust liberally with pepper.

2. Preheat the grill with all the burners on high for 10 minutes and the lid down.

3. While the grill is preheating, make the sauce. In a small saucepan over medium heat, melt the butter. Add the shallots and cook, stirring, until softened, about 3 minutes. Add the broth, wine, and green peppercorns and cook over medium-high heat for 5 to 7 minutes, stirring occasionally. Whisk in the mustard, remove the pan from the heat, and reserve until serving time.

4. With all the burners still on high, place the steak on the grill, close the lid, and sear one side of the steak for about 4 minutes; then turn off the center burner and turn the other burners to medium. Turn the steak (so the seared side is up), moving it directly over the center burner. Close the lid and finish cooking the steak, turning it one more time. After searing, a 2-inch-thick Chateaubriand will take 10 to 13 minutes to cook rare (140°F), 13 to 15 minutes for medium (160°F), and 15 to 19 minutes for well done (170°F).

5. Transfer the steak to a carving board, cover it loosely with aluminum foil, and let rest for 10 to 15 minutes. Meanwhile, reheat the sauce.

6. To serve, slice the meat as you prefer. Pour a couple of tablespoons of warm sauce over each portion and serve.

SERVES 6 TO 8

Chateaubriand with Honey Mustard Glaze

Ask almost anyone why they like their gas grill and they'll tell you it's all about convenience and saving time. With that in mind, it's a good idea to have a few good recipes up your sleeve that don't require a long marinating process. This is one of them.

HONEY MUSTARD GLAZE

1/2 cup hot sweet honey mustard

1 tablespoon freshly ground black pepper

1 tablespoon canola oil

1 Chateaubriand (about 2 pounds), cut 1 3/4 to 2 inches thick

1. Preheat the grill with all the burners on high for 10 minutes and the lid down.

2. Combine the glaze ingredients in a small bowl. Spread half the glaze on one side of the steak. Take the steak and the remaining glaze (and the spreading utensil) out to the grill.

3. Once the grill is hot, turn all the burners to medium. Place the steak, mustard side down, on the grill, spread the remaining glaze on the top of the steak, close the lid, and cook for a total of 14 to 16 minutes, turning once midway through, for medium-rare.

4. Remove to a platter and loosely tent with aluminum foil for 10 minutes before slicing.

SERVES 4

HOW MUCH IS ENOUGH?

COUNT ON EACH PERSON EATING ABOUT ONE-THIRD TO ONE-HALF POUND OF BEEF, NOT INCLUDING BONES.

Beefsteak with Salsa Verde

Think salsa verde, but think Italian, not Mexican. This blended green sauce from Italy is a veritable flavor explosion, the perfect complement to a big grilled steak. Because the steak is not marinated, favor a more tender cut of beef, such as Chateaubriand, big New York strip, rib-eye, or hanger steak. Grill to the desired degree of doneness, cut into 3/8-inch-thick slices, top with the salsa verde, and you've got yourself quite a meal.

SALSA VERDE

4 to 5 cups packed fresh parsley leaves

4 to 6 cloves garlic, to your taste, peeled

Juice of 1 lemon, with some of the pulp, if you can coax it out

2 tablespoons capers, drained

2 teaspoons anchovy paste or mashed anchovies (optional)

1/2 cup olive oil

4 to 5 pounds Chateaubriand, New York strip, rib-eye, or hanger steaks, cut 1 to 1^1/$_2$ inches thick

Olive oil

Kosher salt and freshly ground black pepper to taste

1. Combine the salsa verde ingredients in a food processor or blender and process until the sauce has the consistency of a milkshake. Because of the salty nature of the capers and anchovies, no additional salt is needed. Pour into a bowl, cover, and refrigerate until needed.

2. Preheat the grill with all the burners on high for 10 minutes and the lid down.

3. Coat the steaks evenly with olive oil; dust with salt and pepper. With all the burners still on high, sear each side of the steaks, with the lid closed, for 5 minutes.

4. After searing, turn all the burners to medium, close the lid, and cook the steaks another 6 to 8 minutes, turning them midway through, for rare to medium-rare.

5. Transfer to a platter and loosely tent with aluminum foil for about 10 minutes. Carve into slices and top with the salsa verde.

SERVES 6 TO 8

Steaks with Roquefort Butter

This timeless combination—a great steak, hot off the grill, with a dollop of Roquefort butter melting on top—is as good today as it ever was. If real French Roquefort cheese is not available, substitute a domestic blue cheese.

4 steaks (filet mignon, strip, rib eye, or another favorite)

Olive oil

Freshly ground black pepper

ROQUEFORT BUTTER

6 tablespoons (³/₄ stick) butter, at room temperature

2 ounces Roquefort cheese

1 clove garlic, pressed

1. Brush the steaks with olive oil and dust them liberally with pepper.

2. Preheat the grill with all the burners on high for 10 minutes and the lid down.

3. While the grill is preheating, in a small bowl, combine the butter, Roquefort, and garlic, mixing thoroughly with a fork. Set aside until serving time.

4. Once the grill is hot, place the steak on the grill and close the lid. Sear one side of the steaks, about 2 minutes for 1-inch-thick steaks and 4 minutes for 1¹/₂-inch steaks.

5. After searing, turn off the center burner and turn the other burners to medium. Turn the steaks (so the seared side is up), placing them directly over the center burner. Close the lid and finish cooking the steaks, turning them one more time. After searing, 1-inch-thick steaks will take 4 to 5 minutes to cook to rare, 5 to 7 minutes for medium, and 7 to 9 for well done. Allow slightly more time for 1¹/₂-inch steaks.

6. Serve hot off the grill with a tablespoon or so of the Roquefort butter on top.

SERVES 4

Strip Steaks with Grilled Potato Skins

Whether you call them New York strip steaks or Kansas City strip steaks, almost every beef lover calls them good. In Pasadena, California, there was a legendary steak house called Monty's that not only served a great strip steak, but also may have invented the grilled potato skin. To many potato lovers, the skin is the best part, made even better by grilling.

4 large Idaho or russet potatoes

4 strip steaks, cut 1 to 1^1/2 inches thick

Olive oil

Freshly ground black pepper to taste

Butter, sour cream, chopped fresh chives, and salt and pepper for topping (optional)

1. Preheat the oven to 350°F. Scrub the potatoes well under cold running water. Using the tip of a sharp knife, poke a few steam vents in each potato. Bake the potatoes until fork tender, about 1 hour. Remove from the oven and let cool.

2. Brush the steaks with olive oil and dust liberally with pepper.

3. Preheat the grill with all the burners on high for 10 minutes and the lid down.

4. While the grill is preheating, cut a slit lengthwise in each baked potato and remove all but ^{1}/4 inch or so of the flesh. Flatten each potato with the heel of your hand.

5. With the burners still on high, place the steaks on the grill and close the lid. Sear only one side of the steaks, about 2 minutes for 1-inch-thick steaks and 4 minutes for 1^1/2-inch steaks.

6. After searing the steaks, turn off the center burner and turn the other burners to medium. Turn the steaks (so the seared side is up), placing them directly over the center burner, with the potato skins next to them. Close the lid and finish cooking the steaks, turning them and the potatoes once, at the same time. After searing, 1-inch-thick steaks will take 4 to 5 minutes to cook to rare, 5 to 7 minutes for medium, and 7 to 9 minutes for well done; 1^1/2-inch steaks will take somewhat longer. You can remove the potato skins from the grill when you remove the steaks.

7. Serve the steaks hot off the grill with the potato skins on the side. Top the skins with plenty of butter, sour cream, chives, and salt and pepper if desired.

SERVES 4

Rib-Eye Steaks with Chili Butter

Real steak lovers swear by the rib-eye steak for taste and texture. Though not the most refined of cuts, it's what many people want when they're hungry for a big steak with lots of big steak flavor.

CHILI BUTTER

1/2 cup (1 stick) salted butter, at room temperature

1 tablespoon chili powder

1 large clove garlic, pressed

Juice of 1 lime

4 rib-eye steaks, cut 1 to 1 1/2 inches thick

Olive oil

Freshly ground black pepper to taste

1. Combine the chili butter ingredients in a small bowl, whipping with a fork until well blended. Cover and refrigerate until needed.

2. Brush the steaks with olive oil and dust liberally with pepper.

3. Preheat the grill with all the burners on high for 10 minutes and the lid down.

4. With the burners still on high, place the steaks on the grill, close the lid, and sear one side of the steaks, about 2 minutes for 1-inch-thick steaks and 4 minutes for 1 1/2-inch steaks.

5. After searing, turn off the center burner and turn the other burners to medium. Turn the steaks (so the seared side is up), placing them directly over the center burner. Close the lid and finish cooking the steaks, turning one more time. After searing, 1-inch-thick steaks will take 4 to 5 minutes to cook to rare, 5 to 7 minutes for medium, and 7 to 9 minutes for well done. Allow slightly more time for 1 1/2-inch steaks.

6. Serve the steaks hot off the grill, with a couple of tablespoons of the chili butter on top of each one.

SERVES 4

PRIME IS FINE

THE VERY BEST BEEF—LABELED *PRIME*—IS DEEP RED, HAS CREAMY WHITE FAT, AND IS STREAKED THROUGH WITH THIN BANDS OF FAT, KNOWN AS MARBLING.

Porterhouse Steak for Two with Cambozola Butter

When you're in the mood for something over the top, this recipe is for you. I've had people taste the Cambozola butter and watch as their eyes rolled back in their heads and they nearly swooned. Just keep the number of your friendly cardiologist nearby. As unlikely as it seems, Cambozola is a German import, which my cheese shop describes as "blue brie." And, yes, it's rated triple cream.

CAMBOZOLA BUTTER

5 ounces Cambozola cheese

5 ounces European-style butter, at room temperature (regular salted butter can be substituted, but try to find butter from Europe if you can)

4 to 5 large cloves garlic, to your taste, pressed

1 tablespoon anchovy paste

1 porterhouse steak (1 1/2 to 2 pounds), cut 1 1/2 inches thick

1 tablespoon olive oil

Kosher salt and freshly ground black pepper to taste

1. Combine the Cambozola butter ingredients in a bowl and mix thoroughly with a fork. Allow the flavors to mellow for an hour before serving.

2. Preheat the grill with all the burners on high for 10 minutes and the lid down.

3. Rub the steak with the olive oil. Sprinkle liberally with salt and pepper. With all the burners still on high, sear the steak, with the lid up, 4 to 5 minutes per side.

4. After searing, immediately turn all the burners to medium and cook the steak, with the lid down, another 2 to 3 minutes per side for medium-rare.

5. Remove from the grill; top with as much of the butter as desired. Serve immediately.

NOTE Cambozola Butter can be served as is right from the bowl, or for a more formal presentation, place the butter on a piece of plastic wrap, shape into a log-shaped roll, wrap, refrigerate, and cut into nice round slices before serving.

SERVES 3 TO 4

T-Bone Picante

The dry rub in this recipe transforms an ordinary T-bone into a spicy steak with a Southwestern accent. Team it with Cowpoke Beans (page 357) and steamed rice for a hearty, mouthwatering meal.

HOT-AND-SWEET DRY RUB

$1/4$ cup paprika

2 tablespoons chili powder

2 tablespoons ground cumin

2 tablespoons dark brown sugar

2 tablespoons kosher salt

1 tablespoon granulated sugar

1 tablespoon crumbled dried oregano

1 tablespoon freshly ground black pepper

1 tablespoon ground white pepper

2 teaspoons cayenne pepper (optional: omit if you don't want the meat spicy hot)

4 T-bone steaks, cut 1 to $1^1/2$ inches thick

1. Combine the dry rub ingredients in a small bowl and mix well. Evenly dust the steaks with the mixture and rub it in with your fingers. Cover the steaks with plastic wrap and refrigerate for 1 to 2 hours. Store any leftover dry rub in a tightly covered jar in the freezer.

2. Preheat the grill with all the burners on high for 10 minutes and the lid down.

3. With the burners still on high, place the steaks on the grill, close the lid, and sear one side of the steaks, about 2 minutes for 1-inch-thick steaks and 4 minutes for $1^1/2$-inch steaks.

4. After searing, turn off the center burner and turn the other burners to medium. Turn the steaks (so the seared side is up), placing them directly over the center burner. Close the lid and finish cooking the steaks, turning one more time. After searing, 1-inch-thick steaks will take 4 to 5 minutes to cook to rare, 5 to 7 minutes for medium, and 7 to 9 minutes for well done. Allow slightly more time for $1^1/2$-inch steaks. Serve hot off the grill.

SERVES 4

Whole Tenderloin of Beef with Béarnaise Sauce

A tenderloin roast beef falls into the category of "company food," especially when paired with the classic béarnaise sauce. In truth, few things are as easy to cook as a tenderloin roast. However, to cook any roast to perfection, use a meat thermometer: You can't accurately judge doneness by eye alone. Remember to take the roast off the grill when it is about 10 degrees shy of the desired temperature; the roast will continue to cook as it rests on the carving board. Tenderloin roasts come in half and whole sizes; half usually runs 2 to 3 pounds, and whole 4 to 5 pounds. Count on 1/3 to 1/2 pound per person.

Béarnaise sauce, a tarragon-flavored emulsified butter sauce, goes exceptionally well with both beef and lamb. Some people follow the time-honored method of making béarnaise in a double boiler, but I suggest that you use a blender, which is much faster and easier. Since the eggs don't really heat up enough to cook them, salmonella is a possibility; to minimize it, use the freshest eggs possible from a source you trust.

One 4- to 5-pound beef tenderloin, trimmed of silver skin

Olive oil

Cracked black peppercorns to taste

BÉARNAISE SAUCE

1 tablespoon minced shallot or onion

3 tablespoons white wine vinegar

1 teaspoon coarsely ground black pepper

1 teaspoon dried tarragon, or leaves from 2 to 3 sprigs fresh tarragon, minced

3 large egg yolks, at room temperature

1 cup (2 sticks) unsalted butter, melted and still hot

1. Rub the tenderloin with olive oil and sprinkle it liberally with cracked pepper; pat it down so it sticks to the beef.

2. Preheat the grill with all the burners on high for 10 minutes and the lid down.

3. Once the grill is hot, turn off the center burner and turn the other burners to medium. Place the roast, fat side up, over the center burner, close the lid, and cook until an instant-read meat thermometer inserted into the thickest part registers 5 to 10 degrees shy of the desired temperature (140°F for rare, 160°F for medium, 170°F for well done). A 4- to 5-pound tenderloin will take 50 to 70 minutes to cook to rare.

4. While the tenderloin roasts, prepare the béarnaise sauce. Combine the shallot, vinegar, pepper, and tarragon in a small saucepan, bring to a boil, and continue to boil rapidly until only 1 to 2 teaspoons of liquid remain. Watch carefully, swirling the mixture around almost constantly to avoid scorching. Remove from the heat and allow to cool.

5. Combine the egg yolks and the cooled shallot-and-vinegar mixture in a blender and process until well blended, about 1 minute or so. Turn the blender to high and, with the machine running, add the hot butter, drip by drip at first, gradually increasing it to a steady stream as the mixture begins to thicken. Pour the sauce into a prewarmed thermos bottle. It will keep without curdling or "breaking" for 2 hours or more.

6. When the roast is done, transfer to a carving board, cover loosely with aluminum foil, and allow to rest for 10 minutes or so.

7. Carve the meat into thick (like individual filet mignon steaks) or thin slices as desired. Serve with a small amount of the delightfully rich and flavorful béarnaise sauce.

SERVES 12 TO 15

Standing Rib Roast with Horseradish Sauce

A gas grill makes preparation of this "company meal" a snap. Also, grilling outside keeps the kitchen (and the cook) cool and produces a roast superior to any oven dweller. If you buy your meat from an old-fashioned market, have the butcher cut off the short ribs and the chine (backbone), loosen the feather bones, and tie the whole roast with string. Prepackaged rib roasts are usually offered this way.

One 4- to 6-pound standing rib roast

Salt and freshly ground black pepper to taste

HORSERADISH SAUCE

$^1/_2$ cup sour cream

$^1/_4$ cup prepared horseradish

$^1/_4$ cup mayonnaise

1 tablespoon red wine vinegar

$^1/_2$ teaspoon kosher salt

1 teaspoon freshly ground black pepper

1. Preheat the grill with all the burners on high for 10 minutes and the lid down.

2. While the grill is preheating, dust the roast liberally with salt and pepper.

3. Once the grill is hot, turn off the center burner and turn the other burners to medium. Place the roast over the center burner, close the lid, and cook until an instant-read meat thermometer inserted into the thickest part (away from any bones) registers 5 to 10 degrees shy of the desired temperature (140°F for rare, 160°F for medium, 170°F for well done). A 4- to 6-pound standing rib roast will take $1^1/_4$ to $1^3/_4$ hours to cook to rare, $1^3/_4$ to $2^1/_4$ hours for medium, and $2^1/_4$ to $2^3/_4$ hours for well done.

4. While the roast cooks, combine the horseradish sauce ingredients in a small bowl and mix well. Refrigerate until serving time.

5. When the roast is done, transfer to a carving board, cover loosely with aluminum foil, and let rest for 10 minutes or so before carving the roast into thick or thin slices as desired. Serve with the horseradish sauce on the side.

SERVES 8 TO 10

Garlic-Studded London Broil

Serve this steak hot off the grill, or cold the next day for out-of-this-world steak sandwiches.

One 3- to 4-pound London broil, about 2 inches thick

3 to 4 cloves garlic, cut into about a dozen slivers total

Olive oil

Freshly ground black pepper to taste

1. Using the tip of a sharp knife, make about 6 incisions on each side of the steak, deep enough to hold a sliver of garlic. Insert a sliver of garlic into each incision. Brush the meat with olive oil and dust it liberally with pepper.

2. Preheat the grill with all the burners on high for 10 minutes and the lid down.

3. With the burners still on high, place the steak on the grill, close the lid, and sear one side of the steak for about 4 minutes.

4. After searing the steak, turn off the center burner and turn the other burners to medium. Turn the steak (so the seared side is up), placing it directly over the center burner. Close the lid and finish cooking, turning it one more time. After searing, a 2-inch-thick London broil will take 10 to 13 minutes to reach rare (140°F), 13 to 15 minutes for medium (160°F), and 15 to 19 minutes for well done (170°F).

5. Transfer the meat to a carving board, cover loosely with aluminum foil, and let rest for 10 to 15 minutes before slicing it as you prefer.

SERVES 6 TO 8

London Broil with Black Bean and Corn Salsa

Grilling a large, 3- to 4-pound steak and then slicing it is one of the easiest—and fastest—ways to feed a table full of hungry eaters. The black bean and corn salsa adds a Southwestern "cowboy" touch.

BLACK BEAN AND CORN SALSA

3/4 cup canned black beans, rinsed and drained

3/4 cup frozen corn kernels, thawed

1/4 cup minced onion

1/4 cup diced green bell pepper

3 tablespoons minced fresh cilantro

2 tablespoons vegetable oil

1 tablespoon fresh lime juice

1/4 teaspoon kosher salt

Freshly ground black pepper to taste

One 3- to 4-pound London broil, about 2 inches thick

Olive oil

Freshly ground black pepper to taste

1. Combine the salsa ingredients in a medium-size bowl. Cover and refrigerate until serving time.

2. Brush the steaks with olive oil and dust liberally with pepper.

3. Preheat the grill with all the burners on high for 10 minutes and the lid down.

4. With the burners still on high, place the steaks on the grill, close the lid, and sear one side of the steak for about 4 minutes.

5. After searing, turn off the center burner and turn the other burners to medium. Turn the steak (so the seared side is up), placing it directly over the center burner. Close the lid and finish cooking, turning it one more time. After searing, a 2-inch-thick London

broil will take 10 to 13 minutes to reach rare (140°F), 13 to 15 minutes for medium (160°F), and 15 to 19 minutes for well done (170°F).

6. Transfer the meat to a carving board, cover loosely with aluminum foil, and let rest for 10 to 15 minutes.

7. Slice the meat thin, top each portion with some salsa, and serve.

SERVES 6 TO 8

London Broil with Sherried Mushrooms

There are some flavor combinations that will never go out of style, and this is one of them. Grilling the mushrooms first, before sautéing, gives them a hint of smokiness that combines memorably with the grilled steak.

One 3- to 4-pound London broil, about 2 inches thick

2 cloves garlic, each clove cut into 4 even slivers

1 tablespoon soy sauce

1 tablespoon vegetable oil

Kosher salt and freshly ground black pepper to taste

SHERRIED MUSHROOMS

1 pound fresh mushrooms, wiped clean and stems trimmed

6 to 8 bamboo skewers, soaked in water for 30 minutes and drained

2 tablespoons butter

1/2 cup medium-dry sherry

1/4 teaspoon dried thyme

1 tablespoon finely chopped fresh parsley

Kosher salt and freshly ground black pepper to taste

1. Preheat the grill with all the burners on high for 10 minutes and the lid down.

2. With the tip of a sharp knife, make 8 incisions in the steak, deep enough to accommodate the garlic slivers. Insert the garlic into the incisions. Place the steak on a platter and rub the soy sauce and vegetable oil on both sides. Sprinkle liberally with salt and pepper on both sides.

3. Place the mushrooms on the bamboo skewers, pushing the skewers through the middle of the stem and the middle of the cap.

4. With all the burners still on high, place the steak on the grill, close the lid, and sear one side of the steak for about 4 minutes. Turn off the center burner and turn the other burners to medium. Turn the steak seared side up, placing it directly over the center burner. Close the lid and finish cooking, turning it one more time. After searing, a 2-inch-thick London broil will take 10 to 13 minutes to reach rare (140°F), 13 to 15 minutes for medium (160°F), and 15 to 19 minutes for well done (170°F).

5. Transfer the meat to a carving board, cover it loosely with aluminum foil, and let rest for 10 to 15 minutes.

6. In the meantime, turn all of the burners to low. Place the skewered mushrooms on the grill, close the lid, and cook for a total of 10 minutes, turning the mushrooms once after 5 minutes.

7. Melt the butter in a medium-size skillet over medium-high heat. Remove the mushrooms from the skewers, cut into fairly thick slices, and add to the skillet, along with the sherry, thyme, parsley, and salt and pepper to taste. Cook, stirring, until the sherry has evaporated, 5 to 8 minutes. Remove from the heat.

8. Slice the steak as you prefer, arrange the slices on a platter, and top with the sautéed mushrooms. Serve immediately.

SERVES 4 TO 6

Teriyaki Beef with Green Onions and Mushrooms

When you need a tasty meal in a hurry, this will do the trick. Not only are excellent bottled teriyaki sauces widely available, but this recipe is intensely flavored, so much so that a long marination time is not required. Serve this over steamed white rice.

One 2- to 3-pound London broil, 1 to 1^1/$_2$ inches thick

3 bunches green onions (white part only), cut into 1^1/$_4$-inch pieces

1 pound fresh mushrooms, wiped clean and stems trimmed

One 12-ounce bottled teriyaki sauce of your choice

12 bamboo skewers, soaked in water for 30 minutes and drained

1. To make slicing the steak much easier, put it in the freezer for 30 to 45 minutes, until it starts to get firm, then cut into ^{1}/$_4$-inch-thick slices.

2. About 30 minutes before grilling, combine the sliced beef, green onions, mushrooms, and teriyaki sauce in a large bowl. Toss the beef and vegetables to coat well.

3. Preheat the grill with all the burners on high for 10 minutes and the lid down.

4. While the grill is preheating, thread the marinated beef onto the skewers, alternating with pieces of green onion and mushrooms. The strips of meat should weave among the vegetables.

5. Once the grill is hot, turn all the burners to medium. Place the skewers on the grill, close the lid, and cook for 8 to 12 minutes, turning once. Serve hot off the grill.

SERVES 6 TO 8

Indonesian-Style Beef Satay

Spicy foods are refreshing when the temperature is rising through the roof. This recipe is a somewhat improbable combination of several Indonesian cuisines. It's excellent with ice-cold beer.

One 2- to 3-pound London broil, 1 to 1^1/$_2$ inches thick

PEANUT SAUCE

^{1}/$_2$ cup peanut butter (chunky or smooth)

1 cup chicken or vegetable broth

2 tablespoons soy sauce

1 tablespoon brown sugar

1 to 2 teaspoons Tabasco sauce, to your taste

GINGER-SAKE MARINADE

^{1}/$_2$ cup sake

^{1}/$_4$ cup soy sauce

3 tablespoons vegetable oil

^{1}/$_4$ cup peeled and grated fresh ginger

^{1}/$_4$ cup chopped green onions

1 or 2 fresh chile peppers, to your taste, seeded and minced, or 1 to 2 teaspoons red pepper flakes

12 bamboo skewers, soaked in water for 30 minutes and drained

Lettuce leaves

Cooked Asian rice noodles, chilled, or steamed white rice

Chopped fresh cilantro and mint

1. To make slicing the steak much easier, put it in the freezer for 30 to 45 minutes, until it starts to get firm.

2. In a medium-size saucepan, combine the peanut sauce ingredients and whisk over medium-high heat until it thickens. Remove from the heat and set aside until serving time.

3. Combine the marinade ingredients in a 1-gallon zippered-top plastic bag. Cut the steak into $1/4$-inch-thick slices, add to the marinade, seal, and refrigerate for 15 to 30 minutes.

4. Preheat the grill with all the burners on high for 10 minutes and the lid down.

5. While the grill is preheating, thread or weave the marinated beef onto the skewers, keeping the meat as flat as possible.

6. Once the grill is hot, turn all the burners to medium. Place the skewers on the grill, close the lid, and cook for 8 to 12 minutes, turning once.

7. Meanwhile, gently reheat the peanut sauce and transfer to a serving bowl. Arrange the lettuce leaves on a large platter. Place the rice or noodles in one serving bowl, the cilantro in another, and the mint in another.

8. Serve the skewers and accompaniments family style. Each person takes one lettuce leaf, fills it partially with noodles or steamed rice, a couple of slices of grilled beef, some peanut sauce, and the cilantro and mint, then folds the leaf around the filling like a tortilla.

SERVES 6 TO 8

Chili-Rubbed Beef Fajitas with Peppers and Onions

This is a great in-a-hurry meal that seems to please just about everyone. The dry rub on the steak eliminates the need to marinate the meat, and the peppers and onions cook up in no time.

CHILI RUB

1 tablespoon chili powder

1 teaspoon ground cumin

1 teaspoon garlic salt

1 teaspoon freshly ground black pepper

1 teaspoon dried oregano, crumbled

One 1^1/$_2$- to 2-pound boneless top sirloin steak, 1 inch thick

EXTRAS

6 plum tomatoes

1 medium-size red onion, cut into ^{3}/$_8$-inch-thick slices

1 red, yellow, or orange bell pepper, seeded and quartered

Flour tortillas

Salsa of your choice

Leaves from 1 bunch fresh cilantro, chopped

1. Combine the rub ingredients in a small bowl, and then pat the rub on both sides of the steak. Cover the steak with plastic wrap and put it in the refrigerator for 30 to 60 minutes.

2. Preheat the grill with all the burners on high for 10 minutes and the lid down.

3. Once the grill is hot, turn all the burners to medium. Place the whole plum tomatoes, onion slices, and bell pepper quarters on the grill, close the lid, and cook for about 6 minutes total, turning once midway through. Remove to a shallow bowl and loosely tent with aluminum foil.

4. Keep all the burners on medium. Place the sirloin steak on the grill and cook, with the lid down, for about 10 minutes total for medium-rare, turning once midway through.

5. Wrap the tortillas in foil and put them on the grill for about 1 minute, just to heat through.

6. Carve the steak into thin strips. Cut the tomatoes into quarters and the pepper into strips, and separate the onion into rings. Place some of each in a warm tortilla, add some salsa and cilantro, roll up, and enjoy!

SERVES 3 TO 4

Vietnamese-Style Sliced Steak in Lettuce Leaf Wraps

Wrapping bite-size pieces of spicy grilled food in cool, crisp lettuce leaves is so good that, once you try it, you'll think twice about tortillas, pita bread, other bread-like products. For some reason, these treats taste great during hot summer weather. Ice-cold beer is the drink of choice.

One 1¹/₂-pound boneless top sirloin steak, about 1 inch thick, cut into ³/₈-inch-thick strips

VIETNAMESE-STYLE MARINADE

2 tablespoons soy sauce (or fish sauce, if you have it)

3 to 4 cloves garlic, to your taste, minced or pressed

1 tablespoon toasted sesame oil

Juice of 1 large fresh lime (about 2 tablespoons)

2 tablespoons Thai sweet chili sauce

6 to 8 bamboo skewers, soaked in water for 30 minutes and drained

EXTRAS

About 2 cups fresh bean sprouts

Leaves from 1 bunch fresh cilantro, chopped

About 1 cup shredded carrots

About 1 cup salted dry-roasted peanuts, chopped

Sriracha sauce or other hot pepper sauce (optional)

8 to 10 large lettuce leaves (iceberg works best)

1. Place the sirloin slices in a 1-gallon zippered-top plastic bag. Add the marinade ingredients, seal, squish around to coat the beef, and let marinate in the refrigerator for about 1 hour.

2. Preheat the grill with all the burners on high for 10 minutes and the lid down.

3. While the grill is heating, thread the beef, accordion-style, onto the skewers.

4. Once the grill is hot, turn all the burners to medium. Place the skewered steak on the grill and cook, with the lid down, 6 to 8 minutes total, turning once midway through.

5. Place some steak strips, bean sprouts, cilantro, shredded carrots, and chopped peanuts, along with a squirt or two of sriracha sauce if desired in each lettuce leaf, roll up, and enjoy!

SERVES 4

Hanger Steaks with Caramelized Onions, Mushrooms, Chèvre, and Arugula

For years, hanger steak was either ground up for hamburger meat or, more recently, sent to Japan, where it is prized for its strong beef flavor and great texture. It's beginning to catch on in these parts as "the steak the butcher takes home." This combination—steak, onions, mushrooms, chèvre, and arugula—qualifies as a meal in itself, and a very tasty one at that.

1 hanger steak (about 1 1/2 pounds)

2 tablespoons olive oil

Kosher salt and freshly ground black pepper to taste

2 medium-size yellow onions, cut into 1/4-inch-thick slices

1/2 pound fresh mushrooms, wiped clean, stems trimmed, and thinly sliced

2 teaspoons balsamic vinegar

6 to 8 ounces chèvre, plain or flavored

2 to 3 cups arugula

1 tablespoon extra-virgin olive oil

1 tablespoon red wine vinegar

1. Preheat the grill with all the burners on high for 10 minutes and the lid down.

2. Rub the steak with 1 tablespoon of the olive oil. Sprinkle liberally with salt and pepper.

3. With all the burners still on high, place the steak on the grill, close the lid, and sear the steak for 4 to 5 minutes per side.

4. After searing, immediately turn all the burners to medium and cook the steak, with the lid down, another 3 to 4 minutes per side for medium-rare.

5. Remove to a platter and loosely tent with aluminum foil for about 10 minutes.

6. Pour the remaining 1 tablespoon olive oil into a large skillet over medium-high heat. Add the onions and mushrooms and cook, stirring, until softened, 7 to 10 minutes. Sprinkle the balsamic vinegar over the mixture. Remove from the heat and set aside.

7. Cut the chèvre into $3/8$-inch-thick slices.

8. Place the arugula in a large bowl. Toss with the extra-virgin olive oil and red wine vinegar and season with salt and pepper.

9. Cut the hanger steak into $3/8$-inch-thick slices. Put the dressed arugula on a large platter in an even layer. Lay slices of steak over the arugula. Insert a slice of chèvre between each slice of steak. Top with the warm onion-mushroom mixture and serve immediately.

SERVES 3 TO 4

Flat Iron Steak with Black, White, and Green Peppercorns

Flat iron steaks are tender enough to be grilled without prior marinating. Coated with a little olive oil and a generous grind of multicolored peppercorns, these steaks make for a delicious grilled meal that can be created in a hurry.

2 to 3 tablespoons ground pepper mixture—red, white, and green—to your taste

1 flat iron steak (about 2 pounds), $1^1/2$ to 2 inches thick

1 tablespoon olive oil

Kosher salt to taste

1. Prepare the pepper rub by grinding (or pounding in a mortar and pestle) the three types of pepper in a small bowl and mixing.

2. Coat the steak with the olive oil on both sides. Pat the pepper mixture on both sides of the steak; salt both sides to your taste. Cover the steak with plastic wrap and marinate in the refrigerator for 30 to 60 minutes.

3. Preheat the grill with all the burners on high for 10 minutes and the lid down.

4. Turn all the burners to medium. Place the flat iron steak on the grill, close the lid, and cook 12 to 16 minutes, turning once midway through, for medium-rare.

5. Transfer to a platter and loosely tent with aluminum foil for 10 minutes before slicing.

SERVES 4

Skirt Steak with Tequila Marinade

I like skirt steaks, but they definitely benefit from a little extra time in the marinade. This is a full-flavored marinade, nicely complemented by Cowpoke Beans (page 357), your favorite salsa, and perhaps some steamed rice.

TEQUILA MARINADE

^{1}/2 cup tequila

Juice of 1 lime

1 tablespoon vegetable oil

1 teaspoon chili powder

^{1}/2 teaspoon kosher salt

4 skirt steaks (about 3 pounds)

1. Combine the marinade ingredients in a 1-gallon zippered-top plastic bag. Add the skirt steaks, seal, squish around to coat, and let marinate in the refrigerator for 2 to 3 hours.

2. Preheat the grill with all the burners on high for 10 minutes and the lid down.

3. Once the grill is hot, turn off the center burner and turn the other burners to medium. Place the skirt steaks over the center burner, close the lid, and grill for 10 minutes; then turn and grill for another 5 to 7 minutes for medium-rare. Serve immediately.

SERVES 4 TO 6

Everybody's Favorite Flank Steak

Flank steaks, which can be tough if they aren't marinated before grilling, are one of the tastiest (and leanest) cuts of beef. Given their large surface area, they take well to marinades, and they cook up in a hurry, too. Serve thin-sliced flank steak with Rosemary Potato Wedges (page 307), or make it into delicious steak sandwiches.

THE BEST EVER FLANK STEAK MARINADE

$1/2$ cup dry sherry

$1/4$ cup vegetable or olive oil

$1/4$ cup soy sauce

$1^1/2$ teaspoons ground ginger

1 to 2 teaspoons freshly ground black pepper, to your taste

2 cloves garlic, pressed

1 small onion, minced

One 2- to 3-pound flank steak

1. In a 1-gallon zippered-top plastic bag, combine the marinade ingredients. Add the flank steak, turning it several times to coat both sides, seal, and let marinate in the refrigerator for at least 1 and up to 3 hours, turning the bag over once or twice.

2. Preheat the grill with all the burners on high for 10 minutes and the lid down.

3.   Once the grill is hot, with all the burners still on high, place the flank steak on the grill and cook, with the lid up, for 6 to 8 minutes total for rare to medium-rare, turning it once midway through. Adjust the cooking time slightly up for well-done steak.

4.   Transfer the steak to a cutting board, cover loosely with aluminum foil, and let rest for 5 to 10 minutes before cutting into thin slices and serving hot or at room temperature.

SERVES 4 TO 6

Red Rooster–Soy Marinated Flank Steak

This is my standby marinade, whether I'm in a hurry or not. It works with almost anything, from pork to chicken and tofu. That said, it's particularly well suited to beef. When there's no time to marinate, it'll flavor a flank steak to perfection in an hour. Cook to medium-rare, slice the meat thinly on the bias, and you'll have a table full of happy eaters. The secret to the marinade is the intensely flavored sriracha sauce (otherwise known as "red rooster" sauce because of the rooster on the label), a widely available Vietnamese specialty.

RED ROOSTER–SOY MARINADE

$1/3$ cup sriracha sauce ("red rooster" sauce)

$1/3$ cup soy sauce

2 teaspoons toasted sesame oil

2 to 3 cloves garlic, to your taste, minced or pressed

One $1^1/2$-pound flank steak

1.   Combine the marinade ingredients into a 1-gallon zippered-top plastic bag. Add the flank steak, turning it several times to coat both sides, seal, and let marinate in the refrigerator for at least 1 and up to 4 hours, turning the bag over once or twice.

2.   Preheat the grill with all the burners on high for 10 minutes and the lid down.

3. With all the burners still on high, place the flank steak on the grill and cook, with the lid up, for 6 and 8 minutes total for rare to medium-rare, turning once midway through.

4. Remove the steak to a platter and loosely tent with aluminum foil for 5 to 10 minutes before slicing.

SERVES 3 TO 4

THINKING AHEAD

AS LONG AS YOU'RE COOKING ONE FLANK STEAK, YOU MIGHT AS WELL COOK TWO: LEFTOVERS MAKE A FIRST-RATE SLICED STEAK SANDWICH THE FOLLOWING DAY.

Spicy Flank Steak

This Asian-inspired recipe is well suited to flank steak. Sometimes I eat it hot off the grill with plenty of steamed rice; other times I allow it to cool, slice it, and use it on top of an Asian-style beef salad.

GINGER-GARLIC MARINADE

One 4-inch chunk unpeeled fresh ginger, grated

$1/4$ cup soy sauce

$1/4$ cup water

2 tablespoons vegetable oil

2 tablespoons rice vinegar

2 to 3 large cloves garlic, to your taste, pressed

$1/2$ teaspoon cayenne pepper

One 2- to 3-pound flank steak

Chopped fresh mint and cilantro for garnish (optional)

1. Gather the grated ginger in your hands and squeeze the juice into a nonreactive baking dish. Add the remaining marinade ingredients and mix well. Placed the flank steak in the marinade, turning it several times to coat well, cover, and let marinate in the refrigerator for 2 to 3 hours, turning the steak over several times.

2. Preheat the grill with all the burners on high for 10 minutes and the lid down.

3. With the burners still on high, place the flank steak on the grill and cook, with the lid up, for a total of 6 to 8 minutes for rare to medium-rare, turning it once midway through. Adjust the cooking time slightly up for well-done steak.

4. Transfer the steak to a carving board, cover loosely with aluminum foil, and let rest for 5 to 10 minutes before cutting into thin slices. Garnish with the mint and cilantro if desired, and serve.

SERVES 4 TO 6

GOING AGAINST THE GRAIN

ALWAYS CARVE FLANK STEAK ACROSS THE GRAIN. FOR THE MOST ATTRACTIVE SLICES, HOLD YOUR KNIFE AT A 45-DEGREE ANGLE AS YOU SLICE THE MEAT.

Flank Steak Sandwiches with Grilled Bell Peppers and Onions

Thin slices of flank steak and a mound of grilled peppers and onions make a delicious sandwich—a classic combination that's hard to put down.

SHERRY-SOY MARINADE

$1/2$ cup dry sherry

$1/4$ cup vegetable or olive oil

$1/4$ cup soy sauce

1 to 2 teaspoons freshly ground black pepper

One 2- to 3-pound flank steak

2 medium-size onions

Vegetable oil

2 large green bell peppers

Kosher salt and freshly ground black pepper to taste

Sliced bread or buns, warmed

1. In a 1-gallon zippered-top plastic bag, combine the marinade ingredients. Add the flank steak, turning it several times to coat well, seal, and let marinate in the refrigerator for at least 1 and up to 3 hours, turning the bag over once or twice.

2. Preheat the grill with all the burners on high for 10 minutes and the lid down.

3. While the grill is preheating, peel the onions, cut into 3/8-inch-thick slices, and coat them with oil. Wash and dry the bell peppers, then coat them with oil.

4. With all the burners still on high, place the flank steak on the grill, close the lid, and sear the flank steak 1 to 2 minutes per side.

5. After searing, turn off the center burner and turn the other burners to medium. Move the flank steak directly over the center burner and surround it with the onion slices and bell peppers. Close the lid and cook, turning the meat and vegetables once. The onion slices will be done when they are soft and slightly brown, 6 to 8 minutes; the peppers will be done when they have collapsed on themselves, 10 to 20 minutes. The meat should cook for a total of 18 to 20 minutes for medium; adjust the cooking time slightly up or down for rare or well-done meat.

6. Transfer the steak to a cutting board, cover loosely with aluminum foil, and let rest for 5 minutes.

7. While the steak is resting, remove the stems and seeds from the grilled peppers, then slice 3/8 inch thick. Combine the pepper and onion slices in a bowl and toss with a little salt and pepper.

8. Cut the flank steak into thin slices, then serve the slices of steak topped with the pepper-and-onion mixture on warm sliced bread or buns.

SERVES 4 GENEROUSLY

Tried-and-True
Marinated Beef Kebabs

Most beef cut for kebabs tends to be a little on the tough side; the marinade in this recipe will not only tenderize the meat, but also will give it a flavor that everyone seems to love.

SHERRIED KEBOB MARINADE

$1/2$ cup dry sherry

$1/4$ cup soy sauce

3 tablespoons vegetable oil

2 cloves garlic, pressed

1 small onion, minced

$1 1/2$ teaspoons ground ginger

2 pounds flank, round, or chuck steak, cut into 1-inch cubes

12 bamboo skewers, soaked in water for 30 minutes and drained

1. Combine the marinade ingredients in a 1-gallon zippered-top plastic bag. Add the beef cubes, making sure they are all submerged, seal, and let marinate in the refrigerator for at least 2 to 3 hours or overnight.

2. Preheat the grill with all the burners on high for 10 minutes and the lid down.

3. While the grill is preheating, thread the marinated beef onto the skewers, with the sides of the pieces touching.

4. Once the grill is hot, turn all the burners to medium. Place the skewers on the grill, close the lid, and cook 8 to 12 minutes, turning the skewers once or twice. Serve hot off the grill.

SERVES 4 GENEROUSLY

Skewered Beef Bourguignon

This recipe may sound like one of those well-intentioned but nevertheless ill-advised concoctions from a home arts magazine, circa 1962, but rest assured that it is as tasty as it is up-to-date.

BOURGUIGNON MARINADE

2 cups dry red wine

1/4 cup extra-virgin olive oil

2 bay leaves

1 teaspoon kosher salt

1/2 teaspoon dried thyme

1/2 teaspoon dried rosemary

1/2 teaspoon freshly ground black pepper

3 pounds boneless beef chuck or tri-tip roast, cut into 2-inch chunks

16 small to medium-size fresh mushrooms, wiped clean and stems trimmed

16 small white boiling onions, parboiled for 2 minutes, drained, and peeled

4 strips bacon, partially cooked (don't let them get crispy, just limp), drained, and cut into 4 pieces per slice

2 dozen bamboo skewers, soaked in water for 30 minutes and drained

Buttered parsleyed noodles

1. Combine the marinade ingredients in a 1-gallon zippered-top plastic bag. Add the beef cubes and mushrooms, making sure they're submerged, seal, and let marinate in the refrigerator for 4 to 6 hours.

2. Preheat the grill with all the burners on high for 10 minutes with the lid down.

3. While the grill is preheating, thread the beef, mushrooms, onions, and bacon onto the skewers, alternating each as you go.

4. Once the grill is hot, turn all the burners to medium. Place the kebabs on the grill and cook, with the lid down, for 8 to 12 minutes, turning the skewers once or twice.

5. Transfer the kebabs to a work surface, remove the skewers, and serve on top of the noodles.

SERVES 6 TO 8

Chuck Wagon Chuck Roast

This hearty fare is great for serving a crowd. There's no need to marinate this steak; just baste it frequently during the cooking process. For an unusual but delicious salad course, try combining fresh orange and red onion slices on a bed of lettuce leaves. Dress with a simple oil-and-vinegar mixture and garnish with chopped fresh cilantro if desired. And remember, we're in chuck wagon mode here, so when it comes to side dishes, think about Cowpoke Beans (page 357), "Baked" Potatoes on the Grill (page 305), or even cornbread.

BEER AND CHILI BASTING SAUCE

$3/4$ cup beer

$1/2$ cup vegetable oil

2 tablespoons chili powder

2 teaspoons ground cumin

1 teaspoon dried oregano

1 teaspoon kosher salt

1 teaspoon freshly ground black pepper

One 4- to 6-pound bone-in chuck roast, $1^1/2$ to 2 inches thick

1. Preheat the grill with all the burners on high for 10 minutes and the lid down.

2. While the grill is preheating, combine the basting sauce ingredients in a small bowl. Coat the roast liberally with the sauce.

3. Once the grill is hot, turn off the center burner and turn the other burners to medium. Place the roast over the center burner, close the lid, and cook until a meat thermometer inserted into the thickest part registers 5 to 10 degrees shy of the desired temperature (140°F for rare, 160°F for medium, 170°F for well done), brushing the roast with the basting sauce every 15 minutes or so. Turn the roast once midway through. A 4- to 6-pound chuck roast will take 1 to 1^1/$_4$ hours to cook to rare, 1^1/$_4$ to 1^3/$_4$ hours for medium, and 1^3/$_4$ to 2 hours for well done.

4. Transfer the roast to a carving board, cover loosely with aluminum foil, and let rest for 10 minutes or so before cutting on the diagonal into thin slices.

SERVES 6 TO 8

Boneless Chuck Roast with Bourbon and Coke

This recipe was inspired by one invented for short ribs by my good friend Lou Jane Temple. The combination may strike you as a little odd, but it really works—and it's certainly a conversation starter. And, no, you can't drink the marinade afterward!

One 2- to 2^1/$_2$-pound boneless chuck roast

BOURBON AND COKE MARINADE

1 can Coke (not diet; you need the sugar)

3 ounces good bourbon

1 tablespoon vegetable oil

6 cloves garlic, minced or pressed

1 tablespoon soy sauce

1 tablespoon Worcestershire sauce

1 teaspoon mustard seeds

1 teaspoon caraway seeds

1/2 teaspoon allspice berries

Kosher salt and freshly ground black pepper to taste

1. Place the chuck roast in a 1-gallon zippered-top plastic bag.

2. Combine the marinade ingredients in a medium-size bowl, pour into the bag, seal, and let marinate in the refrigerator for 2 to 3 hours, turning the bag once or twice.

3. Preheat the grill with all the burners on high for 10 minutes and the lid down.

4. With all the burners still on high, place the chuck on the grill, close the lid, and sear for 5 minutes per side.

5. After searing, turn all the burners to medium. Close the lid and cook the roast another 6 to 8 minutes for medium-rare, turning once midway through.

6. Remove the steak to a platter, loosely tent with aluminum foil, and let rest for 10 minutes before slicing.

SERVES 4

THEY'RE NOT JUST GREAT FOR PAINT

SMALL PAINTBRUSHES, SOLD IN HARDWARE STORES, ARE EXCELLENT FOR BASTING.

Sherry and Garlic Marinated Chuck Roast

When most people think of chuck roast, they think "tough." The boneless version, however, is not only smaller than the bone-in variety, it is surprisingly tender and extremely flavorful.

SHERRY-GARLIC MARINADE

1/2 cup dry sherry

1/4 cup vegetable oil

1/4 cup soy sauce

2 cloves garlic, pressed

1 small onion, minced

1/4 teaspoon freshly ground black pepper

One 4- to 6-pound boneless chuck roast

1. Combine the marinade ingredients in a 1-gallon zippered-top plastic bag. Add the chuck roast, turn to coat well, seal, and let marinate in the refrigerator for at least 3 to 4 hours or overnight if desired, turning the roast several times.

2. Preheat the grill with all the burners on high for 10 minutes and the lid down.

3. Once the grill is hot, turn off the center burner and turn the other burners to medium. Place the roast over the center burner, close the lid, and cook for 1 to 1 1/2 hours, turning it once. The roast is done when an instant-read meat thermometer inserted into the thickest part registers 5 to 10 degrees shy of the desired temperature (140°F for rare, 160°F for medium, 170°F for well done). A 4- to 6-pound chuck roast will take 1 to 1 1/4 hours to cook to rare, 1 1/4 to 1 3/4 hours for medium, and 1 3/4 to 2 hours for well done.

4. Transfer the roast to a carving board, cover loosely with aluminum foil, and let rest for 10 minutes or so before cutting on the diagonal into thin slices.

SERVES 6 TO 8

Chuck Roast with Argentine Squirt Sauce

A friend of mine remembered seeing a travel show on television about Argentina. They're big beef lovers there, and all of a sudden this Argentine cowboy is grilling a bunch of steaks on a big outdoor grill and squirting them with a combination of salt, water, and cayenne. Theatrics aside, this really is a good, simple, flavorful idea. Try it! Most folks think of chuck roast as a tough customer, but the boneless cuts seem to have most of the tougher sections trimmed away, leaving a very tasty large steak.

ARGENTINE SQUIRT SAUCE

2 cups water

1 cup kosher salt

2 tablespoons cayenne pepper

One 2- to 2^1/2-pound boneless chuck roast, 1^1/2 inches thick

1 tablespoon vegetable oil

1. Combine the squirt sauce ingredients in a large squirt bottle. Shake until the salt has dissolved. Coat the chuck roast evenly with the vegetable oil.

2. Preheat the grill with all the burners on high for 10 minutes and the lid down.

3. With all the burners still on high, place the roast on the grill and sear, with the lid up, 5 minutes per side. A couple of times during the searing process, squirt the roast with the sauce. This will cause quite a bit of hissing, spitting, and steaming.

4. After searing, turn all the burners to medium, close the lid, and cook the roast for another 6 to 8 minutes, turning once midway through, for rare to medium-rare.

5. Remove the roast to a platter, loosely tent with aluminum foil, and let rest for 10 minutes before slicing.

SERVES 4

Real Tasty Beef Brisket

There are few things better than a well-prepared beef brisket—it's guaranteed to turn any event into a party. But few things are more mysteriously difficult to cook well. With the following procedure, we think we've got you covered, not incidentally because the gas grill seems to be particularly well suited to beef brisket. Because of the long cooking time (6 to 7 hours), this recipe almost demands a stay-at-home cook, or one on a weekend party schedule. Also, be sure you have enough propane to undertake this daylong project. *Note:* If you want to serve truly authentic, Kansas City–style brisket, do it this way: Wrap 2 or 3 thin slices of brisket in a single slice of squishy white sandwich bread, add a little coleslaw, a few dill pickle chips, and a squeeze or two of your favorite bottled barbecue sauce, fold it in half, and enjoy.

SWEET, HOT, AND SOUR BASTING SAUCE

1/4 cup paprika

2 tablespoons chili powder

2 tablespoons ground cumin

2 tablespoons kosher salt

2 tablespoons dark brown sugar

1 tablespoon granulated sugar

1 tablespoon crumbled dried oregano

1 tablespoon freshly ground black pepper

1 tablespoon ground white pepper

2 teaspoons cayenne pepper (optional)

1/2 cup cider vinegar

1/2 cup water

1/2 cup soy sauce

1/4 cup Worcestershire sauce

One 5- to 6-pound beef brisket, fat trimmed to about 1/4 inch on one side

1. To make the basting sauce, combine the dry ingredients in a medium-size bowl and mix until thoroughly blended. *Note:* If there are people in the crowd who really don't care for heat (as in *picante*, not *caliente*), omit the cayenne altogether. Add the vinegar, water, soy sauce, and Worcestershire sauce and mix well. Brush some of the basting sauce over the brisket.

2. Preheat the grill with all the burners on high for 10 minutes and the lid down.

3. Once the grill is hot, turn off the center burner and turn the other burners to medium. Place the brisket, fat side up, over the center burner, close the lid, and cook, without turning the meat, for 6 hours. Baste the brisket with the sauce once or twice an hour.

4. Remove the brisket from the grill and wrap it in aluminum foil. Return the foil-wrapped brisket to the grill, in the same position as before but upside down, and cook for another hour. The meat should be completely fork tender.

5. Remove the brisket from the grill and let rest on a cutting board, still covered, for at least 30 minutes before cutting into thin slices.

SERVES 8

The Classic Burger

This all-American original too often turns out disappointing when cooked at home. The problem, in most cases, is making the burger too thick, or using meat that's too lean. If you're really watching your fat intake, by all means use lean ground beef; otherwise, use ground chuck (which yields a much juicier burger) and don't make the patties any thicker than ³/4 inch. For a truly delicious burger, grill ¹/4-inch-thick slices of onion, ¹/2-inch slices of tomato, and buttered hamburger buns while you're grilling the burgers. Outstanding!

1 pound ground chuck (or lean ground beef if desired)

¹/2 teaspoon kosher salt

¹/2 teaspoon freshly ground black pepper

1. Preheat the grill with all the burners on high for 10 minutes and the lid down.

2. While the grill is preheating, mix together the ground beef, salt, and pepper in a medium-size bowl with your hands and shape into 4 patties, each $1/2$ to $3/4$ inch thick.

3. Once the grill is hot, turn all the burners to medium. Place the burgers on the grill and cook, with the lid down, for 3 to 4 minutes per side for medium-rare, 4 to 5 minutes per side for medium, and about 6 minutes per side for well done, turning them once. Serve hot off the grill.

SERVES 4

WATCH THAT SPATULA!

RESIST THE TEMPTATION TO PRESS DOWN WITH YOUR SPATULA ON HAMBURGER PATTIES AS THEY'RE GRILLING: IT DOES NOTHING BUT SQUEEZE FLAVORFUL JUICES OUT OF THE MEAT.

The Commissioner's Best Beef Ribs

This recipe is for those cooks tired of the same old tomato-based barbecue sauce. Trim the extra fat off the ribs: You don't need it, and trimming it can reduce the chance of flare-ups. Crush the fennel seeds in a mortar or coffee grinder; all you are trying to accomplish is the release of the flavor of the seeds. Add more garlic if you wish—the more you use, the better the rub sticks to the ribs. Again, if you're looking for something different, beef ribs are hard to beat and, better yet, hard to do wrong on a gas grill.

WET GARLIC RUB

2 to 3 cloves garlic, to your taste, minced or pressed

1 tablespoon olive oil

1^1/2 teaspoons freshly ground black pepper

1^1/2 teaspoons dry mustard

1^1/2 teaspoons fennel seeds, crushed

1 teaspoon kosher salt

^{1}/2 teaspoon ground cloves

4 pounds beef ribs (also sold as "dinosaur bones")

1. In small bowl, combine the rub ingredients and mix well.

2. Spread the rub on both sides of the beef ribs (it's easiest to use your hands for this step). Wrap the ribs tightly with plastic wrap and let marinate in the refrigerator for 2 to 4 hours.

3. Preheat the grill with all the burners on high for 10 minutes and the lid down.

4. Once the grill is hot, leave the back burner on high and turn the other burners to medium-low. Place the beef ribs over the burners on medium-low, close the lid, and cook for a total of about 40 minutes, turning every 10 minutes or so. Serve hot off the grill.

SERVES 4 TO 6

Sweet, Hot, and Sour Basted Beef Ribs

Old-timers used to say, "The closer to the bone, the sweeter the meat." That's certainly the case with these ribs.

1 recipe Sweet, Hot, and Sour Basting Sauce (page 208)

4 pounds beef ribs (also sold as "dinosaur bones")

1. About 30 minutes before grilling, brush the ribs with the basting sauce. If there is any left, use it up in the first basting of the ribs on the grill.

2. Preheat the grill with all the burners on high for 10 minutes and the lid down.

3. Once the grill is hot, turn off the center burner and turn the other burners to medium. Place the beef ribs over the center burner, close the lid, and cook for about 1 hour, turning and basting with the sauce every 15 minutes or so. Serve hot off the grill.

SERVES 4 TO 6

Savory Short Ribs of Beef

Anyone who really knows beef knows that short ribs are mighty fine eating. Put away the knives and forks—this is definitely a dish to eat with your hands.

RED WINE AND SOY MARINADE

$1/2$ cup dry red wine

$1/4$ cup soy sauce

3 tablespoons vegetable oil

2 cloves garlic, pressed

$1/2$ teaspoon freshly ground black pepper

$1/4$ teaspoon dried thyme

4 pounds short ribs

1. Combine the marinade ingredients in a 1-gallon zippered-top plastic bag. Add the short ribs, submerging them in the marinade, seal, and let marinate in the refrigerator for 2 to 3 hours.

2. Preheat the grill with all the burners on high for 10 minutes and the lid down.

3. Once the grill is hot, turn off the center burner and turn the other burners to medium. Position the short ribs over the center burner, close the lid, and cook for $1^1/4$ to $1^1/2$ hours, turning the ribs every 10 to 15 minutes. Serve hot off the grill.

SERVES 4 TO 6

Grilled Liver Steaks

Although liver is not to everyone's taste, you may be able to convert a few people with this recipe. Most liver lovers agree that medium is about as "done" as you want to cook liver; any more and it toughens and becomes dry. Serve with Grilled Onion Slices (page 301) and strips of crisp bacon. "Baked" Potatoes on the Grill (page 305) and a spinach salad also make wonderful companions.

1 pound liver steak (beef or calf), about 1 inch thick

3 tablespoons butter, melted

Kosher salt and freshly ground black pepper to taste

1. Preheat the grill with all the burners on high for 10 minutes and the lid down.

2. While the grill is preheating, rub the liver steak with the melted butter and sprinkle with salt and pepper.

3. Once the grill is hot, turn off the center burner and turn the other burners to medium. Place the liver over the center burner, close the lid, and cook for 15 to 20 minutes, turning once or twice. Check for the desired degree of doneness by discreetly slicing into the liver steak with a sharp knife.

4. When the liver is done, slice it into individual portions and serve.

SERVES 4

6

Lamb and Veal

Although lamb and veal aren't quite as popular for grilling as beef and pork, many cuts are greatly enhanced by grilling. Just remember to treat these tender meats with care: Overcooked lamb or veal is tough. ✳ As with all meats, be sure to remove the lamb or veal from the refrigerator about 30 minutes before grilling.

Lamb

According to the USDA, lamb labeled *genuine lamb, lamb,* or *spring lamb* must be less than one year old. Sheep that are between one and two years old are classified as yearlings. Furthermore, the term *spring lamb* identifies lamb processed between the first Monday in March and the first Monday in October. In general, the paler the meat, the younger—and the more tender—the lamb.

A special program administered by the USDA encourages ranchers to raise leaner lamb. After being graded by USDA inspectors, this special lamb is given a red, white, and blue sticker proclaiming it as Certified Fresh American Lamb. About the top third of lamb produced in this country receives this designation. Domestic lamb, which is usually grain fed, tends to be more tender than imported, grass-fed lamb, much of which is from New Zealand.

There is often a thin, parchment-like membrane called a fell covering the fat on lamb. The butcher usually removes it from chops, but you'll find it covering larger cuts. Don't remove the fell, because it helps keep the meat from drying out.

Because lamb is so tender, it is very tasty served rare. Remember that lamb, like all meats, continues to cook after it is taken off the grill. Remove lamb, especially large cuts such as roasts, when its internal temperature registers approximately 10 degrees shy of the desired temperature. Place the meat on a carving board, cover it loosely with a foil tent, and let it rest for 10 to 15 minutes before carving. The resting period allows the meat not only to reach the level of doneness you desire, but also to reabsorb the flavorful juices, yielding a more succulent dish.

Lamb is considered rare at 140°F, medium at 160°F, and well done at 170°F.

Veal

The most delicate veal comes from milk-fed calves, butchered when they are between eight and twelve weeks old. The meat is pale pink and the fat (of which there should be little) is satiny white. A lower grade of veal, but still a good one, comes from grass-fed calves, usually butchered when they are four or five months old. The meat is darker pink than that of milk-fed veal, but it should never be red.

Veal is considered rare at 140°F and medium at 160°F; because veal is so lean, it should never be cooked well done. Most chefs aim for an internal temperature of about 150°F, or medium-rare.

Roast Leg of Lamb
with White Beans   218

Greek Butterflied
Leg of Lamb with
Lemon and Oregano   220

Marsha's Miracle
Butterflied Leg of Lamb   221

Lamb Tenderloin
with Artichoke Sauce   222

Little Debbie's
Rack of Lamb   223

Garlic-and-Rosemary
Rack of Lamb   224

Lamb Chops with Mint
Chimichurri Sauce   226

Lamb Chops with
Blackberries and
Lavender   227

Lamb Chops with
Fresh Mint Sauce   228

Lamb Chops with
Creamy Fresh Dill Sauce   229

Marinated Greek
Lamb Shoulder Chops   230

Lamb Shanks in
Guinness and
Apricot Nectar   232

Lamb Kebabs with
Spicy Yogurt Marinade   233

Mediterranean Lamb
Shish Kebabs   234

Lamb Souvlaki Burgers   235

Lamb Patties with
Mozzarella and Mint   237

Veal Paprika Chops with
Sour Cream and Chives   238

Grilled Veal Chops with
Lemon-Caper Sauce   239

Veal Chops with
Basil-Mustard Sauce   240

Grilled Veal Saltimbocca   241

Roast Leg of Lamb with White Beans

The combination of roast leg of lamb and white beans is a favorite in French households, particularly in Normandy. If you or your family and friends prefer a lamb with a flavor that's not so strong, have your butcher trim the leg of all its fat. Compensate for the loss of fat by rubbing the leg with softened butter.

One 4- to 6-pound leg of lamb

2 cloves garlic, cut into 8 slivers total

3 tablespoons butter (if the leg has been trimmed of fat), softened

Kosher salt and freshly ground black pepper

WHITE BEANS

3 tablespoons olive oil

1 medium-size onion, minced

1 medium-size carrot, minced

Two 15-ounce cans small white beans, drained and rinsed

One 15-ounce can chicken or vegetable broth

2 to 3 large cloves garlic, to your taste, pressed

1 bay leaf

1 teaspoon dried thyme

1 teaspoon kosher salt

1/2 teaspoon freshly ground black pepper

Chopped fresh parsley for garnish (optional)

1. Preheat the grill with all the burners on high for 10 minutes and the lid down.

2. While the grill is preheating, use the point of a sharp knife to make 8 incisions deep enough to hold the garlic across the top of the leg of lamb. Insert a garlic sliver into each incision. If the leg has been trimmed of fat, rub the softened butter on the lamb. Sprinkle the lamb with salt and pepper.

3. Once the grill is hot, turn off the center burner and turn the other burners to medium. Place the lamb over the center burner, close the lid, and cook, rotating the lamb every half hour or so, for 2 to 2^1/$_2$ hours. This yields a leg of lamb cooked to medium, 160°F. If you want a different degree of doneness, adjust the cooking time up or down accordingly. The desired internal temperatures for lamb are 140°F for rare, 160°F for medium, and 170°F for well done. Remove the leg from the grill when an instant-read meat thermometer, inserted deep into the meat in the thickest part away from the bone, registers 10 degrees shy of the desired final temperature.

4. While the lamb cooks, prepare the white beans. In a large saucepan, heat the olive oil over medium-high heat. Add the onion and carrot and cook, stirring, until the onion is softened and transparent, about 4 minutes. Add the beans, broth, garlic, and seasonings. Bring to a boil, reduce the heat to medium-low, and simmer, uncovered, for about 20 minutes, stirring occasionally. When done, the beans should be neither too soupy nor too thick. Remove from the heat.

5. Transfer the leg of lamb to a carving board, loosely tent with aluminum foil, and let rest for 10 minutes or so; it will continue to "cook" to the desired degree of doneness. Meanwhile, reheat the beans, adding more broth, if necessary, to maintain the right consistency.

6. To serve, carve the lamb into fairly thin slices. Arrange them on a serving platter along with the white beans; pour any juices that may have accumulated on the carving board over the sliced lamb and beans. Garnish with a little parsley if desired.

SERVES 6 TO 8

ROASTS ARE THE MOST

ROASTS ARE OFTEN CONSIDERED "COMPANY'S COMING" FOOD, SPECIAL-OCCASION FOOD THAT'S DIFFICULT TO COOK. IN TRUTH, A ROAST IS ONE OF THE EASIEST FOODS TO COOK: SIMPLY SEASON IT, PUT IT ON THE GRILL, COOK IT UNTIL IT REACHES THE DESIRED TEMPERATURE, AND SLICE IT. THAT'S IT.

Greek Butterflied Leg of Lamb with Lemon and Oregano

An exceptional dish to serve to a crowd, a butterflied leg of lamb is easy to grill, easy to carve, and, with its special marinade, especially flavorful. It goes great with Garlicky Grilled Tomatoes (page 313) and Rosemary Potato Wedges (page 307). *Note:* It takes time to properly butterfly a leg of lamb, so order it from your butcher in advance.

One 4- to 6-pound leg of lamb, boned, trimmed, and butterflied

1 recipe Greek-Style Marinade (page 230)

1.   Place the butterflied leg of lamb in a large nonreactive container, pour the cooled marinade over it, cover, and let marinate in the refrigerator for 4 to 6 hours, or overnight if desired.

2.   Preheat the grill with all the burners on high for 10 minutes and the lid down.

3.   While the grill is preheating, drain the marinade from the container into a small saucepan. Bring to a boil for 2 minutes, remove from the heat, and set aside for basting.

4.   Once the grill is hot, turn off the center burner and turn the other burners to medium. Place the lamb over the center burner, close the lid, and cook for 45 to 55 minutes for rare (140°F), 55 to 65 minutes for medium (160°F), or 1 1/4 hours for well done (170°F), inserting an instant-read thermometer into the thickest part to measure the temperature. Turn the lamb several times, basting it each time with the marinade. Remove the meat from the grill when it is 10 degrees shy of the desired final internal temperature.

5.   Transfer the lamb to a carving board, loosely tent with aluminum foil, and let rest for 10 minutes or so before carving into fairly thin slices. Arrange them on a serving platter, pour over any juices that may have accumulated on the carving board, and serve.

SERVES 6 TO 8

Marsha's Miracle Butterflied Leg of Lamb

I first had this lamb at my friend Marsha Maher's house. It was so good I asked if I could have the recipe. Normally very generous with her culinary talent, this time she declined—and then she started to laugh. "No, I can't tell you—really I can't," she said, laughing harder. I finally got the recipe out of her and came to understand why she was laughing. And so will you when you check out the ingredients. But the results are no laughing matter—this is really delicious. Marsha's daughter, also an excellent cook, says you can sex up the marinade with the addition of pressed garlic and fresh rosemary, but it really isn't necessary.

One 16-ounce bottle Kraft Creamy French Dressing (Marsha says, "Accept no substitutes.")

6 cloves garlic (optional), minced or pressed

1 tablespoon dried rosemary (optional), crumbled

One 4-pound leg of lamb, boned, trimmed, and butterflied

1. Pour the French dressing into a 1-gallon zippered-top plastic bag; add the garlic and rosemary if using. Add the lamb, seal, squish around to coat with the dressing, and let marinate in the refrigerator for at least 4 hours and preferably overnight.

2. Preheat the grill with all the burners on high for 10 minutes and the lid down.

3. When the grill is hot, turn off the center burner and turn the other burners to medium. Place the lamb over the center burner, close the lid, and cook, turning the lamb every 12 to 15 minutes, 45 to 55 minutes for rare (140°F), 55 to 65 minutes for medium (160°F), or 1 1/4 hours for well done (170°F), inserting an instant-read thermometer into the thickest part to measure the temperature. Remove the meat from the grill when it is 10 degrees shy of the desired final internal temperature.

4. Remove to a platter, loosely tent with aluminum foil, and let rest for 10 minutes or so before slicing.

SERVES 6 TO 8

YOU DON'T ALWAYS NEED HEAT TO COOK

REMEMBER THAT ALL FOOD CONTINUES TO COOK AFTER IT IS TAKEN OFF THE GRILL. YOUR BEST BET IS TO REMOVE MEAT WHEN IT IS 5 TO 10 DEGREES SHY OF THE DESIRED DEGREE OF DONENESS.

Lamb Tenderloin
with Artichoke Sauce

Two of the hallmarks of spring, lamb and artichokes, are a great combination of flavors, and this recipe makes the most of them. If you can't find lamb tenderloin, have your butcher bone and tie together lamb loin chops.

ARTICHOKE SAUCE

One 13-ounce can artichoke hearts, about half the water drained off

2 tablespoons mayonnaise

1 tablespoon olive oil

$1/4$ teaspoon kosher salt

1 clove garlic, peeled

1 tablespoon butter

1 pound lamb tenderloin or boned and tied lamb loin chops (about $1^1/2$ pounds), about $1^1/2$ inches thick

Freshly ground black pepper

1 teaspoon olive oil

1 tablespoon Dijon mustard

1. Combine the artichoke hearts and their reserved water and the mayonnaise, olive oil, salt, and garlic in a blender on low speed until smooth. Transfer to a small saucepan over medium heat; whisk in the butter when the sauce is hot. Remove from the heat and set aside until needed.

2. Preheat the grill with all the burners on high for 10 minutes and the lid down.

3. While the grill is preheating, coat the lamb with the olive oil, dust it with the pepper, and then evenly spread the mustard over both sides.

4. When the grill is hot, leave the back burner on high and turn the other burners to low. Place the lamb over the burners on low, close the lid, and cook about 16 minutes, turning once midway through, for medium-rare.

5. Remove the lamb to a platter, loosely tent with aluminum foil, and let rest for 10 minutes. Meanwhile, reheat the sauce to just below the boiling point. Slice the lamb and serve topped with the sauce. Enjoy!

SERVES 4

Little Debbie's Rack of Lamb

There's a long Middle Eastern tradition of combining pomegranates and lamb, and for good reason. Dealing with pomegranates used to involve a lot of work and mess. Luckily, pomegranate juice is now commonly available and makes quick work of this delicious marinade.

2 racks of lamb (each 1^1/$_2$ to 1^3/$_4$ pounds)

POMEGRANATE MARINADE

1^1/$_2$ cups pomegranate juice

^{1}/$_4$ cup olive oil

2 tablespoons ground coriander

1 teaspoon ground white pepper

5 to 6 cloves garlic, to your taste, peeled

1. Place the racks in a 2-gallon zippered-top plastic bag.

2. Combine the marinade ingredients in a large measuring cup, pour into the bag, seal, and squish around to coat the lamb. Let marinate in the refrigerator for at least 4 to 6 hours and preferably overnight.

3. Preheat the grill with all the burners on high for 10 minutes and the lid down.

4. When the grill is hot, turn off the center burner and turn the other burners to medium. Place the racks over the center burner, close the lid, and cook for 30 and 40 minutes, depending on desired degree of doneness; 30 minutes will be on the rare side, and 40 minutes more toward medium. Turn the racks once midway through cooking. Remove the meat from the grill when it is 10 degrees shy of the desired final internal temperature.

5. Remove to a platter, loosely tent with aluminum foil, and let rest for 10 minutes before carving into individual chops.

SERVES 4

Garlic-and-Rosemary Rack of Lamb

This rack of lamb, infused with the classic combination of garlic and rosemary, is very easy to grill to perfection—and it never fails to make a memorable impression. *Note:* When you purchase the lamb, ask your butcher to make a cut for the garlic and rosemary along the length of each rack, between the meat and the rib bones, but not all the way through to the other side.

2 racks of lamb (each 1^1/2 to 1^3/4 pounds)

4 to 6 cloves garlic, to your taste, pressed

1 tablespoon dried rosemary, crumbled

Kosher salt and freshly ground black pepper to taste

Olive oil

1. Preheat the grill with all the burners on high for 10 minutes and the lid down.

2. While the grill is preheating, spread the garlic, rosemary, salt, and pepper in the openings between the meat and the rib bones in each rack, making an even layer with your fingers. Rub a little olive oil over the outside of each rack; dust the lamb with more salt and pepper.

3. Once the grill is hot, turn off the center burner and turn the other burners to medium. Place the racks over the center burner, close the lid, and cook for 30 and 40 minutes, depending on desired degree of doneness; 30 minutes will be on the rare side, and 40 minutes more toward medium. Turn the racks once midway through cooking. Remove the meat from the grill when it is 10 degrees shy of the desired final internal temperature: rare 140°F, medium 160°F, well done 170°F.

4. Place the lamb on a carving board, loosely tent with aluminum foil, and let rest for 10 minutes or so before carving the racks into individual rib chops. Arrange them on a serving platter, pour any juices that may have accumulated on the carving board over the chops, and serve.

SERVES 4

Lamb Chops with Mint Chimichurri Sauce

Lamb and mint go together like the proverbial horse and carriage. But for all of those who, like me, grew up eating overcooked lamb with that bright green mint jelly, this sauce is definitely not your mother's mint sauce. Prepare to be delighted.

4 to 6 full-size lamb chops (3 to 4^1/$_2$ pounds), about 1 inch thick

MINT CHIMICHURRI SAUCE

1 cup packed fresh Italian parsley leaves

^{1}/$_2$ cup packed fresh mint leaves

^{1}/$_2$ cup dry white wine

^{1}/$_2$ cup olive oil

^{1}/$_4$ cup white wine vinegar

1 teaspoon kosher salt

2 jalapeños, seeded

3 cloves garlic, peeled

1. Place the lamb chops in a 1-gallon zippered-top plastic bag.

2. Combine the sauce ingredients in a medium-size bowl, pour into the bag, seal, and squish around to coat the chops. Let marinate in the refrigerator for 2 to 4 hours.

3. Preheat the grill with all the burners on high for 10 minutes and the lid down.

4. When the grill is hot, turn all the burners to medium. Remove the lamb chops from the sauce, reserving the sauce. Place the lamb chops on the grill, close the lid, and cook for a total of 8 to 12 minutes, turning once midway through; 8 minutes will be rare to medium-rare, 12 minutes medium to medium-well.

5. Transfer the chops to a platter, loosely tent with aluminum foil, and let rest for 10 minutes. Meanwhile, bring the reserved marinade to a boil in a medium-size saucepan for 2 minutes.

6. Serve the lamb chops with a spoonful of sauce on top, and be prepared for a flavor treat.

SERVES 4 TO 6

Lamb Chops with Blackberries and Lavender

This is a very pleasant and unusual combination of flavors, inspired by a trip to the Pacific Northwest and a visit to Bruce Bennet's herb garden. Naturally, it's best made with fresh, in-season berries. You can use untreated lavender flowers as a garnish on the finished dish, but use the more pungent leaves for the marinade.

8 lamb loin chops (about 3 pounds)

BLACKBERRY AND LAVENDER MARINADE

2 cups fresh blackberries

$1/2$ cup sweet red vermouth

$1/4$ cup fresh lavender leaves, finely chopped

1 teaspoon kosher salt

$1/4$ teaspoon Worcestershire sauce

4 to 6 cloves garlic, to your taste, minced or pressed

1. Place the lamb chops in a 1-gallon zippered-top plastic bag.

2. Combine the marinade ingredients, mashing the berries, in a medium-size bowl. Pour the marinade into the bag, seal, and squish around to coat the chops. Let marinate in the refrigerator for at least 3 to 4 hours and preferably overnight.

3. Preheat the grill with all the burners on high for 10 minutes and the lid down.

4. When the grill is hot, turn all the burners to medium. Place the lamb chops on the grill, close the lid, and cook for 4 to 6 minutes per side for medium-rare. Adjust the time slightly up or down if you desire a different degree of doneness.

5. Transfer the chops to a platter, loosely tent with aluminum foil, and let rest for 10 minutes before serving.

SERVES 4

Lamb Chops with Fresh Mint Sauce

For those of us brought up on well-done lamb and store-bought mint jelly, serving lamb medium-rare with an authentic mint sauce will come as a pleasant change. Not overcooking the lamb greatly benefits its flavor, and a piquant, minty sauce is, for most people, quite an improvement over mint jelly.

FRESH MINT SAUCE

1/2 cup white wine vinegar

2 tablespoons minced fresh mint

1 tablespoon light brown sugar

Olive oil

8 lamb loin chops (about 3 pounds)

Kosher salt and freshly ground black pepper to taste

1. Combine the mint sauce ingredients in a small, lidded jar. Shake well until the brown sugar is dissolved. Taste and adjust the amounts of vinegar and brown sugar if you desire.

2. Preheat the grill with all the burners on high for 10 minutes and the lid down.

3. While the grill is preheating, rub a little olive oil on both sides of each chop and dust with salt and pepper.

4. Once the grill is hot, turn all the burners to medium. Place the chops on the grill and cook, with the lid up, 4 to 6 minutes per side for medium-rare, turning them once. Adjust the time slightly up or down if you desire a different degree of doneness.

5. Serve the chops hot off the grill, passing the mint sauce at the table.

SERVES 4

Lamb Chops with Creamy Fresh Dill Sauce

The flavors of lamb and fresh dill do wonderful things for each other. This outstanding dish is just right when you're trying to impress your guests. Serve with Skewered Herbed Potatoes (page 307) and Grilled Marinated Asparagus (page 282).

CREAMY FRESH DILL SAUCE

2 tablespoons butter

2 tablespoons minced shallots

$1/3$ cup dry white wine

2 tablespoons minced fresh dill

$1/4$ teaspoon kosher salt

$1/3$ cup heavy cream

Olive oil

8 lamb loin chops (about 3 pounds)

Kosher salt and freshly ground black pepper to taste

Fresh sprigs dill for garnish (optional)

1. Melt the butter in a small saucepan. Add the shallots and cook, stirring, over medium heat until softened, about 3 minutes. Add the wine, bring to a boil, and reduce the heat to low. Add the dill and salt and slowly drizzle in the cream. Let simmer (do not boil) for 5 to 10 minutes, stirring constantly. Remove from the heat and set aside until serving time.

2. Preheat the grill with all the burners on high for 10 minutes and the lid down.

3. While the grill is preheating, rub a little olive oil on both sides of each chop and dust with salt and pepper.

4. Once the grill is hot, turn all the burners to medium. Place the chops on the grill and cook, with the lid up, for 4 to 6 minutes per side for medium-rare, turning them once. Adjust the time slightly up or down if you desire a different degree of doneness.

5. While the chops are on the grill, gently reheat the dill sauce. Do not let it come to a boil.

6. Serve the chops hot off the grill with a little sauce drizzled on top and a sprig of dill to garnish if desired. Pass additional sauce at the table.

SERVES 4

Marinated Greek Lamb Shoulder Chops

Lamb shoulder (or sirloin) chops cook up beautifully on a gas grill, and the Greek marinade adds a wonderful dimension to the lamb. This is especially good when served with a Greek salad made from lettuce, feta cheese, black olives, tomatoes, and cucumbers, and dressed with a simple vinaigrette.

GREEK-STYLE MARINADE

3/4 cup dry white or rosé wine

1/4 cup extra-virgin olive oil

6 bay leaves

1 small onion, minced

4 cloves garlic, pressed

8 strips lemon zest, about 1 inch long

1 tablespoon dried oregano, crumbled

4 lamb shoulder or sirloin chops, about 1 inch thick

1. Combine the marinade ingredients in a small saucepan and bring to a boil. Remove from the heat and let cool to room temperature.

2. Place the lamb chops in a 1-gallon zippered-top plastic bag, pour in the cooled marinade, seal, and let marinate in the refrigerator for 4 to 6 hours or overnight if desired.

3. Preheat the grill with all the burners on high for 10 minutes and the lid down.

4. Once the grill is hot, turn all the burners to medium. Place the chops on the grill and cook, with the lid up, for 10 to 16 minutes total, turning once. This will yield chops cooked to medium; adjust the time slightly up or down if you desire a different degree of doneness. Serve hot off the grill.

SERVES 4

Lamb Shanks in Guinness and Apricot Nectar

I was pleasantly surprised to find that it's possible to produce tender lamb shanks on the grill. Normally associated with a long (like, really long) cooking time in the oven, these lamb shanks benefit from marinating overnight and grilling over low heat. The marinade combination of Guinness Stout and apricot nectar was the brainchild of the talented chef Amy Newman, when she was "cheffing" at the legendary Café Lulu in Kansas City, Missouri.

8 large lamb shanks, or 1 per person

GUINNESS AND APRICOT NECTAR MARINADE

1/3 cup canola oil

Three 12-ounce cans Guinness Stout

Three 11.5-ounce cans apricot nectar

4 to 6 cloves garlic, to your taste, minced or pressed

1 tablespoon dried rosemary, crumbled

Kosher salt and freshly ground black pepper to taste

1. Place the lamb shanks in a 2-gallon zippered-top plastic bag.

2. Combine the marinade ingredients in a large bowl, pour into the bag, seal, and squish around to coat the shanks. Let marinate in the refrigerator for 24 hours, turning the bag occasionally.

3. Preheat the grill with all the burners on high for 10 minutes and the lid down.

4. When the grill is hot, turn the back burner to medium and the other burners to low. Place the lamb shanks over the burners on low and cook, with the lid down, for a total of 30 minutes, turning every 10 minutes or so.

5. Remove the shanks to a platter, loosely tent with aluminum foil, and let rest for 10 to 15 minutes before serving.

SERVES 8

Lamb Kebabs with Spicy Yogurt Marinade

There's something about yogurt that not only tenderizes meat, but also boosts every flavor you add to it. These kebabs are excellent combined with a good Indian mango chutney, such as Major Grey's.

1^1/$_2$ to 2 pounds boneless lamb, trimmed of fat and cut into 1-inch chunks

SPICY YOGURT MARINADE

1 cup plain yogurt

2 tablespoons vegetable oil

1 tablespoon fresh lemon juice

2 teaspoons ground cumin

1 teaspoon cayenne pepper

1 teaspoon kosher salt

1 teaspoon ground white pepper

2 to 3 cloves garlic, to your taste, minced or pressed

6 to 8 bamboo skewers, soaked in water for 30 minutes and drained

1. Place the lamb chunks in a 1-gallon zippered-top plastic bag.

2. Combine the marinade ingredients in a large measuring cup, pour into the bag, seal, and squish around to coat the lamb. Let marinate in the refrigerator for at least 3 to 4 hours or overnight.

3. Preheat the grill with all the burners on high for 10 minutes and the lid down.

4. While the grill is preheating, thread the lamb cubes onto the skewers, with their sides barely touching.

5. When the grill is hot, turn all the burners to medium. Place the skewered lamb on the grill, close the lid, and cook for a total of 8 to 12 minutes, turning once midway through.

6. Remove to a platter, loosely tent with aluminum foil, and let rest for 10 minutes before serving.

SERVES 4

Mediterranean Lamb Shish Kebabs

It's hard to go wrong with lamb shish kebabs, marinated and grilled to order. An excellent choice as a dinner-party main course, lamb kebabs can be paired with a rice pilaf and Marinated Eggplant with Tomatoes and Fontina Cheese (page 289). First-class dining!

MEDITERRANEAN MARINADE

$^1/_2$ cup extra-virgin olive oil

$^1/_4$ cup dry white wine

2 tablespoons red wine vinegar

4 cloves garlic, pressed

1 tablespoon dried rosemary

2 teaspoons freshly ground black pepper

1 teaspoon dried thyme

2 pounds boneless lamb, trimmed of fat and cut into 1$^1/_4$-inch cubes

12 bamboo skewers, soaked in water for 30 minutes and drained

1. Combine the marinade ingredients in a 1-gallon zippered-top plastic bag. Add the cubed lamb, seal, squish around to coat, and let marinate in the refrigerator for 4 to 6 hours or overnight if desired.

2. Preheat the grill with all the burners on high for 10 minutes and the lid down.

3. While the grill is preheating, thread the lamb cubes onto the skewers, with their sides barely touching.

4. When the grill is hot, turn all the burners to medium. Place the skewered lamb on the grill, close the lid, and cook for a total of 8 to 12 minutes, turning once midway through. This will yield lamb cooked to medium-rare; adjust the time slightly up or down if you desire a different degree of doneness. Serve hot off the grill.

SERVES 4

Lamb Souvlaki Burgers

Here's the Greek version of the American hamburger: seasoned ground lamb patties, grilled, slipped inside warm pita bread, and topped off with a tangy yogurt-cucumber sauce known as *tzatziki*. For a cheese-souvlaki burger, add a little crumbled feta cheese inside the pita.

TZATZIKI SAUCE

1/2 cup plain yogurt

1/4 cup peeled, seeded, and chopped cucumber

1/2 teaspoon dillweed

1/2 teaspoon dried mint, crumbled

1 1/2 pounds ground lamb

1/4 cup minced onion

2 teaspoons dried oregano, crumbled

2 teaspoons freshly ground black pepper

1 teaspoon kosher salt

4 regular-size pita breads

1 cup shredded lettuce

1 large ripe tomato, chopped

4 green onions, chopped

1. Combine the *tzatziki* sauce ingredients in a small bowl. Refrigerate until serving time.

2. In a large bowl, combine the ground lamb, onion, oregano, pepper, and salt, using your hands to mix thoroughly. Shape into 4 oval patties, each about $3/4$ inch thick.

3. Preheat the grill with all the burners on high for 10 minutes and the lid down.

4. While the grill is preheating, open the pita pockets, so they will be ready for the lamb patties.

5. Once the grill is hot, turn all the burners to medium. Place the lamb patties on the grill and cook, with the lid up, for 14 to 18 minutes, turning them once. This will yield patties cooked to medium; adjust the time slightly up or down if you desire a different degree of doneness.

6. A couple of minutes before the lamb patties are done, put the pita breads on the grill to warm.

7. To serve, put one patty in each pita bread, add the lettuce, tomato, and green onion, and top with the *tzatziki* sauce.

SERVES 4

Lamb Patties with Mozzarella and Mint

These tasty morsels are unlike any hamburger you've ever eaten. First of all, they're made with ground lamb, the cheese is on the inside instead of on top, and the mint and garlic place them, deservedly, in the gourmet category.

1 1/2 pounds ground lamb

1 1/2 tablespoons finely chopped fresh mint

1/2 teaspoon kosher salt

1/2 teaspoon red pepper flakes

4 to 6 cloves garlic, to your taste, minced or pressed

3/4 cup shredded mozzarella cheese

Freshly ground black pepper to taste

OPTIONAL EXTRAS

Warm pita bread

Chopped fresh tomatoes

Tzatziki Sauce (page 235)

1.   Preheat the grill with all the burners on high for 10 minutes and the lid down.

2.   While the grill is preheating, in a large bowl mix together the ground lamb, mint, salt, red pepper flakes, and garlic. Do not overmix. Using your hands, form into 3 or 4 patties, about 1 inch thick. Using a sharp paring knife and approaching from the side, cut and form a pocket in the middle of the lamb patty. Stuff the pocket with 1 or 2 tablespoons of the mozzarella. Reseal the opening. Sprinkle both sides with salt and black pepper.

3.   When the grill is hot, turn the back burner to medium and the other burners to low. Place the lamb patties over the burners on low and cook, with the lid down, about 7 minutes per side for medium, adjusting the time up or down to your desired degree of doneness.

4.   Serve with warm pita bread, chopped tomatoes, and *tzatziki* sauce if desired.

SERVES 4

Veal Paprika Chops with Sour Cream and Chives

Here's an elegant, easy alternative when you're in the mood for something a little different. The veal chops cook up perfectly on the grill, and the addition of sour cream and chives somehow seems (and tastes) just right. Serve with buttered egg noodles and sautéed carrots and you've got quite a meal!

4 veal chops (about $1/2$ pound each), $1^1/2$ inches thick

1 tablespoon olive oil

2 teaspoons paprika

2 teaspoons ground white pepper

$1/2$ cup sour cream for garnish

1 tablespoon chopped fresh chives for garnish

1. Preheat the grill with all the burners on high for 10 minutes and the lid down.

2. While the grill is preheating, coat the veal chops evenly on both sides with the olive oil. Dust liberally with the paprika and white pepper.

3. With all the burners still on high, place the veal chops on the grill and cook, with the lid up, for 6 minutes per side for medium-rare. Don't overcook.

4. Remove to a platter, loosely tent with aluminum foil, and let rest for 5 to 10 minutes before serving with a dollop of sour cream with a sprinkle of chives on top. Delicious!

SERVES 4

DON'T RUN OUT OF GAS!

IT'S A GOOD IDEA TO KEEP A SPARE TANK OF GAS FOR YOUR GRILL ON HAND. YOU'LL THANK YOURSELF THE DAY YOU RUN OUT OF GAS AFTER ALL THE STORES HAVE CLOSED. BE SURE TO STORE THE EXTRA TANK OUTDOORS, IN A SAFE LOCATION, WHERE THE TEMPERATURE WILL NEVER EXCEED 125°F.

Grilled Veal Chops with Lemon-Caper Sauce

Veal chops and the grill were made for each other. The chops cook up quickly, and with the addition of a zesty lemon-caper sauce, are special enough to serve for a dinner party.

LEMON-CAPER SAUCE

1/4 cup (1/2 stick) butter

1 tablespoon fresh lemon juice

1 tablespoon capers, or more to your taste, drained and rinsed

4 veal chops, about 1 inch thick

Olive oil

Freshly ground black pepper to taste

1. Melt the butter in a small saucepan. Remove the pan from the heat and let the butter cool partially. Stir in the lemon juice and capers, and set aside until serving time.

2. About 30 minutes before grilling, rub the chops with olive oil and dust liberally with pepper.

3. Preheat the grill with all the burners on high for 10 minutes and the lid down.

4. With all the burners still on high, place the chops on the grill, close the lid, and sear on one side for about 2 minutes.

5. After searing, turn off the center burner and turn the other burners to medium. Turn the chops over (so the seared side is up), placing them directly over the center burner, and close the lid. After searing, 1-inch-thick chops will take 4 to 5 minutes to cook to rare and 5 to 7 minutes for medium; cooking veal to well done is not recommended, because the meat will be very dry. Turn the chops one more time. Meanwhile, warm the lemon-caper sauce if desired.

6. Serve the veal hot off the grill, topped with the lemon-caper sauce.

SERVES 4

Veal Chops with Basil-Mustard Sauce

Veal chops are special grilled fare, suitable for the most discerning of diners. They're best when at least 1 inch thick; any thinner and they're difficult to cook without drying them out. This sauce is an elegant accompaniment.

BASIL-MUSTARD SAUCE

1 tablespoon butter

2 tablespoons minced shallots

$1/2$ cup chicken broth

20 large fresh basil leaves, minced

$1^1/2$ teaspoons Dijon mustard

$1/3$ cup heavy cream

4 veal chops, about 1 inch thick

Olive oil

Freshly ground black pepper to taste

1.   Melt the butter in a small saucepan. Add the shallots and cook, stirring, over medium heat until softened. Pour in the broth and bring to a boil. Reduce the heat to low, stir in the basil, mustard, and cream, and let simmer for 5 to 10 minutes (do not let it boil). Remove from the heat and set aside until serving time.

2.   About 30 minutes before grilling, rub the chops with olive oil and dust liberally with pepper.

3.   Preheat the grill with all the burners on high for 10 minutes and the lid down.

4.   With all the burners still on high, place the chops on the grill, close the lid, and sear on one side for about 2 minutes.

5.   After searing, turn off the center burner and turn the other burners to medium. Turn the chops over (so the seared side is up), placing them directly over the center burner, and close the lid. After searing, 1-inch-thick chops will take 4 to 5 minutes to cook to rare and 5 to 7 minutes for medium; cooking veal to well done is not recommended, because the meat will be very dry. Turn them one more time. Meanwhile, warm the basil-mustard sauce over low heat.

6. Serve the chops hot off the grill, topped with the sauce.

SERVES 4

Grilled Veal Saltimbocca

The Depot Restaurant, a local favorite for generations of Napa Valley residents, has been serving up soul-satisfying Italian specialties for the past 60 years. One of Chef Clemente's signature dishes is his veal saltimbocca—thin slices of veal wrapped around a slice of prosciutto and provolone cheese, sautéed, and finished off with a little Marsala wine. I was curious to see if I could re-create his classic on the gas grill and was very pleased with the results. I think you will be, too. This is excellent with Risotto (page 345) or Polenta (page 348).

MARSALA SAUCE

1 1/2 cups Marsala wine

1/4 cup (1/2 stick) butter

1 tablespoon fresh lemon juice

8 thin slices prosciutto

8 thin slices provolone cheese

8 large fresh sage leaves

1 to 1 1/2 pounds veal scaloppine (8 slices)

1. Combine the Marsala, butter, and lemon juice in a medium-size saucepan over medium-high heat. Whisking, reduce by half, about 10 minutes or so. Remove from the heat until needed.

2. Preheat the grill with all the burners on high for 10 minutes and the lid down.

3. While the grill is preheating, place a slice of prosciutto, a slice of provolone, and a sage leaf, in that order, in the middle of each slice of veal. Fold the two short sides of the veal in slightly; fold the long ends over the short ends, forming a small packet. Secure the packet with a toothpick.

4. When the grill is hot, turn all the burners to medium. Place the saltimbocca on the grill, folded side down, and cook, with the lid up, 2 to 3 minutes per side. Do not overcook.

5. Remove to a platter, loosely tent with aluminum foil, and let rest for 5 minutes. Meanwhile, reheat the sauce. Top the saltimbocca with sauce and serve immediately.

SERVES 4

7

Pork, Ham, and Sausage

Barbecue purists may scoff at gas grills, but it is possible to get delicious pork barbecue from a gas grill. For the best-tasting barbecue, however, you may want to experiment with those wood chips you always thought you'd like to use someday. Soak the wood chips in warm water for about 30 minutes. Then place them in a small, disposable aluminum pan and cover with aluminum foil, or put them in a doubled piece of heavy-duty aluminum foil, folded over to make a secure packet. Pierce the foil in several places to allow the smoke to escape. The chips are placed over the burner(s) that remain on, while you cook the meat over the burner that is off. Keep the lid of the grill down and your pork will be bathed in delicious smoke.

Over the years, changes in tastes have influenced the types of pigs being bred. It was not long ago that huge, very fatty pigs were desirable. Today's pigs, however, are smaller and much leaner—yielding meat far lower in calories than that of old. A 3-ounce serving of a trimmed pork loin chop contains about 170 calories and about 7 grams of fat. (If you are watching calories and fat, be aware that the leanest pork cuts are the boneless pork loin roast and pork tenderloin.)

When buying pork, look for meat that is a pale pinkish gray, with very white (not yellow) fat and not too much of it—the darker the flesh, the older the animal.

Pork has become not only leaner, but also much more savory, because the recommended internal cooking temperature has been reduced. Fear of trichinosis caused generations of cooks to overcook pork until it was dry and tasteless. The USDA has now determined that the parasite that causes trichinosis is destroyed at 137°F. At 160°F—the point at which pork is done to the medium stage—there is absolutely no cause for concern regarding trichinosis. Pork cooked to medium may still be slightly pink, but the juices should run clear. Pork is considered well done at 170°F.

As with all meats, remove pork from the refrigerator about 30 minutes before grilling to allow the meat to come close to room temperature.

PORK AND SMOKE

WOOD CHIPS ADD A DELICIOUS SMOKE FLAVOR TO GRILLED FOODS. HICKORY ADDS THE MOST INTENSE FLAVOR—IT'S GREAT TO USE WITH PORK. OTHER GOOD WOOD CHOICES FOR PORK ARE APPLE, CHERRY, MAPLE, PECAN, AND WALNUT.

Authentic Barbecued
Spareribs 246

Baby Back Ribs 246

Barbecued Country-
Style Pork Ribs 248

Sweet-and-Sour
Pork Chops 249

Hot-and-Sweet
Pork Chops with
Asian Pear–Apple Sauce 250

Grilled Tacos al Pastor 251

Spicy Hoisin Pork
Brochettes 253

Cured Pork Tenderloin
with Rémoulade 254

Dijon Mustard–Slathered
Pork Tenderloin 255

Jamaican Jerked
Pork Tenderloin 256

Pork Tenderloin
Barbecue 257

Tenderloin of Pork
with Mushrooms
and Raspberries 259

Pork Tenderloin with
Apples and Onions 260

Skewered Mexican
Pork Strips 262

Caribbean Skewered
Pork with Garlic and
Fresh Lime 264

Skewered Pork with
Spicy Peanut Marinade 265

Pork Loin with Dijon-
Mascarpone Sauce 266

Rolled Pork Loin Roast
Florentine 267

Pork Loin Normandy 268

Burnt-End Sandwiches 269

Whole Fresh Ham 270

Whole Cured Ham
on the Grill 271

Ham Steaks with Grilled
Fresh Pineapple Spears 272

Chinese-Style
Pork Burgers 273

Bratwurst in Beer 274

Grilled Bockwurst with
Sauerkraut, Applesauce,
and Cornbread 275

Sausage-and-Cheese
Quesadillas 276

Grilled Italian Sausages
with Polenta 277

Grilled Choucroute 278

Authentic Barbecued Spareribs

There's nothing much better than barbecued spareribs. The technique described in this recipe will produce the type of ribs you thought you could only get at a real barbecue joint. Allow 1 pound of ribs per person.

2 slabs pork ribs, full-slab or loin (a.k.a. baby back ribs), 4 to 6 pounds total

1 recipe Sweet, Hot, and Sour Basting Sauce (page 208)

Bottled barbecue sauce of your choice, heated

1. About 30 minutes before grilling, remove the ribs from the refrigerator. Pour some of the basting sauce into a bowl, and brush the ribs liberally with it. Use any leftover sauce during the first basting of the ribs on the grill.

2. Preheat the grill with all the burners on high for 10 minutes and the lid down.

3. Once the grill is hot, turn off the center burner and turn the other burners to medium. Place the ribs over the center burner, close the lid, and cook for $1^1/2$ hours, turning the ribs every 20 minutes or so and basting them with the sauce.

4. Remove the ribs from the grill, cut the slabs into individual ribs, and serve with your favorite bottled barbecue sauce (heated on the stove ahead of time) drizzled on top.

SERVES 4 TO 6

Baby Back Ribs

Who doesn't like baby back pork ribs? Follow this procedure and they'll turn out great every time: spicy, tender, and perfectly cooked. After years of cooking all kinds of ribs, I've determined that it makes a significant difference if you apply the dry rub to the ribs the night before you are going to grill them. Applying the dry rub spices in layers, right from the spice jars, is a trick I learned from watching some winning contestants at the Kansas City American Royal Barbecue

Contest. The best way to do this is to cut off a length of plastic wrap slightly more than twice as long as the ribs. Place the ribs on the center of the plastic wrap, coat them with liberal layers of the dry rub spices (on both sides), then fold the plastic wrap tightly around the ribs. Tear off a similar length of aluminum foil and wrap the ribs in a second protective layer. Keep the ribs in the refrigerator overnight, until ready to grill.

4 to 5 pounds baby back ribs

BARBECUE RUB

1 to 1^1/2 tablespoons kosher salt

1 to 1^1/2 tablespoons freshly ground black pepper

1 to 1^1/2 tablespoons cayenne pepper (optional)

1 to 1^1/2 tablespoons chili powder

1 to 1^1/2 tablespoons ground cumin

1 to 1^1/2 tablespoons paprika

1 to 1^1/2 tablespoons ground white pepper

Bottled barbecue sauce of your choice

1. Lay the slab of baby back ribs on a large piece of plastic wrap, as described above. Liberally dust both sides of the ribs with the salt, black pepper, cayenne if desired, chili powder, cumin, paprika, and white pepper, layering one spice on top of the other. Wrap the ribs in the plastic wrap and then wrap again in aluminum foil. Allow to marinate in the refrigerator at least 6 hours and preferably overnight.

2. Preheat the grill with all the burners on high for 10 minutes and the lid closed.

3. When the grill is hot, turn off the center burner and turn the other burners to medium. Unwrap the ribs, place them over center burner, close the lid, and cook for 1^1/2 to 2 hours, turning every 20 minutes or so.

4. At the end of the cooking time, turn all the burners off. Baste the ribs with a liberal coating of your favorite barbecue sauce, close the lid, and allow the ribs to rest in the still-warm grill for 10 to 15 minutes before serving up.

SERVES 2 TO 4, DEPENDING ON WHO'S EATING!

Barbecued Country-Style Pork Ribs

This succulent, meaty cut of pork is the essence of simplicity to grill, but satisfies the burliest of appetites. Just don't overcook them, please! Remember, the USDA says you only have to cook pork to 137°F for it to be safe to eat. Keep your instant-read meat thermometer at the ready and take the ribs off the grill as soon as they reach the magic mark. You'll be amazed at the difference not overcooking pork makes. Serve with mashed potatoes and applesauce.

3 to 4 pounds country-style pork ribs

About 1/2 cup dry rub of your choice

Kosher salt and freshly ground black pepper to taste

Bottled barbecue sauce of your choice

1. Sprinkle the ribs liberally with the dry rub, salt, and pepper. Place them in a 1-gallon zippered-top plastic bag, seal, and let marinate in refrigerator for at least 2 hours and preferably overnight.

2. Preheat the grill with all the burners on high for 10 minutes and the lid down.

3. Once the grill is hot, turn off the center burner and turn the other burners to medium-low. Arrange the ribs diagonally so they are not directly over the lit burners. Close the lid and cook, turning every 12 minutes or so until an instant-read meat thermometer inserted into the thickest part of a rib registers 137°F, 35 to 45 minutes.

4. Turn off all the burners. Swab all the sides of the ribs with your favorite barbecue sauce. Close the lid and allow the ribs to rest for 10 minutes before serving.

SERVES 6

Sweet-and-Sour Pork Chops

The intense sweet-and-sour flavors typical of many Chinese sauces and marinades combine well with pork. Serve these chops with plenty of steamed rice and perhaps some coleslaw made with Chinese cabbage and rice vinegar.

SWEET-AND-SOUR MARINADE

$1/2$ cup soy sauce

$1/4$ cup hoisin sauce

$1/4$ cup distilled white vinegar

$1/4$ cup honey

$1/4$ cup pineapple juice

2 cloves garlic, pressed

3 tablespoons peanut or vegetable oil

6 pork loin or rib chops, $3/4$ to 1 inch thick

1. Combine the marinade ingredients in a 1-gallon zippered-top plastic bag. Add the pork chops, coating them well, seal, and let marinate in the refrigerator for 1 to 2 hours.

2. Preheat the grill with all the burners on high for 10 minutes and the lid down.

3. Once the grill is hot, turn off the center burner and turn the other burners to medium. Place the pork chops over the center burner, close the lid, and grill just until cooked through, 25 to 30 minutes total, turning them once. Serve hot off the grill.

SERVES 6

Hot-and-Sweet Pork Chops with Asian Pear–Apple Sauce

This is a very simple and delicious dish. The hoisin sauce in the marinade just caramelizes on the outside of the chops and complements the flavor of the succulent pork. On a whim, I decided to try making the traditional pork accompaniment, applesauce, out of Asian pears and apples instead of just apples: It's wonderful!

HOT-AND-SWEET MARINADE

1/2 cup soy sauce

1/2 cup sriracha sauce ("red rooster" sauce)

1/3 cup hoisin sauce

1 tablespoon sesame oil

4 bone-in pork chops (about 2 1/2 pounds), about 1 1/2 inches thick

Asian Pear–Apple Sauce (recipe follows)

1. Combine the marinade ingredients in a measuring cup and pour into a 1-gallon zippered-top plastic bag. Add the pork chops, seal, and squish around to coat the chops. Let marinate for 1 to 2 hours in the refrigerator.

2. Preheat the grill with all the burners on high for 10 minutes and the lid down.

3. Once the grill is hot, turn off the center burner and turn the other burners to medium. Place the pork chops over the center burner, close the lid, and grill just until cooked through, about 7 minutes per side.

4. Transfer the chops to a platter, loosely tent with aluminum foil, and let rest 5 to 10 minutes before serving with the sauce.

SERVES 4

ASIAN PEAR–APPLE SAUCE

1. Count on 2 Asian pears for every Fuji apple. Peel and core the Asian pears and apples, then cut into 1-inch chunks. Place in a saucepan with about $1/2$ inch water. Add a pinch of salt and cook over medium-low heat, covered, until the fruit is soft, 10 to 15 minutes.

2. Remove from the heat and mash with a potato masher. Resist the temptation to add cinnamon or any other spices, as it tastes great just the way it is. Serve warm on the side of the pork chops.

Grilled Tacos al Pastor

I've taken some liberties with this recipe. As aficionados of Mexican cuisine know, *tacos al pastor* are made from thin slices of marinated pork, stacked and cooked on a sort of vertical rotisserie. These popular tacos, as interpreted in Mexico City, add fresh pineapple slices to the mix with great success. I've replaced the traditional pasilla and guajillo chiles with the readily available canned chipotle chiles in adobo sauce. These are intensely flavorful tacos *and* they are spicy—*muy picante*!

3 pounds boneless pork chops

CHIPOTLE MARINADE

One 7-ounce can chipotle chiles in adobo sauce

$1/3$ cup red wine vinegar

3 cloves garlic, peeled

$1/2$ teaspoon ground cumin

$1/2$ teaspoon kosher salt

6 to 8 bamboo skewers, soaked in water for 30 minutes and drained

2 cups peeled and cored fresh pineapple, cut into 1-inch chunks

Soft corn tortillas

Pico de gallo (a salsa typically made of finely chopped onions, tomatoes, and hot or bell peppers); substitute chopped onion if not available

Coarsely chopped fresh cilantro

2 limes, cut into wedges

1. Cut the pork chops into 1-inch cubes and place in a 1-gallon zippered-top plastic bag.

2. Combine the marinade ingredients in a blender and blend until smooth. Pour into the bag, seal, and squish around to coat the pork. Let marinate in the refrigerator for 1 to 2 hours.

3. Thread the pork chunks onto the skewers, alternating with pieces of pineapple.

4. Preheat the grill with all the burners on high for 10 minutes and the lid down.

5. When the grill is hot, turn off the center burner and turn the other burners to low. Arrange the skewers diagonally over the center burner so no portion is directly over heat. Cook, with the lid down, for a total of 20 to 30 minutes, turning once after about 12 minutes.

6. Heat the tortillas briefly on the grill. To serve, place a skewer on top of a tortilla and garnish with pico de gallo, chopped cilantro, and squeezes of lime juice.

SERVES 6

Spicy Hoisin Pork Brochettes

Hoisin sauce contains enough sugar to caramelize nicely during the relatively short grilling time. If you have the time, marinate overnight in the refrigerator for the fullest flavor.

SPICY HOISIN MARINADE

$1/3$ cup hoisin sauce

2 tablespoons sake

2 tablespoons Thai sweet chili sauce

2 tablespoons soy sauce

1 teaspoon toasted sesame oil

1 teaspoon peeled and finely grated fresh ginger

3 to 4 cloves garlic, to your taste, finely minced or pressed

$1^{1}/_{2}$ to 2 pounds boneless pork chops, cut into $1/_{2}$-inch-thick strips

6 to 8 bamboo skewers, soaked in water for 30 minutes and drained

1. Combine the marinade ingredients in a small bowl, then pour into a 1-gallon zippered-top plastic bag. Add the pork cubes, seal, squish around to coat well, and let marinate in the refrigerator for at least 2 hours and preferably overnight.

2. Preheat the grill with all the burners on high for 10 minutes and the lid down.

3. While the grill is heating, thread the pork on the skewers, with the sides of the cubes just touching.

4. When the grill is hot, turn all the burners to medium. Place the skewered pork on the grill, close the lid, and cook 10 to 12 minutes, turning once midway through. Serve hot off the grill.

SERVES 4

Cured Pork Tenderloin with Rémoulade

Don't let the word *cured* make you think that this recipe is difficult; it isn't. Curing a pork tenderloin makes the meat both firmer and more succulent. Read through the following instructions and you'll see just how easy it is. Slice the meat thin, serve it warm or cold with the rémoulade, and you've got the perfect centerpiece for a big party buffet.

CURE

8 cups water

1/2 cup sugar

1/2 cup kosher salt

2 pork tenderloins (each 3/4 to 1 pound), trimmed of any fat and silver skin

Vegetable oil

Freshly ground black pepper to taste

RÉMOULADE

1/2 cup mayonnaise

3 tablespoons Dijon mustard

1 tablespoon chopped sweet pickle

1 tablespoon chopped capers

1 tablespoon chopped fresh parsley

1/2 teaspoon dried tarragon

1. The night before you plan to grill the pork, combine the cure ingredients in a large container and stir to completely dissolve the sugar and salt. Add the tenderloins, cover, and refrigerate overnight.

2. About 30 minutes before grilling time, remove the tenderloins from the cure, blot them as dry as you can, rub the meat with a little vegetable oil, and dust with pepper.

3. Preheat the grill with all the burners on high for 10 minutes and the lid down.

4. While the grill is preheating, mix the rémoulade ingredients together in a small bowl, and refrigerate until serving time.

5. Once the grill is hot, turn off the center burner and turn the other burners to medium. Place the tenderloins over the center burner, close the lid, and cook for 25 to 35 minutes, turning once or twice.

6. Transfer the tenderloins to a carving board, carve into thin slices, and serve with the rémoulade on the side.

SERVES 6 TO 8

Dijon Mustard–Slathered Pork Tenderloin

Dijon mustard and pork make for a great flavor combination. Because of the intensity of the mustard, there's no need for a long marination time. This is excellent served with Orzo with Basil (page 350) and applesauce.

DIJON MUSTARD SLATHER

1/2 cup Dijon mustard

3 tablespoons extra-virgin olive oil

3 cloves garlic, pressed

1/4 teaspoon freshly ground black pepper

2 pork tenderloins (each 3/4 to 1 pound), trimmed of any fat and silver skin

1. Combine the slather ingredients in a medium-size nonreactive container and mix well. Add the pork tenderloins, turning to coat them thoroughly with the slather. Cover and let marinate in the refrigerator for 30 to 60 minutes.

2. Preheat the grill with all the burners on high for 10 minutes and the lid down.

3. Once the grill is hot, turn off the center burner and turn the other burners to medium. Remove the pork from the slather, place over the center burner, close the lid, and cook for 25 to 35 minutes, turning once or twice.

4. Transfer the tenderloins to a carving board, carve into thin slices, and serve.

SERVES 6 TO 8

Jamaican Jerked Pork Tenderloin

Anyone who has traveled to Jamaica can tell you that jerk pork more than rivals Southern-style American barbecue. The flavors are intensely hot, sweet, and aromatic—all at the same time! I don't even try to replicate those flavors at home because I prefer the real stuff: jerk seasoning that has been bottled at the source, in Jamaica. If you can't find jerk seasoning, try my favorite: Walkerswood Jamaican Jerk Seasoning, from St. Ann, Jamaica, available from the gourmet foods section of www.amazon.com.

Bottled Jamaican jerk seasoning of your choice

Vegetable oil

2 pork tenderloins (each 3/4 to 1 pound), trimmed of any fat and silver skin

Chopped fresh cilantro for garnish (optional)

1. Combine the jerk seasoning and vegetable oil according to the label directions to make a paste-like marinade. Coat the tenderloins with the jerk-seasoning paste, cover tightly with plastic wrap, and refrigerate for 1 to 3 hours.

2. Preheat the grill with all the burners on high for 10 minutes and the lid down.

3. Once the grill is hot, turn off the center burner and turn the other burners to medium. Place the tenderloins over the center burner, close the lid, and cook for 25 to 35 minutes, turning every 10 minutes or so.

4. Transfer the tenderloins to a carving board, loosely tent with aluminum foil, and let rest for 10 minutes before slicing thinly. Garnish with cilantro if desired, and serve.

SERVES 6 TO 8

THE SELF-CLEANING GRILL

AFTER YOU'VE FINISHED GRILLING THE LAST OF YOUR MEAL, TURN ALL THE BURNERS ON HIGH, CLOSE THE GRILL'S LID, AND COME BACK IN 5 TO 10 MINUTES. WHEN YOU RETURN, ANY BITS OF FOOD THAT REMAINED WILL HAVE BURNED OFF AND THE GRILL WILL BE READY FOR NEXT TIME.

Pork Tenderloin Barbecue

This is a simple variation on that North Carolina specialty, the pulled-pork sandwich. It makes an excellent centerpiece for a buffet meal, along with warm hamburger buns, Not-Your-Mother's Coleslaw (page 352), and Homemade French Fries (page 360). This is a dish that everyone—even finicky youngsters—seems to love.

HOT-AND-SWEET DRY RUB

$1/4$ cup paprika

2 tablespoons chili powder

2 tablespoons ground cumin

2 tablespoons kosher salt

2 tablespoons firmly packed dark brown sugar

1 tablespoon granulated sugar

1 tablespoon crumbled dried oregano

1 tablespoon freshly ground black pepper

1 tablespoon ground white pepper

2 teaspoons cayenne pepper (optional)

2 pork tenderloins (each 3/4 to 1 pound), trimmed of any fat and silver skin

Hamburger buns, warmed

Bottled barbecue sauce of your choice, heated

Dill pickle chips

Coleslaw

1. Combine the dry rub ingredients in a 1-gallon zippered-top plastic bag, omitting the cayenne if you don't want the meat spicy-hot. Add the pork tenderloins and cover with the dry rub, coating the meat thoroughly. Seal and let marinate in the refrigerator for 2 to 4 hours.

2. Preheat the grill with all the burners on high for 10 minutes and the lid down.

3. Once the grill is hot, turn off the center burner and turn the other burners to medium. Place the tenderloins over the center burner, close the lid, and cook for 25 to 35 minutes, turning once or twice.

4. Transfer the tenderloins to a carving board and cut into thin slices. Serve on warm hamburger buns, topped with heated barbecue sauce, dill pickle chips, and some coleslaw.

SERVES 6 TO 8

RUBBING IN FLAVOR

USING DRY SPICE RUBS IS ONE OF THE EASIEST AND FASTEST WAYS TO FLAVOR ANY FOOD FOR THE GRILL.

Tenderloin of Pork with Mushrooms and Raspberries

Here's a candidate for your next dinner party. It goes together quickly but tastes like you spent all day on it. The combination of mushrooms and raspberries is an unusual one and pairs perfectly with the pork. This is excellent with a big mound of mashed potatoes, and what are mashed potatoes without some fresh peas?

FRESH HERB MARINADE

$1/4$ cup olive oil

1 teaspoon finely chopped fresh thyme

1 teaspoon finely chopped fresh sage

$1/2$ teaspoon kosher salt

Freshly ground black pepper to taste

2 pork tenderloins ($1^1/2$ to 2 pounds total), trimmed of any fat and silver skin

MUSHROOM AND RASPBERRY SAUCE

2 tablespoons olive oil

$1/2$ cup thinly sliced fresh mushrooms

1 tablespoon finely chopped shallot

$3/4$ cup beef broth

$3/4$ cup chicken broth

2 teaspoons raspberry vinegar

$1/4$ cup frozen raspberries, thawed and mashed

$1^1/2$ tablespoons brandy

1 tablespoon soy sauce

Fresh raspberries for garnish (optional)

1.   Combine the marinade ingredients in a 1-gallon zippered-top plastic bag. Add the pork tenderloins, seal, and let marinate in the refrigerator for 2 to 3 hours.

2. In a large skillet over medium heat, heat the olive oil, then add the mushrooms and shallot and cook, stirring, until the shallot is softened, about 2 minutes. Add both broths and the vinegar, mashed raspberries, brandy, and soy sauce and cook, stirring, until reduced by one third. Remove from the heat.

3. Preheat the grill with all the burners on high for 10 minutes and the lid down.

4. When the grill is hot, leave the back burner on high and turn the other burners to low. Place the tenderloins over the burners on low, close the lid, and cook 7 to 10 minutes per side, for a total cooking time of 14 to 20 minutes.

5. Remove to a platter, loosely tent with aluminum foil, and let rest for 10 minutes. Meanwhile, reheat the sauce.

6. Slice the tenderloins as you prefer, arrange the slices on a platter, and pour the sauce over the top. Garnish with fresh raspberries if available.

SERVES 4

Pork Tenderloin with Apples and Onions

Boneless, lean, and uniform in size, pork tenderloins are ideal for grilling. And they're tender, to boot! Try grilled pork tenderloins topped with this apple and onion "sauce" once, and you're almost certain to make it again; it's an instant classic. The brining step is optional, but it markedly improves the pork's flavor and texture.

BRINE

2 cups water

1/2 cup kosher salt

1/3 cup sugar

2 pork tenderloins (each 3/4 to 1 pound)

1 tablespoon vegetable oil

Kosher salt and ground white pepper to taste

APPLE AND ONION SAUCE

2 tablespoons butter

2 tablespoons vegetable oil

2 medium-size onions, sliced in half from top to bottom, then cut into thin half-moons

3 large green apples, such as Granny Smith, peeled, cored, and cut into 3/8-inch-thick slices

One 14-ounce can chicken broth

1/2 cup sour cream

1 teaspoon sweet paprika

1 bunch fresh chives, finely chopped

1. Pour the water into a 1-gallon zippered-top plastic bag. Add the salt and sugar, seal, and mix with your hands until the sugar and salt have dissolved. Add the pork tenderloins, seal, and let brine in the refrigerator for 4 to 6 hours.

2. Preheat the grill with all the burners on high for 10 minutes and the lid down.

3. Remove the tenderloins from the brine and pat dry. Coat all sides with the vegetable oil and a liberal sprinkling of salt and white pepper.

4. When the grill is hot, leave the back burner on high and turn the other burners to low. Place the tenderloins over the burners on low heat, close the lid, and cook 7 to 10 minutes per side, for a total cooking time of 14 to 20 minutes.

5. Remove to a platter and loosely tent with aluminum foil.

6. While the tenderloins are resting, melt the butter with the vegetable oil in a large skillet over medium-high heat. Reduce the heat to medium, add the onions and apples, and cook, stirring, until the onions are softened, 5 to 7 minutes. Add the broth and just bring to a boil. Add the sour cream and stir until smooth. Remove from the heat.

7. Slice the tenderloins as you prefer, arrange the slices on a platter, and pour the sauce over the top. Sprinkle with the paprika and chopped chives and serve immediately.

SERVES 4

Skewered Mexican Pork Strips

Marinated strips of pork tenderloin, grilled to succulent perfection, are the center-piece for a "build-your-own-burrito" dinner. Folded inside a warm flour tortilla with beans, tomato and avocado slices, and chopped red onion—not to mention your favorite hot sauce or salsa—this spicy skewered pork is a real hit.

MEXICAN MARINADE

$1/3$ cup fresh lime juice

$1/3$ cup apple juice

3 tablespoons vegetable oil

2 cloves garlic, pressed

$1^1/2$ teaspoons chili powder

1 teaspoon ground cumin

1 teaspoon hot pepper sauce

2 pork tenderloins (each $3/4$ to 1 pound), trimmed of any fat and silver skin

12 bamboo skewers, soaked in water for 30 minutes and drained

10-inch flour tortillas

Tomato slices

Avocado slices

Diced red onion

Cowpoke Beans (page 357)

Sour cream (optional)

Hot pepper sauce or salsa of your choice

1. Combine the marinade ingredients in a 1-gallon zippered-top plastic bag. Cut the pork tenderloins lengthwise into $3/8$-inch-thick strips. Cut the strips again lengthwise into strips $3/4$ to 1 inch wide. Cut these strips again so that they are about $2^1/2$ inches long. Place the strips in the marinade, taking care to submerge them, seal, and let marinate in the refrigerator for 2 to 4 hours.

2. Preheat the grill with all the burners on high for 10 minutes and the lid down.

3. While the grill is preheating, drain the marinade from the bag into a small saucepan. Bring to a boil for 2 minutes, remove from the heat, and set aside for basting. Weave the marinated pork strips fairly tightly onto the skewers.

4. Once the grill is hot, turn off the center burner and turn the other burners to medium. Place the skewered pork over the center burner. Wrap the flour tortillas in aluminum foil and place them next to the pork. Close the lid and cook for 10 to 15 minutes, turning the skewers once and basting at that time with the boiled marinade if desired.

5. Assemble all the ingredients for the burritos, remove the skewered pork and the tortillas from the grill, and enjoy!

SERVES 4 TO 6

TAKE YOUR TEMPERATURE!

MEAT THERMOMETERS ARE INVALUABLE AIDS IN ALL GRILLING. IT'S A GOOD IDEA TO KEEP A COUPLE ON HAND, IN CASE ONE BREAKS OR DISAPPEARS—A COMMON OCCURRENCE.

Caribbean Skewered Pork with Garlic and Fresh Lime

Because of the intensity of the simple yet tasty marinade in this recipe, the pork need not marinate long. This dish is great for those occasions when you have little time but still want to serve something with lots of taste.

GARLIC AND FRESH LIME MARINADE

2/3 cup fresh lime juice

1/3 cup vegetable oil

6 to 8 cloves garlic, to your taste, pressed

2 pork tenderloins (each 3/4 to 1 pound), trimmed of any fat and silver skin

12 bamboo skewers, soaked in water for 30 minutes and drained

1. Combine the marinade ingredients in a 1-gallon zippered-top plastic bag. Cut the pork tenderloins lengthwise into 3/8-inch-thick strips. Cut the strips again lengthwise into strips 3/4 to 1 inch wide. Cut these strips again so that they are about 2 1/2 inches long. Place the strips in the marinade, taking care to submerge them, seal, and let marinate in the refrigerator for 30 minutes.

2. Preheat the grill with all the burners on high for 10 minutes and the lid down.

3. While the grill is preheating, weave or thread the pork onto the skewers.

4. Once the grill is hot, turn off the center burner and turn the other burners to medium. Place the skewered pork over the center burner, close the lid, and cook for 10 to 15 minutes, turning the skewers once. Serve hot off the grill.

SERVES 6 TO 8

Skewered Pork with Spicy Peanut Marinade

My inspiration for this dish comes from the many excellent Thai dishes that feature peanuts and hot spices. This skewered pork recipe is both fast and delicious.

SPICY PEANUT MARINADE

1/2 cup dry or medium-dry sherry

1/4 cup soy sauce

1/4 cup vegetable oil

2 to 4 cloves garlic, to your taste, pressed

1/4 cup peanut butter (chunky or smooth)

2 teaspoons red pepper flakes

2 pork tenderloins (each 3/4 to 1 pound), trimmed of any fat and silver skin

12 bamboo skewers, soaked in water for 30 minutes and drained

1. Combine the marinade ingredients in a 1-gallon zippered-top plastic bag. Cut the pork tenderloins lengthwise into 3/8-inch-thick strips. Cut the strips again lengthwise into strips 3/4 to 1 inch wide. Cut these strips again so that they are about 2 1/2 inches long. Place the strips in the marinade, taking care to submerge them, seal, and let marinate in the refrigerator for 1 to 2 hours.

2. Preheat the grill with all the burners on high for 10 minutes and the lid down.

3. While the grill is preheating, weave or thread the pork onto the skewers.

4. Once the grill is hot, turn off the center burner and turn the other burners to medium. Place the skewered pork over the center burner, close the lid, and cook for 10 to 15 minutes, turning the skewers once. Serve hot off the grill.

SERVES 6 TO 8

Pork Loin with Dijon-Mascarpone Sauce

Pork has long been paired with slightly sweet, fruity sauces or marinades. This sauce, a combination of mascarpone cheese, Dijon mustard, and apple juice concentrate, follows that tradition, but breaks some new ground at the same time. I've made this dish many times and it's always been met with raves.

DIJON-MASCARPONE SAUCE

1 cup mascarpone

$^1/_2$ cup frozen apple juice concentrate, thawed

$^1/_3$ cup Dijon mustard

$^1/_3$ cup finely chopped fresh chives

One 3- to 4-pound bone-in pork loin roast

1 tablespoon vegetable oil

Kosher salt and ground white pepper to taste

Finely chopped fresh chives for garnish (optional)

1. In a medium-size bowl, combine the sauce ingredients. Cover and refrigerate until needed. Rub the pork roast with the vegetable oil; dust with salt and white pepper.

2. Preheat the grill with the burners on high for 10 minutes and the lid down.

3. When the grill is hot, turn off the center burner and turn the other burners to medium. Place the pork roast over the center burner, close the lid, and cook until an instant-read meat thermometer inserted in the center registers 140°F, 1 to 1$^3/_4$ hours.

4. Remove the roast to a platter, loosely tent with aluminum foil, and let rest for 10 minutes.

5. Remove the sauce from the refrigerator. Carve the roast and serve with a dollop of the sauce on top, garnished with more chopped chives if desired.

SERVES 4 TO 6

Rolled Pork Loin Roast Florentine

This is an impressive centerpiece to serve with Skewered Herbed Potatoes (page 307), Grilled Onion Slices (page 301), and some homemade chunky applesauce.

One 3- to 5-pound rolled boneless pork loin roast

1/4 cup dried rosemary, crumbled

8 to 10 cloves garlic, to your taste, each cut lengthwise into 4 slivers

Kosher salt and freshly ground black pepper

1/4 cup olive oil

1. About an hour before you are ready to cook the pork roast, cut the string that holds the roast together and sprinkle 1 tablespoon of the crumbled rosemary, 8 or 10 of the garlic slivers, and salt and pepper over the inside of the unrolled roast. Roll the roast back up and tie with fresh cotton string. Using the tip of a sharp knife, make as many incisions, evenly spaced around the roast, as you have remaining garlic slivers. Insert the slivers into the incisions and rub the outside of the roast with the olive oil. Sprinkle the remaining 3 tablespoons rosemary over the outside of the roast, pressing it in with the heel of your hand; dust with more salt and pepper. Cover the roast with plastic wrap and refrigerate until ready to grill.

2. Preheat the grill with all the burners on high for 10 minutes and the lid down.

3. Once the grill is hot, turn off the center burner and turn the other burners to medium. Place the pork roast over the center burner, close the lid, and cook for 1 1/2 to 2 1/2 hours, depending on the size of the roast. With a cut of meat this size, it's essential to use an instant-read meat thermometer. The roast will be cooked to medium (when the pork is at its most succulent) when it reaches 160°F and well done at 170°F. Once the roast has come within 10 degrees of the desired final temperature, remove it from the grill.

4. Place the roast on a carving board, loosely tent with aluminum foil, and let rest for 10 minutes or so, during which time the pork will continue to "cook" to the desired degree of doneness; then cut the strings off the roast and carve into fairly thin slices. Serve with any juices that may have accumulated on the carving board.

SERVES 6 TO 10

Pork Loin Normandy

Apples and pork is a favorite combination from the Normandy region of France. Using thawed frozen apple juice concentrate in the marinade is a quick way to add intense apple flavor to the meat. Serve this dish with Sauerkraut-and-Potato Casserole (page 362).

ROSEMARY-APPLE MARINADE

One 6-ounce can frozen apple juice concentrate, thawed

$1/2$ cup minced onion

$1/2$ cup dry white wine

3 tablespoons vegetable oil

2 tablespoons soy sauce

$1/2$ teaspoon dried rosemary, crumbled

Freshly ground black pepper to taste

One 3- to 5-pound rolled boneless pork loin roast

1. Combine the marinade ingredients in a 1-gallon zippered-top plastic bag. Add the pork roast, seal, turn to coat, and let marinate in the refrigerator for 2 to 4 hours.

2. Preheat the grill with all the burners on high for 10 minutes and the lid down.

3. Once the grill is hot, turn off the center burner and turn the other burners to medium. Place the roast over the center burner, close the lid, and cook for $1^1/2$ to $1^3/4$ hours, depending on the size of the roast. With a cut of meat this size, it's essential to use an instant-read meat thermometer. The roast will be cooked to medium (when the pork is at its most succulent) when it reaches 160°F and well done at 170°F. Once the roast has come within 10 degrees of the desired final temperature, remove it from the grill.

4. Place the roast on a carving board, loosely tent with aluminum foil, and let rest for 10 minutes or so, during which time the pork will continue to "cook" to the desired degree of doneness; then cut the strings off the roast and carve into fairly thin slices. Serve along with any juices that may have accumulated on the carving board.

SERVES 6 TO 10

Burnt-End Sandwiches

Burnt-end sandwiches are indigenous to Kansas City, Missouri, a town that takes its barbecue seriously. Most of the barbecue joints there serve some variation on the sandwich, most often cut from a barbecued beef brisket. Snead's, a longtime barbecue haven in Kansas City, developed the burnt-end sandwich into a culinary classic. It features toasted white bread cut into triangles and topped with a few burnt-end pieces, some coleslaw, a couple of dill pickle chips, and a squirt of barbecue sauce. Fold it over and . . . oh, my—good eatin'!

BONE-IN OR BONELESS?

NOTHING BEATS A BONELESS ROAST FOR EASY CARVING AND SERVING. BUT A BONE-IN ROAST WILL GRILL MORE QUICKLY.

In this version, we've replaced the brisket with a boneless pork loin rib-end roast, although boneless country-style ribs would also do nicely. The reason for this substitution is simple: Pork loin ends are much smaller cuts of meat than the beef brisket, so it's easier to produce more burnt ends with them, not to mention that pork tends to be more succulent than beef.

One 2- to 4-pound pork loin end roast

1 recipe Sweet, Hot, and Sour Basting Sauce (page 208)

White bread, toasted

Dill pickle chips

Coleslaw

Bottled barbecue sauce of your choice

1. About 30 minutes before grilling, remove the pork from the refrigerator and brush it liberally with some of the basting sauce.

2. Preheat the grill with all the burners on high for 10 minutes and the lid down.

3. Once the grill is hot, turn off the center burner and turn the other burners to medium. Place the pork over the center burner, close the lid, and cook, without turning it, for $1^1/2$ to 2 hours, basting with the sauce every 20 minutes or so, until a meat thermometer inserted into the pork registers 150 to 155°F.

4. Transfer the pork to a carving board and cut so that each piece has some burned ends. Serve the pork buffet style, letting each guest make a sandwich with the toast, pork, pickles, coleslaw, and barbecue sauce, à la Snead's.

SERVES 4 TO 8

Whole Fresh Ham

It's a mystery why the pork roast known as the fresh ham isn't served more often. As far as pork goes, it's probably the most flavorful and succulent cut there is. A whole fresh ham runs to 15 pounds, but it is most often offered at the meat counter cut in half, divided into the butt end and the shank end. Obviously, these are roasts to feed a crowd. Consider serving the meat with homemade applesauce, hominy, or the ever-popular mountain of mashed potatoes. The only seasonings a fresh ham requires are some salt and plenty of freshly ground black pepper.

One 6- to 7-pound fresh ham, butt or shank end

Kosher salt and freshly ground black pepper to taste

1. Preheat the grill with all the burners on high for 10 minutes and the lid down.

2. While the grill is preheating, wipe the roast with a paper towel and sprinkle liberally with salt and plenty of pepper.

3. Once the grill is hot, turn off the center burner and turn the other burners to medium. Place the ham over the center burner, close the lid, and cook for 3 to 4 hours, rotating the ham every hour or so. With a cut of meat this size, it's essential to use a meat thermometer. It will be cooked to medium (when the pork is at its most succulent) when it reaches 160°F and well done at 170°F. Once the roast has come within 10 degrees of the desired final temperature, remove it from the grill.

4. Place the roast on a carving board, loosely tent with aluminum foil, and let rest for 10 minutes or so, during which time the pork will continue to "cook" to the desired degree of doneness; then carve the meat into fairly thin slices and serve along with any juices that may have accumulated on the carving board.

SERVES 12 TO 14

Whole Cured Ham on the Grill

When you cook a ham on the grill, the object is not so much to "grill" it as it is to heat it, while imparting some of that smoky, outdoor flavor so difficult to achieve in an indoor oven. There's the added benefit, of course, of relieving some of the congestion in the kitchen—especially when there's already a hungry crowd assembled at your house for dinner.

MAPLE-SHERRY GLAZE

$^1/_2$ cup soy sauce

$^1/_4$ cup medium-dry sherry, such as amontillado

$^1/_4$ cup pure maple syrup or honey

$^1/_4$ cup vegetable oil

2 teaspoons ground ginger

2 cloves garlic, pressed

1 teaspoon Tabasco sauce

One 10- to 15-pound fully cooked canned ham or smoked and cured whole ham

1. Combine the glaze ingredients in a small bowl.

2. Preheat the grill with all the burners on high for 10 minutes and the lid down.

3. Once the grill is hot, turn off the center burner and turn the other burners to medium. Place the ham over the center burner, fat side up, close the lid, and cook for 15 to 18 minutes per pound, until an instant-read meat thermometer inserted into the center of the ham registers 140°F. Cook a smoked and cured ham to 160°F, because it has not been fully precooked (if the ham is fully precooked, it will say so; if you have any doubt, ask your butcher). Rotate the ham every half hour or so. Baste liberally with the glaze during the last 30 minutes of cooking.

4. Transfer the ham to a carving board, loosely tent with aluminum foil, and let rest for 15 minutes before carving into thin slices.

SERVES 20 TO 30

Ham Steaks with Grilled Fresh Pineapple Spears

A big ham steak is one of the easiest and tastiest foods you can cook on the grill. It's a real crowd-pleaser, because it's hard to find anyone, including youngsters, who dislikes the taste of ham. Combine this dish with grilled pineapple and you've got the makings of a memorable meal.

ASIAN-STYLE BARBECUE MARINADE

1/4 cup soy sauce

2 tablespoons hoisin sauce

2 tablespoons dry sherry

2 tablespoons vegetable oil

1 teaspoon ground ginger

1 teaspoon Tabasco sauce

1 ham steak, about 1 inch thick

Grilled Fresh Pineapple Spears (page 332)

1. Combine the marinade ingredients in a 1-gallon zippered-top plastic bag. Add the ham steak, turn to coat it well, seal, and let marinate in the refrigerator for 30 to 60 minutes.

2. Preheat the grill with all the burners on high for 10 minutes and the lid down.

3. Once the grill is hot, turn off the center burner and turn the other burners to medium. Remove the ham steak from the marinade, reserving the marinade, and place it over the center burner. Close the lid and cook for 12 minutes, turning once and basting with the leftover marinade.

4. When the ham is heated through, transfer it to a warm serving platter, surround with the pineapple spears, and serve. Your family will love you.

SERVES 3 TO 4

KEEPING IT PRETTY

TO KEEP HAM STEAKS FROM CURLING ON THE GRILL, CUT SLASHES THROUGH THE FAT AROUND THE EDGES AT 1-INCH INTERVALS.

Chinese-Style Pork Burgers

As unusual as these "hamburgers" are, it's amazing how quickly people take to them. Be sure to toast the buns on the grill before serving the burgers.

1 pound lean ground pork

1 large egg, beaten

$1/4$ cup fine dry bread crumbs

2 tablespoons minced green onions (white part only)

1 clove garlic, pressed

$1/2$ teaspoon kosher salt

$1/2$ teaspoon freshly ground black pepper

4 hamburger buns

Hoisin sauce

Green onions, cut in half lengthwise, then cut into 1-inch pieces

Bean sprouts

1. Combine the ground pork, beaten egg, bread crumbs, minced green onions, garlic, salt, and pepper in a medium-size bowl, mixing well with your hands. Shape into 4 patties, each about $3/4$ inch thick. Refrigerate until grilling time.

2. Preheat the grill with all the burners on high for 10 minutes and the lid down.

3. Once the grill is hot, turn all the burners to medium. Place the pork patties on the grill and cook, with the lid down, for a total of 14 to 18 minutes, turning them once. They are done when the juices run clear.

4. A couple of minutes before the pork patties are done, put the buns on the grill to warm.

5. Place one patty in each bun, top with a tablespoon or so of hoisin sauce, sprinkle with green onion slivers and bean sprouts, and serve.

SERVES 4

Bratwurst in Beer

This is a good recipe for an informal get-together: It's easy, inexpensive, and tasty. Serve the bratwurst on good-quality buns, with plenty of sauerkraut, chopped onions, and a variety of mustards. German potato salad and steamed green beans, served at room temperature, dressed with a simple oil-and-vinegar vinaigrette, make excellent side dishes.

Two 12-ounce cans beer

12 bratwursts

1. Preheat the grill with all the burners on high for 10 minutes and the lid down.

2. Once the grill is hot, turn off the center burner and turn the other burners to medium. Place a disposable aluminum roasting pan over the center burner and pour the beer into the pan. Place the sausage over the burners on medium. Close the lid and cook, turning the sausages frequently, until lightly browned, 10 to 12 minutes.

3. As they brown, move the bratwursts into the pan with the beer. Once all the sausages are in the pan, close the lid and cook for another 20 to 25 minutes.

4. Serve the bratwursts directly form the pan. Leave any leftovers in the pan, so that the last brat will be as hot and juicy as the first; they won't be left over for long!

SERVES 6 TO 8

THE GRILLER'S FRIEND

KEEP PLENTY OF ALUMINUM FOIL NEARBY WHEN YOU'RE GRILLING, ESPECIALLY THE HEAVY-DUTY VARIETY; IT CAN BE A GRILLER'S BEST FRIEND.

Grilled Bockwurst with Sauerkraut, Applesauce, and Cornbread

When teamed with sauerkraut, applesauce, and cornbread hot from the oven, bockwurst—mild white sausages made from pork and veal—makes an excellent cool-weather meal. Store-bought sauerkraut and applesauce are both excellent products, and the packaged cornbread mixes rival the homemade versions. So the only real cooking involved in this meal is to simply grill the sausages and bake the cornbread!

8 bockwursts

2 pounds sauerkraut, heated

Applesauce

Cornbread

A variety of mustards

1. Preheat the grill with all the burners on high for 10 minutes and the lid down.

2. Once the grill is hot, turn off the center burner and turn the other burners to medium. Place the sausages over the center burner, close the lid, and cook, turning frequently, until lightly browned, 12 to 18 minutes.

3. Place the grilled bockwursts on top of the hot sauerkraut and serve with applesauce on the side, a basket of cornbread, and mustard.

SERVES 4

Sausage-and-Cheese Quesadillas

The addition of chorizo sausage turns these quesadillas into a hearty main dish.

1 pound uncooked chorizo sausage

8 large flour tortillas

1 tablespoon vegetable oil

4 cups finely shredded Monterey Jack or mild cheddar cheese (or a combination of both)

Hot sauce or salsa of your choice (optional)

Chopped fresh cilantro for garnish (optional)

1. Remove the chorizo from the casings. Crumble the sausage into a skillet and cook, stirring, over medium heat until fully cooked, 15 to 30 minutes. Remove the sausage from the skillet using a slotted spoon and drain on several layers of paper towel.

2. While the sausage is cooking, preheat the grill with all the burners on high for 10 minutes and the lid down.

3. While the grill is preheating, assemble the quesadillas. Lightly brush one side of each tortilla with vegetable oil. Place 4 tortillas, oiled side down, side by side on your work surface. Divide the cheese among the 4 tortillas and layer evenly. Sprinkle the chorizo on top. Top each circle with another tortilla, this time with the oiled side facing up. Press down lightly on each quesadilla to compress the cheese and sausage.

4. Once the grill is hot, turn all the burners to low. Using a metal spatula, carefully place the quesadillas on the grill. Watch closely: As soon as the cheese begins to melt, turn each quesadilla over and brown the other side. The quesadillas are done when they are lightly toasted on both sides and the cheese is completely melted.

5. Cut the quesadillas into wedges and serve warm. If desired, top them with your favorite hot sauce or sprinkle them with cilantro if desired.

SERVES 4

Grilled Italian Sausages with Polenta

Depending on your diners' tastes, choose hot or mild Italian sausage. If you haven't tried it, try to find a brand of "instant" polenta, which cooks in five minutes and is every bit as good as the regular polenta. This dish goes exceptionally well with spinach sautéed with garlic in olive oil and splashed with a little sherry vinegar.

^{1}/2 recipe Polenta (page 348)

8 mild or hot Italian sausages (about 2 pounds)

1. Cook the polenta according to the recipe directions. Keep warm on a large platter, covered with aluminum foil, in a preheated 225°F oven.

2. Preheat the grill with all the burners on high for 10 minutes and the lid down.

3. Once the grill is hot, turn off the center burner and turn the other burners to medium. Place the sausages over the center burner, close the lid, and cook, turning frequently, until browned, 15 to 20 minutes.

4. Place the grilled Italian sausage on top of, or around the sides of, the polenta. Serve hot.

SERVES 4

Grilled Choucroute

As impressive as this dish is (a perennial favorite from the Alsace region of France), you can pull it together and feed 12 people in about 30 minutes. No kidding. All of the smoked meats are fully cooked when you buy them, so it's simply a matter (with the exception of the ham hocks, which benefit from a fairly lengthy steaming prior to grilling) of heating them through and assembling the bed of seasoned sauerkraut. Open some applesauce, warm a loaf of crusty rye bread in the oven, crack open a cold beer, and you've an instant, awesome feast. I prefer to use bagged sauerkraut over canned, but either will do.

2 pounds smoked ham hocks, cut into 1-inch-thick slices (have your butcher do this for you)

8 to 10 cups sauerkraut

2 tablespoons caraway seeds

1 cup dry vermouth

2 to 3 pounds smoked pork chops

2 to 3 pounds assorted precooked sausages, such as Louisiana hot links or andouille, kielbasa, bratwurst, and the like

1. Put the ham hocks in a medium-size saucepan and add about an inch of water. Bring to a boil, reduce the heat to low, cover, and let the ham hocks "steam" for $1^1/2$ hours. Check occasionally to make sure the water has not boiled away; add more as needed. After steaming, place the ham hocks on several layers of paper towels and pat dry.

2. In a colander, briefly rinse the sauerkraut under cold running water. Let drain for a few minutes and place in a large saucepan. Add the caraway seeds and vermouth, bring to a boil, immediately reduce the heat to low, and cover.

3. Preheat the grill with all the burners on high for 10 minutes and the lid down.

4. When the grill is hot, turn all the burners to medium-low. Arrange the smoked chops, sausages, and ham hocks on the grill and close the lid. Remember, all you need to do is thoroughly heat the meats, so the total cooking time will be 10 to 12 minutes. Turn the chops, sausages, and ham hocks every 4 to 5 minutes.

5. Mound the sauerkraut on the largest platter you have; surround with the grilled meats and serve.

SERVES 12

8

Vegetables and Vegetarian Main Dishes

Homegrown vegetables are naturally good in soups, casseroles, stews, and other kitchen fare, but they are even better hot off the grill. After all, both garden and grill are outdoors. And grilling, the simplest (not to mention the oldest) form of cooking, perfectly suits the ripe flavors of freshly harvested vegetables. ✳ One primary reason most people grow their own vegetables is for the superior flavor of homegrown produce. If that's the case for you, experiment on your grill with all manner of vegetables. You'll find that they need no masking with heavy sauces, no transformation of taste or texture with extra-long cooking times. ✳ The gas grill may not impart the rustic smokiness associated with charcoal grilling, but its consistency of temperature and clean-burning qualities are ideal for cooking vegetables—some would say even better than a charcoal grill.

The following are a few general guidelines for successfully preparing vegetables on the grill:

* With the exception of onions and eggplant (and there are many who would omit eggplant from the list), there's no need to peel vegetables for the grill. Potatoes and carrots easily come clean if you use one of those tough plastic scrubbing pads.

* Vegetables with many layers, such as onions and fennel, are best quartered, leaving some of the stem end intact. Doing so keeps the layers from separating into a lot of hard-to-manage pieces.

* Resist the temptation to parboil or partially cook in the microwave oven any vegetable before grilling. Both techniques alter the texture of the vegetable, resulting in a mushy, inferior dish.

* Skewered small, round vegetables, such as pearl onions, zucchini rounds, mushrooms, and cherry tomatoes, are the devil to keep from twirling around as you turn the skewers on the grill. Your best bet is to thread the vegetables onto two presoaked bamboo skewers, parallel to each other; it works like a charm.

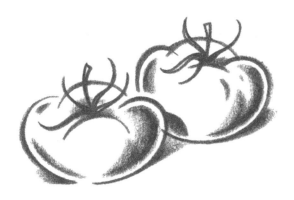

Grilled Marinated Asparagus 282

Grilled Lemon-Sherry Asparagus 283

Grilled Whole Beets with Fresh Ginger-Orange Sauce 284

Buttered Grilled Carrots 285

Good Old Corn on the Cob 285

Corn on the Cob with Lime-Chili Butter 286

Minted Grilled Cucumber Spears 287

Grilled Whole Eggplant 288

Grilled Thyme Eggplant 289

Marinated Eggplant with Tomatoes and Fontina Cheese 289

Eggplant, Tomato, and Pepper Mélange 290

Grilled Eggplant Stacks with Udon Noodles and Fresh Cilantro Sauce 291

Grilled Escarole 294

Grilled Fennel with Anchovy-Garlic Butter 295

Grilled Garlic 296

Grilled Whole Leeks 296

Grilled Marinated Mushrooms 297

Portobello Mushroom Burgers 299

White Onion Kebabs with Rosemary and Balsamic Vinegar 300

Oriental Grilled Green Onions 301

Grilled Onion Slices 301

Grilled Peppers 302

Marinated Roasted Peppers 303

Grilled Cheese-Stuffed Peppers 304

"Baked" Potatoes on the Grill 305

Grilled Potato Skins 306

Skewered Herbed Potatoes 307

Rosemary Potato Wedges 307

Roast Sweet Potatoes with Cilantro-Lime Butter 308

Grilled Summer Squash 309

Grilled Zucchini 310

Honey-Glazed Winter Squash en Brochette 311

Skewered Plum Tomatoes with Garlic and Basil 312

Garlicky Grilled Tomatoes 313

Grilled Pesto Tomatoes 314

Cherry Tomatoes en Brochette 315

Tomatoes Stuffed with Duchess Potatoes 316

Veggie Cheesy Burgers 317

Mixed Vegetable Brochettes 318

Grilled Ratatouille 319

Grilled Marinated Tofu 321

Tofu Kebabs 321

Grilled Polenta with Mushroom "Ragout" 322

Grilled Quesadilla 324

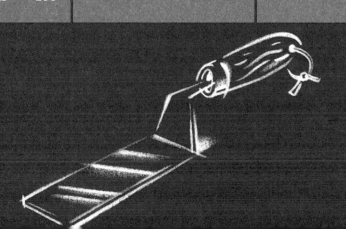

Grilled Marinated Asparagus

Yes, asparagus can be grilled. The trick, of course, is to keep them perpendicular, rather than parallel, to the grill bars. With that caveat, grilling asparagus is strongly recommended; they're quite different in flavor and texture from the steamed version, and very tasty.

2 pounds fresh asparagus, the fatter the better

1 cup homemade or commercial bottled vinaigrette dressing of your choice

Mayonnaise or lemon juice (optional)

1. Preheat the grill with all the burners on high for 10 minutes and the lid down.

2. While the grill is preheating, wash the asparagus under cold running water. Using a vegetable peeler, scrape off the skin from the bottom third of each asparagus spear. With a sharp knife, trim off the tough bottom $1/2$ inch or so from each spear.

3. In a 1-gallon zippered-top plastic bag, combine the asparagus and vinaigrette. Let sit briefly, about 10 minutes.

4. Once the grill is hot, turn off the center burner and turn the other burners to medium. Drain the marinade from the container, reserving it to serve at the table if you wish. Place the asparagus over the center burner perpendicular to the grate, close the lid, and cook until crisp-tender, 5 to 8 minutes total, turning once or twice.

5. Serve the asparagus warm off the grill, with a little mayonnaise, lemon juice, or some of the left-over vinaigrette if desired.

SERVES 4 TO 6

FRESH ON THE GRILL

AS A RULE, NEVER PRECOOK ANY FRUIT OR VEGETABLES BEFORE GRILLING: THE FOOD WILL LOSE BOTH FLAVOR AND TEXTURE IN THE PROCESS.

Grilled Lemon-Sherry Asparagus

I had my doubts about grilled asparagus, but after trying it once I'm a convert. The asparagus will pick up just a hint of smokiness from the grill, without overpowering this vegetable's distinctive flavor. Be sure to place thin asparagus spears perpendicular to the bars on the grill; otherwise you'll have a problem with them falling through the grate.

1 bunch fresh asparagus

LEMON-SHERRY VINAIGRETTE

Juice of 1/2 lemon

2 tablespoons olive oil

1 tablespoon sherry vinegar

Pinch of kosher salt

Freshly ground black pepper to taste

1. Rinse the asparagus under cold running water. If they are fat, use a vegetable peeler to remove the thick skins from the bottom half of each spear.

2. Preheat the grill with all the burners on high for 10 minutes and the lid down.

3. While the grill is preheating, combine the vinaigrette ingredients in a small jar and shake until well combined.

4. When the grill is hot, turn all the burners to medium. Place the asparagus on the grill perpendicular on the grate and cook until crisp-tender, 5 to 8 minutes total, turning once or twice. (Note: If the asparagus spears are thin, reduce the cooking time accordingly.)

5. Remove to a shallow platter and pour the vinaigrette over the spears while they are still hot off the grill. Serve warm, at room temperature, or cold.

SERVES 4

Grilled Whole Beets with Fresh Ginger-Orange Sauce

The flavor combination of oranges, ginger, and beets is outstanding. Grating the ginger with the skin intact, then squeezing it with your hands releases an amazing amount of ginger "juice"—an easy way to get the essence of this special rhizome.

FRESH GINGER-ORANGE SAUCE

1/4 cup fresh orange juice

2 tablespoons mayonnaise

1/4 teaspoon kosher salt

1/2 cup grated unpeeled fresh ginger

2 pounds beets (select the largest beets you can find—each at least as big as a tennis ball)

1. Combine the orange juice, mayonnaise, and salt in a small bowl. Using your hands, gather the grated ginger together in a ball and squeeze it tightly over the mayonnaise mixture. Discard the grated ginger. Stir the sauce, cover, and refrigerate until serving time.

2. Preheat the grill with all the burners on high for 10 minutes and the lid down.

3. While the grill is preheating, scrub the beets. Trim away the tops and roots, but do not peel.

4. Once the grill is hot, turn off the center burner and turn the other burners to medium. Place the beets over the center burner, close the lid, and cook until the tip of a sharp knife easily pierces them, 20 to 40 minutes, depending on their size, turning them occasionally.

5. Remove the beets from the grill, skin, and slice them. Top each portion with the ginger-orange sauce and serve.

SERVES 4

Buttered Grilled Carrots

To many a mind, carrots are best when grilled. There's something about the grilling process and the dry heat that enhances the carrot's natural texture and flavor. Grilled carrots are excellent served with the Fresh Ginger-Orange Sauce from the previous recipe (page 284), or simply buttered lightly and sprinkled with minced parsley.

4 to 8 large carrots (the larger the better)

About $1/4$ cup ($1/2$ stick) butter, melted

Minced fresh parsley (optional)

1. Preheat the grill with all the burners on high for 10 minutes and the lid down.

2. While the grill is preheating, cut the tops from the carrots and scrub under cold running water; do not peel them. Blot dry, then coat them liberally with the melted butter.

3. Once the grill is hot, turn off the center burner and turn the other burners to medium. Place the carrots over the center burner, close the lid, and cook until the tip of a sharp knife easily pierces them at their thickest part, 20 to 30 minutes, turning them occasionally.

4. Serve the carrots hot off the grill with a little extra melted butter and a sprinkling of parsley if desired.

SERVES 4

Good Old Corn on the Cob

Grilling corn right in its husk is the easiest way to cook it—and you don't heat up the kitchen with a big pot of boiling water! Always choose the freshest corn possible, with tightly fitting husks and fresh-looking, dry (not soggy) silks.

4 to 8 ears fresh corn, with husks

1. Preheat the grill with all the burners on high for 10 minutes and the lid down.

2. While the grill is preheating, carefully pull back the husks and remove the silks from each ear. Rinse the corn under cold running water and fold the husks back up around the corn. Tie the tops of the husks together with small pieces of string or with a husk leaf torn in thin strips.

3. Once the grill is hot, turn off the center burner and turn the other burners to medium. Place the corn over the center burner, close the lid, and cook until tender, 25 to 35 minutes, turning it occasionally.

4. Remove the corn from the grill, remove the husks, and serve.

SERVES 4

Corn on the Cob with Lime-Chili Butter

As good as plain grilled corn on the cob is, the addition of fresh lime juice and chili powder takes it to another realm.

LIME-CHILI BUTTER

$1/4$ cup ($1/2$ stick) butter

1 tablespoon fresh lime juice

$1^1/2$ teaspoons chili powder

Kosher salt and freshly ground black pepper to taste

4 ears fresh corn, with husks

1. Combine the lime-chili butter ingredients in a small saucepan over medium heat and cook, stirring occasionally, until the butter is melted. Remove from the heat and set aside.

2. Preheat the grill with all the burners on high for 10 minutes and the lid down.

3. While the grill is preheating, husk the corn and remove the silks. Wash the ears under cold running water. Tear off squares of aluminum foil large enough to wrap each cob of corn completely. Place one cob of corn on each sheet of foil and brush the ear liberally with the lime-chili butter. Wrap the foil tightly around the corn.

4. Once the grill is hot, turn off the center burner and turn the other burners to medium. Place the corn over the center burner, close the lid, and cook 25 to 35 minutes, turning occasionally.

5. Remove the corn from the grill, unwrap the ears, pouring any melted butter back over the cobs, and serve hot.

SERVES 4

COMPOUNDING THE FLAVOR

COMPOUND BUTTERS, MIXTURES OF BUTTER WITH HERBS, SPICES, AND OTHER FLAVORINGS, CAN TRANSFORM SIMPLE GRILLED FARE INTO A SPECIAL TREAT.

Minted Grilled Cucumber Spears

Grilled cucumber has a pleasant, fresh taste and delicate texture. It goes well with all types of Asian food and serves as a welcome relief from any type of spicy food, especially when paired with a little fresh mint, as in this recipe.

2 to 3 cucumbers

2 to 3 tablespoons rice vinegar, to your taste

1/4 cup chopped fresh mint

Kosher salt to taste

1. Preheat the grill with all the burners on high for 10 minutes and the lid down.

2. While the grill is preheating, peel, seed, and cut the cucumbers lengthwise into quarters.

3. Once the grill is hot, turn all the burners to medium. Place the cucumbers on the grill and cook, with the lid down, for about 6 minutes, turning them a few times.

4. Remove the cucumbers to a serving platter, splash with the vinegar, sprinkle with the mint, season with salt, and serve warm.

SERVES 4

Grilled Whole Eggplant

Here's a new and delicious twist that eggplant lovers will, well, love. My friend Marsha Maher introduced it to me. It's one of those procedures that you think will never work, but miraculously do.

1 large eggplant

Extra-virgin olive oil

Ground cumin

Juice of $1/2$ lemon

Kosher salt and freshly ground black pepper to taste

1. Preheat the grill with all the burners on high for 10 minutes and the lid down.

2. While the grill is preheating, rinse the eggplant under cold running water.

3. Once the grill is hot, turn all the burners to medium. Place the eggplant on the grill, close the lid, and cook until puffed up like a balloon, 20 and 30 minutes, turning every 5 minutes or so.

4. Remove from the grill. Poke a hole or two in the eggplant skin with the tip of a sharp knife. The eggplant will deflate. Allow to cool to the point where you can handle it, then cut in half with a sharp butcher knife. Using a spoon, scrape the soft flesh away from the skin. Put the flesh in a bowl. Drizzle with extra-virgin olive oil, a dusting of ground cumin, a little lemon juice, and salt and pepper to taste. It's wonderful!

SERVES 2

Grilled Thyme Eggplant

Eggplant cooked on the grill demands only a light basting of olive oil—a fraction of the amount of oil it takes to sauté eggplant in a pan. As a result, you can taste more of the eggplant's unique flavor—and taste less of the oil. This recipe works with either the long, thin Asian eggplant or the traditional fat, oval ones.

1 large purple eggplant or 3 small Asian eggplants

1 lemon, cut in half

$1/4$ cup extra-virgin olive oil

1 tablespoon dried thyme, crumbled

Kosher salt and freshly ground black pepper to taste

1. Peel the eggplant, or leave it unpeeled if you wish. Slice into rounds about $3/8$ inch thick and rub with the lemon halves. Brush both sides of each slice with olive oil, then sprinkle with the thyme and salt and pepper on both sides.

2. Preheat the grill with all the burners on high for 10 minutes and the lid down.

3. Once the grill is hot, turn all the burners to medium. Place the eggplant slices on the grill and cook, with the lid down, until well browned and easily pierced with the tip of a sharp knife, about 6 minutes total, turning them once. Serve hot off the grill.

SERVES 4

Marinated Eggplant with Tomatoes and Fontina Cheese

This is a special vegetable dish, one that some vegetarians might consider a meal in itself! It is superb, however, served as a side dish with grilled chicken or steak—colorful, attractive, and delicious.

2 large eggplants, peeled and sliced $3/8$ inch thick

$1^1/2$ cups homemade or bottled vinaigrette or Italian salad dressing

4 to 5 large ripe tomatoes, sliced $3/8$ inch thick

$3/4$ pound fontina cheese, sliced $1/4$ inch thick

Minced fresh basil or parsley

1. Combine the eggplant slices with the vinaigrette in a large bowl. Set aside to marinate for 30 to 45 minutes.

2. Preheat the grill with all the burners on high for 10 minutes and the lid down.

3. While the grill is preheating, make three-layer stacks with all the eggplant, tomato, and cheese slices: an eggplant slice on the bottom, then a tomato slice, and a cheese slice on top.

4. Once the grill is hot, turn all the burners to medium. Carefully place the stacks on the grill, close the lid, and cook until the eggplant is easily pierced with the tip of a sharp knife and the cheese has melted, about 8 minutes.

5. Serve hot, with a sprinkling of basil.

SERVES 6 TO 8

Eggplant, Tomato, and Pepper Mélange

This dish is as beautiful to look at as it is delicious to eat. It's all about the intense flavors of summer, so it's best to make it when all of the vegetables are at their peak.

1 large purple eggplant or 3 small Asian eggplants

4 large ripe tomatoes

3 bell peppers, preferably 1 red, 1 green, and 1 yellow

1/2 cup extra-virgin olive oil

Kosher salt and freshly ground black pepper to taste

Chopped fresh basil and parsley for garnish

1. Preheat the grill with all the burners on high for 10 minutes and the lid down.

2. While the grill is preheating, peel the eggplant if you wish and slice it into 3/8- to 1/2-inch-thick rounds. Cut the tomatoes into slices and the peppers into rings (removing the seeds) also 3/8 to 1/2 inch thick. After slicing, immediately coat the vegetables liberally with some of the olive oil.

3. Once the grill is hot, turn off the center burner and turn the other burners to medium. Place the eggplant, tomato, and pepper slices over the center burner, close the lid, and cook for 6 to 10 minutes, turning them once, using a metal spatula (the tomatoes will not hold together if turned more than once). The eggplant is done when it is easily pierced with the tip of a sharp knife; the tomatoes simply need to heat through, and the peppers are done when they are wilted but still have a little crunch to them.

4. On a large platter, arrange alternating slices of eggplant, tomatoes, and peppers. Drizzle all over with the remaining olive oil. Dust the slices liberally with salt and pepper and sprinkle with basil and parsley. Serve warm, at room temperature, or even cold the next day.

SERVES 6 TO 8

Grilled Eggplant Stacks with Udon Noodles and Fresh Cilantro Sauce

This is an impressive dish, but surprisingly easy to pull together. The secret to success is advance preparation. If you slice all the vegetables ahead of time, building the stacks is like an assembly line. If you can score some helpers, the process can be a party in itself, with a delicious payoff at the end.

You can use a basting brush to coat the eggplant with the "paint" in this recipe, but an actual small paintbrush (from the hardware store) is a great addition to anyone's arsenal of kitchen equipment. The cilantro sauce can be made ahead of time and kept at room temperature while the noodles and vegetable stacks cook. On a big platter, position each vegetable stack in a twirled "nest" of the udon noodles; top with the cilantro sauce and you've got quite a presentation.

FRESH CILANTRO SAUCE

2 to 3 cups packed fresh cilantro leaves (about 1 large bunch), coarsely chopped

1/3 cup unsalted dry-roasted peanuts

2 cloves garlic, peeled

Juice of 1/2 lime

2 teaspoons mirin

1 teaspoon kosher salt

1 teaspoon sriracha sauce or other hot pepper sauce

1/2 cup peanut oil

SAVORY "PAINT"

3 tablespoons light vegetable oil

3 tablespoons toasted sesame oil

3 tablespoons tamari or other soy sauce

1 tablespoon sriracha sauce or other hot pepper sauce

VEGETABLE STACKS

1 medium-size eggplant, peeled or unpeeled, cut into 3/8-inch-thick rounds

4 slices smoked mozzarella

4 green onions, each cut in half lengthwise and then cut in half crosswise (to fit the size of the mozzarella slice)

3 bell peppers—red, yellow, and green—each one quartered and seeded

4 large white mushrooms

Vegetable oil

One 16-ounce package udon noodles

FOR GARNISH (OPTIONAL)

Chopped salted dry-roasted peanuts

Chopped fresh cilantro

Lime quarters

1. Combine the sauce ingredients, except the peanut oil, in a food processor and process until finely chopped. With the motor running, drizzle the peanut oil through the feed tube until the sauce has a pourable consistency.

2. Combine the "paint" ingredients in a small bowl and paint the eggplant slices on both sides with it.

3. Preheat the grill with all the burners on high for 10 minutes and the lid down.

4. While the grill is preheating, construct each vegetable stack, from top to bottom, with 1 round eggplant, 1 slice smoked mozzarella, the equivalent of 1 green onion, and 1 quarter of each color pepper—red, yellow, and green—arranged in a pinwheel fashion. Hold the entire stack together with a bamboo skewer, topped with a whole mushroom. To prevent sticking, dunk the bottom of each stack in a shallow plate of vegetable oil just before putting it on the grill.

5. When the grill is hot, turn off the center burner and leave the other burners on high. Place the vegetable stacks over the center burner, close the lid, and cook, without moving or turning, for about 20 minutes. Don't overcook: The stack is done when the peppers can be easily pierced with the tip of a sharp knife.

6. Meanwhile, cook the udon noodles according to the package instructions. Drain, then toss the noodles in a bowl with the cilantro sauce. On each serving plate, make a nest of hot noodles and place an eggplant stack in the center. Drizzle with a little of the reserved "paint" over the top. Garnish with chopped peanuts, cilantro, and a wedge of fresh lime.

SERVES 4 GENEROUSLY

Grilled Escarole

Botanically, escarole and endive are one and the same, known in Latin as *Cichorium endivia*. The difference is in the way they are grown: Escarole is grown for its broad outer leaves; endive is the center portion of the plant, usually pale in color. Both forms have a slightly bitter taste most people find appealing. I'm not quite sure where the idea came from to grill whole heads of escarole, but I'm glad it surfaced, as the resulting slight smokiness complements its flavor wonderfully. Once dressed with a little sherry vinegar, salt, and pepper, it becomes a complex combination of tastes, quite delicious with any grilled mild white fish.

2 good-size heads escarole

2 tablespoons sherry vinegar

Kosher salt to taste

1. Preheat the grill with all the burners on high for 10 minutes and the lid down.

2. While the grill is preheating, wash the escarole thoroughly under plenty of cold running water. Do not dry; the extra water will help keep the outer leaves from burning.

3. With all the burners still on high, place the escarole at the edge of the fire, close the lid, and cook about 8 minutes, turning once midway through.

4. Remove from the grill, chop coarsely, and dress with sherry vinegar and salt in a medium-size serving bowl. Serve hot or at room temperature.

NOTE If any of the ends of the escarole leaves burn, simply scrape them off with the edge of a sharp butcher knife before chopping.

SERVES 4

Grilled Fennel with Anchovy-Garlic Butter

Fennel is served far too infrequently in this country. As a vegetable, it is unique for its combination of crisp texture (somewhat like celery) and mild licorice flavor. This dish is excellent with any grilled fish, and the anchovy-garlic butter makes it particularly good for any Mediterranean-inspired meal.

2 fennel bulbs

ANCHOVY-GARLIC BUTTER

1/4 cup (1/2 stick) butter, at room temperature

2 large cloves garlic, pressed

4 anchovy fillets, rinsed

Juice of 1/2 lemon

1 teaspoon freshly ground black pepper

1. Trim the ferny tops from the fennel bulbs. Cut the bulb into 1/2-inch wedges, with the root end left intact so that the fennel will stay together on the grill.

2. Preheat the grill with all the burners on high for 10 minutes and the lid down.

3. While the grill is preheating, combine the anchovy-garlic butter ingredients in a bowl. Using a fork, mash together until the anchovies are in very small bits. Keep at room temperature until serving time.

4. Once the grill is hot, turn all the burners to medium. Place the fennel on the grill, close the lid, and cook until easily pierced with the tip of a sharp knife, 5 to 8 minutes.

5. Serve hot off the grill, with the anchovy-garlic butter spread on top of each slice.

SERVES 4

Grilled Garlic

Grilled whole garlic has become increasingly popular, not only for its delicious, slightly nutty flavor, but for its purported health benefits. Try squeezing the soft cloves of grilled garlic onto slices of crusty Italian bread that have been brushed lightly with olive oil and toasted briefly on the grill. Fantastic!

4 heads of garlic

1/4 cup extra-virgin olive oil

1. Preheat the grill with all the burners on high for 10 minutes and the lid down.

2. While the grill is preheating, peel away as much of the papery skin from the garlic as possible. Slice off 1/4 inch from the top of each bulb. Brush each head liberally with olive oil.

3. Once the grill is hot, turn off the center burner and turn the other burners to medium. Place the whole garlic heads, cut side down, over the center burner, close the lid, and cook until the outside skin has browned and the cloves inside are soft, 30 to 40 minutes.

4. Remove the garlic from the grill and let cool for about 10 minutes, until cool enough to handle. Squeeze the garlic pulp out of the skins and serve.

SERVES 4 TO 8

Grilled Whole Leeks

Leeks, those underused members of the onion family, are wonderful for grilling. Their strong, earthy flavor mellows on the grill, making them a fine mate for any grilled beef. Although a little salt and pepper is all they really need, leeks also benefit from a sprinkling of balsamic vinegar after grilling.

4 leeks

2 tablespoons extra-virgin olive oil

Kosher salt and freshly ground black pepper to taste

2 tablespoons balsamic vinegar (optional)

1. Preheat the grill with all the burners on high for 10 minutes and the lid down.

2. While the grill is preheating, cut off most of the green tops from the leeks and split the leeks in half lengthwise. Leave the root ends intact to help keep them from separating on the grill. Wash well under cold running water and pat dry. Brush the cut leeks with a little olive oil.

3. Once the grill is hot, turn off the center burner and turn the other burners to medium. Place the leeks over the center burner, close the lid, and cook until easily pierced through with the tip of a sharp knife, 20 to 30 minutes, turning them once.

4. Remove from the grill, sprinkle with salt, pepper, and balsamic vinegar if desired, and serve.

SERVES 4

A SPRINKLE AND A SPLASH

A SPRINKLING OF SALT AND SOME FRESHLY GROUND PEPPER AND A SPLASH OF BALSAMIC OR SHERRY VINEGAR IMPROVE THE FLAVOR OF ALMOST ANY GRILLED VEGETABLE.

Grilled Marinated Mushrooms

Although this recipe was originally developed for standard-issue white or brown mushrooms, it works equally well for any of the exotic mushrooms that are becoming available in more and more markets across the country. Common white or brown mushrooms have one advantage, however: they are very easy to grill because they are easy to thread onto skewers. Some of the more delicate, exotic mushrooms are more difficult to handle on the grill—more difficult, but worth the effort nonetheless.

THYME AND RED WINE MARINADE

1/2 cup dry red wine

1/4 cup olive oil

Juice of 1/2 lemon

1 large clove garlic, pressed

2 teaspoons dried thyme, crumbled

1 teaspoon kosher salt

1/2 teaspoon cracked black peppercorns

1 pound fresh mushrooms, wiped clean and stems trimmed

12 bamboo skewers, soaked in water for 30 minutes and drained

1. In a 1-gallon zippered-top plastic bag, combine the marinade ingredients. Toss the mushrooms in the marinade, seal, and let marinate in the refrigerator for 1 to 2 hours, shaking the bag occasionally.

2. Preheat the grill with all the burners on high for 10 minutes and the lid down.

3. While the grill is preheating, thread the mushrooms tightly onto the skewers.

4. Once the grill is hot, turn off the center burner and turn the other burners to medium. Place the skewered mushrooms over the center burner, close the lid, and cook until tender, 8 to 12 minutes, depending on the size of the mushrooms. Turn the mushrooms once.

5. Serve the mushrooms hot off the grill. Alternatively, let them cool to room temperature, slice them if you wish, and serve as an appetizer on pieces of crunchy, toasted bread.

SERVES 3 TO 4

QUALITY IS EVERYTHING

THE SIMPLICITY OF THE GRILLING PROCESS DEMANDS HIGH-QUALITY RAW INGREDIENTS, EVEN MORE SO THAN OTHER, MORE COMPLICATED COOKING METHODS. WHEN YOU GRILL, ALWAYS START WITH THE FRESHEST AND BEST INGREDIENTS.

Portobello Mushroom Burgers

With the rise of vegetarianism in this country comes an increase in the number of new recipes for non–meat eaters. Certainly one of the best is the portobello mushroom burger, which even some carnivores like better than the original "quarter-pound" version.

4 large portobello mushrooms, stems removed

1 lemon, cut in half

2 tablespoons extra-virgin olive oil

Crumbled dried thyme to taste

Kosher salt and freshly ground black pepper to taste

2 tablespoons butter, at room temperature

4 good-quality hamburger buns

Arugula, watercress, or lettuce leaves

Tomato slices

Onion slices

Condiments of your choice, such as Dijon mustard, mayonnaise, or ketchup

1. Preheat the grill with all the burners on high for 10 minutes and the lid down.

2. While the grill is preheating, rub the portobello mushrooms with a soft, damp cloth to clean them, then rub with the lemon halves. Brush them lightly with the olive oil and sprinkle with the thyme, salt, and pepper. Spread the softened butter on each hamburger bun half.

3. Once the grill is hot, turn off the center burner and turn the other burners to medium. Place the mushrooms over the center burner, close the lid, and cook until easily pierced with the tip of a sharp knife, 8 to 10 minutes, turning once. Meanwhile, toast the hamburger buns on the grill for about 2 minutes per side.

4. Place the mushrooms on the buns and serve. Let the diners add the toppings and condiments as they prefer.

SERVES 4

White Onion Kebabs with Rosemary and Balsamic Vinegar

Small white boiling onions are great candidates for grilling: They thread easily onto skewers, cook relatively quickly, and best of all, have an intense onion flavor that goes well with almost any grilled meat.

16 to 24 small white boiling onions

12 bamboo skewers, soaked in water for 30 minutes and drained

$1/4$ cup extra-virgin olive oil

1 tablespoon crushed fresh rosemary

Kosher salt and freshly ground black pepper to taste

2 tablespoons balsamic vinegar (optional)

1. Preheat the grill with all the burners on high for 10 minutes and the lid down.

2. While the grill is preheating, carefully peel the skins from the onions. Thread the onions onto two parallel skewers, with the onions' sides touching. Combine the olive oil and rosemary in a bowl and brush over the onions.

3. Once the grill is hot, turn off the center burner and turn the other burners to medium. Place the skewered onions over the center burner, close the lid, and cook until lightly browned and easily pierced through with the tip of a sharp knife, 15 to 20 minutes, turning occasionally.

4. Remove the onions from the grill, sprinkle with salt and pepper, add a dash of balsamic vinegar if desired, and serve.

SERVES 4

Oriental Grilled Green Onions

Not many people think of grilling green onions (or scallions), but they make an unusual and tasty side dish for grilled beef or lamb and are particularly good with any Asian-inspired recipe.

2 tablespoons toasted sesame oil

1 tablespoon soy sauce

1 teaspoon hoisin sauce

12 green onions, root ends and green tops trimmed slightly

1. Preheat the grill with all the burners on high for 10 minutes and the lid down.

2. While the grill is preheating, combine the sesame oil, soy sauce, and hoisin sauce in a small bowl and brush on the green onions.

3. Once the grill is hot, turn all the burners to medium. Place the green onions perpendicular to the grill bars and cook, with the lid up, until lightly browned, 3 to 4 minutes, turning once. Serve hot off the grill.

SERVES 4

Grilled Onion Slices

These onion slices are not only delicious on hamburgers, but they also make a flavorful side dish to any grilled meat. Brown-skinned onions have the most intense flavor, sweetened somewhat by grilling, but both the milder, white-skinned onions and red onions can be grilled successfully, as well.

$^1/4$ cup extra-virgin olive oil

1 tablespoon dried rosemary or thyme, crumbled

2 to 4 onions, sliced $^3/8$ inch thick

Kosher salt and freshly ground black pepper to taste

1. Preheat the grill with all the burners on high for 10 minutes and the lid down.

2. While the grill is preheating, combine the olive oil and rosemary and brush on the onions.

3. Once the grill is hot, turn all the burners to medium. Place the onion slices on the grill, close the lid, and cook until lightly browned, 2 to 4 minutes, turning them once (using a spatula).

4. Remove the onions from the grill, sprinkle with salt and pepper, and serve hot.

SERVES 4

Grilled Peppers

Any pepper, mild or hot, can be grilled. Although grilling makes peppers less pungent, it does not make hot varieties any less hot. Grilled peppers go with virtually any grilled food and are flavorful enough on their own not to require any adornment, except for salt and pepper. *Note:* You can prepare these peppers for a handful or a houseful: The sheer quantity doesn't matter, as long as you make enough to satisfy everyone.

Whole bell or hot peppers, any variety

Olive oil

Kosher salt and freshly ground black pepper to taste

1. Preheat the grill with all the burners on high for 10 minutes and the lid down.

2. While the grill is preheating, wash the peppers under cold running water, dry, and rub them with a little olive oil.

3. Once the grill is hot, turn off the center burner and turn the other burners to medium. Place the peppers over the center burner, close the lid, and cook until lightly browned and they collapse on themselves, 10 to 20 minutes, turning them occasionally.

4. Remove the peppers from the grill and, when they are cool enough to handle, remove their stems and seeds. Serve hot off the grill, sprinkled with salt and pepper.

EACH LARGE PEPPER SERVES 2

Marinated Roasted Peppers

The gas grill is tops when it comes to roasting peppers quickly and easily. Take the peppers one step further by marinating them and you have a fantastic addition to any pasta dish. They also hold their own as an appetizer when teamed up with some crusty Italian or French bread and a soft cheese, such as Teleme or fresh mozzarella. For a visual, as well as gustatory, treat, roast peppers of all colors: green, red, yellow, and orange.

Unlike grilling most other foods, the point of grilling peppers is to actually char the skin (but not the flesh). You'll need to keep your eye on the peppers while they roast, turning them frequently as the skin on one side or another becomes charred. The more evenly charred the skins are, the easier it will be to remove them.

4 bell peppers, preferably an assortment of colors

1/4 cup olive oil

2 tablespoons red wine vinegar

Kosher salt and freshly ground black pepper to taste

1. Preheat the grill with all the burners on high for 10 minutes and the lid down.

2. With all the burners still on high, place the peppers on the grill and cook, with the lid up, until the skins are blackened all over and the peppers have collapsed on themselves, or even split, 10 to 15 minutes. Keep your eye on them while they roast, turning frequently as the skin on one side or another becomes charred.

3. Transfer the peppers to a brown paper bag or bowl, seal it tightly, and let them "sweat" until soft, 15 minutes or so.

4. Once the peppers have cooled, use a small, sharp knife to remove the stems and skins and to scrape away the seeds and membrane inside the peppers—a messy proposition, but definitely worth it. Do not wash the peeled peppers, because that will greatly diminish their natural flavor.

5. Cut the roasted peppers in thin strips and place them in a bowl. Add the oil, vinegar, and salt and pepper. Set aside for at least 30 minutes at room temperature or refrigerate them in an airtight container for several days. Serve the peppers warm or at room temperature.

SERVES 4 TO 8

Grilled Cheese-Stuffed Peppers

This recipe is a grilled version of the popular Mexican specialty *chiles rellenos*. It is wonderful as an appetizer or as a side dish for grilled beef or chicken.

4 large green chiles (preferably the dark green poblano or pasilla; otherwise, the long green Anaheim variety)

3 medium-size ripe tomatoes

$1/4$ teaspoon ground cumin

$1/4$ teaspoon dried oregano, crumbled

Kosher salt and freshly ground black pepper to taste

1 cup coarsely shredded Monterey Jack cheese

Vegetable oil

1.   Preheat the grill with all the burners on high for 10 minutes and the lid down.

2.   While the grill is preheating, wash and dry the peppers.

3.   With all the burners still on high, place the chiles on the grill and cook, with the lid up, until the skins are blackened all over and the peppers have collapsed on themselves or even split, 10 to 15 minutes. Keep your eye on them while they roast, turning frequently as the skin on one side or another becomes charred.

4.   Transfer the chiles to a brown paper bag or bowl, seal it tightly, and let them "sweat" until soft, 15 minutes or so.

5.   After the peppers have been removed from the grill, turn off the center burner and turn the others to medium. Position the tomatoes over the center burner, close the lid, and cook for about 15 minutes. Do not turn the tomatoes.

6.   Transfer the tomatoes to a small dish and chop them roughly (skins and all). Add the cumin and oregano and season with salt and pepper.

7.   When the peppers are cool enough to handle, peel away the charred outer skin. Make a lengthwise cut in each pepper, leaving the stem end attached, and remove the seeds and

as much of the veins as possible. Stuff each pepper gently with cheese, fold the cut ends together, and seal up the cut with a toothpick or two. Oil the stuffed peppers lightly and place them over the burner that is off. Close the lid and cook just until the cheese is melted, about 8 minutes.

8. Serve the peppers with the seasoned chopped tomatoes as a sauce.

SERVES 4 AS A SIDE DISH, 2 AS A MAIN DISH

SPRAY ON THAT OIL

USING A SIMPLE TRIGGER-PUMP SPRAY BOTTLE FILLED WITH OLIVE OIL IS A FAST AND EASY WAY TO APPLY A THIN COATING OF OIL TO ANY FOOD BEFORE GRILLING.

"Baked" Potatoes on the Grill

If you're planning to serve baked potatoes as a side dish for a grilled entrée, you might as well "bake" the potatoes on the grill, too. It saves time and energy, and avoids heating up the kitchen.

4 Idaho or russet potatoes

Butter, sour cream, and chopped fresh chives for toppings (optional)

Kosher salt and freshly ground black pepper to taste

1. Preheat the grill with all the burners on high for 10 minutes and the lid down.

2. While the grill is preheating, scrub the potatoes well under cold running water and poke a few incisions into each one with the tip of a sharp knife. Wrap each potato in two layers of aluminum foil.

3. Once the grill is hot, turn off the center burner and turn the other burners to medium. Place the potatoes over the center burner, close the lid, and cook until pierced easily with the tip of a sharp knife, 45 to 60 minutes. If you prefer crisp skins, remove the aluminum foil for the last 10 minutes or so of the cooking time.

4. Serve the potatoes hot off the grill with plenty of butter, sour cream, chives, and salt and pepper.

SERVES 4

SLOWER IS BETTER

AS TEMPTING AS IT MAY BE TO COOK FOODS DIRECTLY OVER THE HOT BURNERS, MOST OF THE TIME YOU'LL HAVE GREATER SUCCESS IF YOU TURN ONE BURNER OFF AND COOK THE FOOD INDIRECTLY OVER THE BURNER THAT IS OFF, WITH THE LID DOWN. ALTHOUGH INDIRECT COOKING TAKES A LITTLE LONGER, IT VIRTUALLY GUARANTEES THAT YOU WON'T EVER BURN GRILLED FOOD.

Grilled Potato Skins

This recipe is dedicated to those who say that the best part of a baked potato is the skin. Grilled potato skins have an extra crispiness that many people find irresistible.

4 Idaho or russet potatoes

4 teaspoons butter, melted

Butter, sour cream, and chopped fresh chives for toppings (optional)

Kosher salt and freshly ground black pepper to taste

1. Scrub the potatoes well under cold running water and, using the tip of a sharp knife, poke a few steam vents in each potato. Bake the potatoes in a preheated 350°F oven until fork tender, about 1 hour. Remove from the oven and let cool, then cut a slit in each baked potato and remove all but $1/4$ inch or so of the flesh. Flatten each potato with the heel of your hand. Lightly brush the insides of the potatoes with the melted butter.

2. Preheat the grill with all the burners on high for 10 minutes and the lid down.

3. Once the grill is hot, turn all the burners to medium. Place the potato skins on the grill and cook, with the lid down, for about 10 minutes, turning them once.

4. Serve the skins hot off the grill with plenty of butter, sour cream, chives, and salt and pepper.

SERVES 4

Skewered Herbed Potatoes

Roasted new potatoes, seasoned liberally with fresh herbs and doused with garlic, are hard to resist. This classic flavor combination is well suited to grilled fish or poultry. Remember, threading new potatoes on bamboo skewers makes them much easier to manage than individual ones, loose on the grill.

20 new potatoes, each about the size of a golf ball

$^1/_3$ cup olive oil

3 tablespoons chopped fresh herbs (dill, basil, oregano, thyme, rosemary, mint, or any combination)

2 cloves garlic, pressed

1 teaspoon freshly ground black pepper

Kosher salt to taste

6 bamboo skewers, soaked in water for 30 minutes and drained

1.   Preheat the grill with all the burners on high for 10 minutes and the lid down.

2.   While the grill is preheating, wash and scrub the potatoes under cold running water. Pat dry, but do not peel. Place the potatoes in a bowl and toss with the oil, herbs, garlic, pepper, and salt. Thread 5 potatoes, with their sides touching, on each skewer.

3.   Once the grill is hot, turn off the center burner and turn the other burners to medium. Place the potato skewers over the center burner, close the lid, and cook until easily pierced with the tip of a sharp knife, about 30 minutes, turning every 10 minutes or so. Serve hot off the grill.

SERVES 4

Rosemary Potato Wedges

Brown-skinned baking potatoes that are quartered lengthwise in long wedges and cooked on the grill are like big, crisp French fries, but without all the oil. The addition of a little rosemary makes them the perfect accompaniment for any cut of beef or any type of poultry. If desired, sprinkle a little coarse salt on the potato wedges after grilling—it really sparks the flavors into life.

4 large Idaho or russet potatoes

1/3 cup extra-virgin olive oil

1 tablespoon crushed dried rosemary

Freshly ground black pepper to taste

Coarse or regular table salt (optional)

1. Preheat the grill with all the burners on high for 10 minutes and the lid down.

2. While the grill is preheating, wash and scrub the potatoes under cold running water. Pat dry with paper towels, but do not peel. Cut the potatoes lengthwise in wedges, place in a bowl, and toss with the oil, rosemary, and pepper.

3. Once the grill is hot, turn off the center burner and turn the other burners to medium. Place the potato wedges over the center burner, close the lid, and cook until easily pierced with the tip of a sharp knife, 30 to 40 minutes, turning them every 10 minutes or so.

4. Serve the potatoes hot off the grill, sprinkled with a little coarse salt if desired.

SERVES 4

Roast Sweet Potatoes with Cilantro-Lime Butter

This perfect combination of Southern Hemisphere flavors is guaranteed to turn any sweet-potato hater into a sweet-potato lover.

4 sweet potatoes

1/4 cup (1/2 stick) butter, softened

2 tablespoons fresh lime juice

2 tablespoons chopped fresh cilantro

1. Preheat the grill with all the burners on high for 10 to minutes and the lid down.

2. Scrub the sweet potatoes under cold running water and poke a few incisions into each with the tip of a sharp knife. Wrap each sweet potato in two layers of aluminum foil.

3. Once the grill is hot, turn off the center burner and turn the other burners to medium. Place the potatoes over the center burner, close the lid, and cook until pierced easily all the way through with the tip of a sharp knife, about an hour, turning and rotating them once or twice. If you prefer crisp skins, remove the aluminum foil for the last 10 minutes or so of the cooking time.

4. While the potatoes roast, combine the butter, lime juice, and chopped cilantro. Set aside at room temperature.

5. To serve, remove the potatoes from the foil. Split each one open and top with the flavored butter. Serve hot.

SERVES 4

Grilled Summer Squash

All types of summer squash—zucchini, yellow crooknecks, pattypans, you name it—can be grilled easily. Although convention has dictated that squashes be cut in pieces and threaded onto skewers for grilling, it's actually preferable to cook them whole and slice them later. Both the flavor and texture of any summer squash are enhanced using this method.

4 small summer squashes (1^1/$_2$ to 2 pounds)

^{1}/$_4$ cup olive oil

Chopped fresh parsley

Kosher salt and freshly ground black pepper to taste

1. Preheat the grill with all the burners on high for 10 minutes and the lid down.

2. Wash the squashes under cold running water and pat dry. Trim the tops and bottoms of the squashes, then rub the olive oil all over them.

3. Once the grill is hot, turn off the center burner and turn the other burners to medium. Place the whole squashes over the center burner, close the lid, and cook until easily pierced with the tip of a sharp knife, 12 to 20 minutes (depending on the size and variety of the squash), turning the squashes as needed.

4. Transfer the squashes to a cutting board, slice, toss with the parsley and salt and pepper, and serve.

SERVES 4

Grilled Zucchini

You can never have too many good zucchini recipes because there are times, like late summer, when most gardens produce more zucchini than anyone knows what to do with. I'm not sure what makes this recipe so good, but I do know that it's my favorite way to prepare zucchini, and it's been a big hit with everyone who's tried it.

4 zucchini (1^1/2 to 2 pounds)

^{1}/4 cup olive oil

1 to 2 tablespoons fresh lemon juice, to your taste

1 teaspoon red or white wine vinegar

2 tablespoons finely chopped fresh parsley or basil (or both)

Kosher salt and freshly ground black pepper to taste

1. Preheat the grill for 10 minutes with all the burners on high and the lid closed.

2. Wash the zucchini under cold running water and pat dry. Trim the ends, then slice them lengthwise about ^{1}/4 inch thick. Drizzle 1 tablespoon of the olive oil on both sides of the zucchini slices.

3. Once the grill is hot, turn off the center burner and turn the others to medium. Position the zucchini slices over the center burner, close the lid, and cook the zucchini about 2 minutes per side, just long enough to produce grill marks; the zucchini should still have some crunch to it when you remove the slices from the grill.

4. Transfer the grilled squash to a bowl, toss it in the remaining 3 tablespoons olive oil, the lemon juice, and vinegar. Top with the parsley and dust with salt and pepper. Serve hot or at room temperature.

SERVES 4

GRILL BASKETS

HINGED WIRE BASKETS COME IN VERY HANDY WHEN GRILLING DELICATE PIECES OF FISH OR SLICED VEGETABLES.

Honey-Glazed Winter Squash en Brochette

When cut into cubes of a manageable size (1 to 1½ inches), winter squash grills up beautifully. Naturally sweet winter squash pairs well with grilled ham and pork recipes.

1½ pounds winter squash, peeled, seeded, and cut into 1- to 1½-inch cubes

6 bamboo skewers, soaked in water for 30 minutes and drained

½ cup (1 stick) butter, melted

2 tablespoons honey or pure maple syrup

1. Preheat the grill with all the burners on high for 10 minutes and the lid down.

2. While the grill is preheating, thread the squash cubes onto the skewers, with the cubes' sides touching. Brush liberally with some of the melted butter.

3. Once the grill is hot, turn off the center burner and turn the other burners to medium. Place the skewered squash over the center burner, close the lid, and cook until easily pierced with the tip of a sharp knife, 15 to 20 minutes, turning the skewers once.

4. In a bowl, combine the remaining melted butter with the honey. Remove the squash from the skewers and toss the cubes lightly with the sweetened butter. Serve hot.

SERVES 4

Skewered Plum Tomatoes with Garlic and Basil

The meaty, oval-shaped paste tomatoes (most often the Roma variety, or one of its offspring) are great for grilling. Although they can be grilled whole, they are more attractive on the plate if they are cut in half lengthwise. To hold them securely while they cook, thread them onto two parallel bamboo skewers.

8 plum tomatoes, cut in half lengthwise

12 bamboo skewers, soaked in water for 30 minutes and drained

1/4 cup extra-virgin olive oil

2 cloves garlic, minced

1/4 cup minced fresh basil

Kosher salt and freshly ground black pepper to taste

1. Preheat the grill with all the burners on high for 10 minutes and the lid down.

2. While the grill is preheating, thread the tomato halves, cut side up, onto 2 parallel skewers. Rub the olive oil on both sides.

3. Once the grill is hot, turn off the center burner and turn the other burners to medium. Place the skewered tomatoes over the center burner, close the lid, and cook until heated through and soft to the touch, 8 to 10 minutes, turning them once.

4. Remove the tomatoes from the grill, sprinkle with the garlic and basil, season with salt and pepper, and serve.

SERVES 4

Garlicky Grilled Tomatoes

These tomatoes are delicious as an accompaniment to virtually any grilled meat. They can also serve as the base for a very easy and tasty pasta sauce. To make the sauce, peel the cooked tomatoes if you wish, mince them, and place in a bowl. Add a couple of tablespoons of olive oil, salt, freshly ground black pepper, and chopped herbs if desired. Mix everything well and serve on top of spaghetti for a delightful and fresh-tasting summer pasta.

4 medium-size to large ripe tomatoes

4 cloves garlic, pressed

4 teaspoons extra-virgin olive oil

Kosher salt and freshly ground black pepper to taste

2 to 4 tablespoons minced fresh oregano, basil, or both, to your taste

1. Preheat the grill with all the burners on high for 10 minutes and the lid down.

2. While the grill is preheating, cut off the top $^3/_8$ inch of each tomato. If you have a tomato corer, use it to remove about half of the core; otherwise, use the tip of a very sharp paring knife. Press the equivalent of 1 clove of garlic into the cavity of each tomato. Drizzle about 1 teaspoon of the olive oil over the top of each tomato and dust with salt and pepper.

3. Once the grill is hot, turn off the center burner and turn the other burners to medium. Place the tomatoes, cut side up, over the center burner, close the lid, and cook until heated through and soft to the touch, 10 to 15 minutes, depending on their size and degree of ripeness. Do not turn the tomatoes.

4. Using a spatula, carefully transfer the tomatoes to a serving platter; they do tend to split easily at this point. Sprinkle them liberally with oregano and serve hot.

SERVES 4

Grilled Pesto Tomatoes

Basil-rich pesto and red-ripe tomatoes are natural partners, made even more intensely delicious by grilling. As simple as this side dish is, it is one of the best.

PESTO

2 garlic cloves, peeled

1/4 teaspoon kosher salt

1 tablespoon pine nuts, toasted in a dry skillet over medium heat until lightly browned

2 tablespoons extra-virgin olive oil

3 tablespoons butter, softened

20 large fresh basil leaves

Freshly ground black pepper to taste

4 medium-size to large ripe tomatoes

2 teaspoons extra-virgin olive oil

Kosher salt and freshly ground black pepper to taste

1. To make the pesto, combine the garlic, salt, pine nuts, olive oil, and butter in a food processor or blender and process until smooth. Add the basil and continue to process until smooth. Season the pesto with pepper and set aside.

2. Preheat the grill with all the burners on high for 10 minutes and the lid down.

3. While the grill is preheating, cut off the top $3/8$ inch of each tomato. If you have a tomato corer, use it to remove about half of the core; otherwise, use the tip of a very sharp paring knife. Fill the cavity of each tomato with an equal amount of the pesto, drizzle about $1/2$ teaspoon of the olive oil over the top, and dust with salt and pepper.

4. Once the grill is hot, turn off the center burner and turn the other burners to medium. Place the tomatoes, cut side up, over the center burner, close the lid, and cook until heated through and soft to the touch, 10 to 15 minutes, depending on their size and degree of ripeness. Do not turn the tomatoes.

5. Using a spatula, carefully transfer the tomatoes to a serving platter; they do tend to split easily at this point. Serve at once.

SERVES 4

Cherry Tomatoes en Brochette

Cherry tomatoes are often surprisingly flavorful for their size and, fortunately, are available in a nicely ripened state year-round. Threaded onto skewers, cherry tomatoes are the essence of simplicity to grill.

24 cherry tomatoes

12 bamboo skewers, soaked in water for 30 minutes and drained

1/4 cup olive oil

2 cloves garlic, pressed

Kosher salt and freshly ground black pepper to taste

1. Preheat the grill with all the burners on high for 10 minutes and the lid down.

2. While the grill is preheating, thread the tomatoes onto two parallel skewers. Combine the olive oil and garlic in a bowl and brush onto the tomatoes.

3. Once the grill is hot, turn off the center burner and turn the other burners to medium. Place the skewered cherry tomatoes over the center burner, close the lid, and cook until heated through and soft to the touch, 8 to 10 minutes.

4. Remove the tomatoes from the grill, sprinkle with salt and pepper, and serve.

SERVES 4

MAKING AN OKAY TOMATO GREAT

TO DRAMATICALLY ENHANCE THE FLAVOR AND TEXTURE OF A LESS-THAN-PERFECT OR OUT-OF-SEASON TOMATO, JUST GRILL IT!

Tomatoes Stuffed with Duchess Potatoes

This combination of tomatoes and potatoes topped with cheese is not only unusual, but also beautiful—and delicious.

DUCHESS POTATOES

6 large baking potatoes, peeled

3/4 cup milk

4 to 6 tablespoons (1/2 to 3/4 stick) butter

Kosher salt and freshly ground black pepper to taste

2 large eggs, beaten

8 large ripe tomatoes

1 cup finely shredded Swiss cheese

Chopped fresh parsley for garnish

1. To make the duchess potatoes, boil the potatoes in plenty of salted water until very tender and easily pierced with the tip of a sharp knife, about 30 minutes. Drain well and return the potatoes to the pot. Mash the potatoes, adding the milk and butter, until they have reached a fairly smooth consistency. Season with salt and pepper. Beat in the eggs and set aside briefly to cool.

2. Slice off the top 1/2 inch of each tomato. Using a sharp-edged spoon (a melon baller or serrated grapefruit spoon works well), hollow out the tomatoes by removing the meat, being careful not to pierce the skin. Set aside.

3. Spoon the slightly cooled potatoes into a plastic bag and force them into one of the bag's bottom corners (as in a pastry bag). With a pair of scissors, cut the tip off that corner to create an opening about 3/4 inch wide. Squeeze the duchess potatoes out of the bag and into each hollowed-out tomato, mounding the potatoes slightly on top. Press 1 to 2 tablespoons of the cheese on top of the potatoes in each tomato.

4. Preheat the grill with all the burners on high for 10 minutes and the lid down.

5. Once the grill is hot, turn off the center burner and turn the other burners to medium. Place the stuffed tomatoes over the center burner, close the lid, and cook until the potatoes are heated through and the cheese has melted, 15 to 20 minutes.

6. Using a spatula, carefully transfer the tomatoes to a serving platter; they do tend to split easily at this point. Sprinkle parsley over the tomatoes and serve hot.

SERVES 8

SMOKE AND VEGETABLES

WOOD SMOKE MAY OVERPOWER THE FLAVOR OF MOST VEGETABLES, BUT A PERFORATED ALUMINUM FOIL PACKET OF HERBS, SUCH AS OREGANO OR ROSEMARY, IN THE GRILL WILL ADD A DELICATE FLAVOR.

Veggie Cheesy Burgers

Toasted buttered buns, grilled onions, and melted cheese take these veggie burgers from mundane to mouthwatering. They're great served with a shovelful of Tater-Tots, hot from the oven.

Frozen veggie burger patties, defrosted

Nonstick cooking spray

Kosher salt and freshly ground black pepper to taste

Onion slices, about $1/4$ inch thick

Your favorite cheese, cut into thin slices

Good-quality burger buns, spread liberally with butter

Shredded lettuce (optional)

Sliced tomato (optional)

1. Coat both sides of the patties with cooking spray and dust liberally with salt and pepper.

2. Keeping the onion slices intact, coat both sides liberally with cooking spray.

3. Preheat the grill with all the burners on high for 10 minutes and the lid down.

4. When the grill is hot, turn off the center burner and turn the other burners to medium. Place the patties and onion slices over the center burner, close the lid, and cook for 4 minutes, then turn the patties and onion slices and place a slice of cheese on top of cooked side of the patty. When you flip the patties and onions, place the buns, buttered side down, over the unlit burner. Close the lid and cook for another 4 minutes.

5. Remove from the grill and construct your burger with the grilled onions, lettuce, tomatoes, and whatever else your heart desires.

Mixed Vegetable Brochettes

When you try to combine meat and vegetables on one skewer, one or the other usually turns out imperfect. It is far better to separate the meat from the vegetables on different skewers. That said, it's certainly okay to combine a variety of vegetables on one skewer—the brochettes will be attractive and all the vegetables will be cooked "just right." The types of vegetables listed here should be considered suggestions only—and you decide how much of each to cook, enough to make 12 skewers.

Red, green, or yellow bell peppers, seeded and cut into 1-inch squares

Fresh white mushrooms, wiped clean and stems trimmed

Onions, cut into 1-inch cubes

Zucchini or other summer squash, cut into 1-inch-thick slices

Cherry or yellow pear tomatoes

Eggplant, peeled and cut into 1-inch cubes

12 bamboo skewers, soaked in water for 30 minutes and drained

Olive oil

Kosher salt and freshly ground black pepper to taste

Dried thyme to taste

1. Preheat the grill with all the burners on high for 10 minutes and the lid down.

2. While the grill is preheating, thread the vegetables onto the skewers, keeping them separate—all mushrooms on one set of skewers, all onions on another, and so forth. Pierce the mushrooms sideways through the cap and spear the zucchini through the skin, so that the cut sides face toward the grill. Coat all the vegetables with a liberal amount of olive oil, salt and pepper, and a sprinkling of thyme.

3. Once the grill is hot, turn all the burners to medium. Place the brochettes on the grill, close the lid, and cook for about 10 minutes, turning them occasionally. The eggplant is done when easily pierced with the tip of a sharp knife; the tomatoes simply need to be heated through, and the peppers and onions are ready when wilted but still a little crunchy. Serve hot off the grill.

SERVES 4 TO 6

Grilled Ratatouille

The grilled version of ratatouille—a classic vegetable mixture from the Provence region of France—is actually far more authentic than the more common stovetop version. Not long ago, all ratatouille was cooked over an open grill; indeed, many traditional chefs throughout France still cook the vegetables over the coals. This dish actually tastes better the day after it has been assembled, so you might want to plan ahead.

1 large eggplant, peeled and cut into 1-inch cubes

1 medium-size onion, quartered

3 medium-size zucchini (or any other summer squash), cut into 1/2-inch-thick rounds

2 bell peppers, seeded and cut into 1-inch-wide strips

12 paste or plum tomatoes, or 18 cherry tomatoes

12 to 24 bamboo skewers, soaked in water for 30 minutes and drained

1/2 cup extra-virgin olive oil

3 to 4 cloves garlic, to your taste, minced

1/2 teaspoon dried oregano

1 to 2 tablespoons chopped fresh basil, to your taste

Fresh lemon juice or balsamic vinegar to taste

Kosher salt and freshly ground black pepper to taste

1. Thread the eggplant, onion, zucchini, bell peppers, and tomatoes on separate skewers, using two parallel skewers as needed. Brush the brochettes liberally with some of the olive oil.

2. Preheat the grill with all the burners on high for 10 minutes and the lid down.

3. Once the grill is hot, turn off the center burner and turn the other burners to medium. Place the skewered vegetables over the center burner, close the lid, and cook for 15 to 25 minutes, turning the brochettes as needed. Some vegetables, such as tomatoes, will cook more quickly than the others. With the exception of the onions, which should be thoroughly wilted when done, remove each type of vegetable while it still has a little crunch left.

4. As each type of vegetable is done, slide the pieces off the skewers into a large bowl. Cut in half or quarter the tomatoes before mixing them with the other vegetables. Season the mixture with olive oil, garlic, oregano, and basil. Taste the vegetables, and add lemon juice and salt and pepper. Toss the mixture lightly.

5. Serve the ratatouille immediately or cover the bowl and refrigerate until the next day.

SERVES 6 TO 8

Grilled Marinated Tofu

These days, mixed households of carnivores and vegetarians are not at all unusual. If you invite a group over to your house for a cookout, some of the guests will almost certainly be vegetarians. When you're planning a grilled meal featuring a meat dish, you can avoid a problem by having some tofu (the firm variety) on hand. Simply marinate the tofu (it's a flavor sponge), then grill it alongside the rest of the meal for a delicious entrée.

One 1-pound block firm tofu

1 cup bottled teriyaki sauce

$1/4$ cup vegetable or toasted sesame oil

1. Preheat the grill with all the burners on high for 10 minutes and the lid down.

2. While the grill is preheating, slice the tofu $1/2$ inch thick and put the slices in a shallow dish. Combine the teriyaki sauce and oil in a bowl and pour over the tofu. Let stand at room temperature until grilling time.

3. Once the grill is hot, turn off the center burner and turn the other burners to medium. Place the tofu over the center burner, close the lid, and cook until heated through and lightly "toasted" on the outside, 8 to 10 minutes, turning once (using a metal spatula). Serve immediately.

SERVES 2 TO 3

Tofu Kebabs

Combining meat and vegetables on the same skewer has always caused problems for grillers, simply because the meat usually takes much longer than the vegetables to cook. When it comes to tofu, however, that problem is solved, because tofu and vegetables cook at about the same rate. Marinating all the ingredients in a little teriyaki sauce greatly enhances their flavor.

One 1-pound block firm tofu, cut into 1^1/$_4$-inch cubes

12 cherry tomatoes

2 bell peppers (any color), seeded and cut into 1^1/$_4$-inch squares

12 fresh mushrooms, wiped clean and stems trimmed

12 bamboo skewers, soaked in water for 30 minutes and drained

1^1/$_2$ cups bottled teriyaki sauce

^{1}/$_3$ cup vegetable or toasted sesame oil

1. Preheat the grill with all the burners on high for 10 minutes and the lid down.

2. While the grill is preheating, thread the tofu cubes, cherry tomatoes, bell peppers, and mushrooms in turn onto the skewers. Place the skewered vegetables in a shallow container. Combine the teriyaki sauce and oil in a bowl and pour over the skewers. Let stand at room temperature until grilling time.

3. Once the grill is hot, turn off the center burner and turn the other burners to medium. Place the skewers over the center burner, close the lid, and cook until the tofu is heated through and lightly "toasted" on the outside and the vegetables are just beginning to soften, 8 to 10 minutes, turning the skewers once. Serve immediately.

SERVES 4

Grilled Polenta with Mushroom "Ragout"

This is a great use for leftover polenta and a wonderful main dish for vegetarian diners. It's so good, you may want to plan ahead and make a batch of polenta just for this dish. It's best to make the polenta the night or morning before, as it must be thoroughly cold and set to stand up to grilling.

1 1/2 cups broth (beef, chicken, vegetable, or mushroom)

1/2 cup dry sherry

1/2 teaspoon dried thyme

Freshly ground black pepper to taste

1 pound medium-size fresh white or brown mushrooms, wiped clean and stems trimmed

Nonstick cooking spray or several tablespoons olive oil

1 recipe microwave polenta (page 348), cold and thoroughly firm

2 tablespoons finely chopped fresh parsley

2 tablespoons butter

Squeeze of fresh lemon juice

1. In a medium-size saucepan, combine the broth, sherry, thyme, and pepper. Bring to a boil and continue to boil until reduced by half. Remove from the heat.

2. Rinse the mushrooms under cold running water. Skewer them whole, from the stem end through the cap. Coat the mushrooms on all sides with cooking spray or brush with olive oil.

3. Using a sharp knife, cut the polenta into 8 same-size triangles: Slice diagonally from corner to corner first, then make two more cuts from the center of each side of the pan to the other. Lift the triangles out and place on a large platter or cookie sheet; brush liberally with olive oil or coat both sides with cooking spray.

4. Preheat the grill with all the burners on high for 10 minutes and the lid down.

5. Once the grill is hot, turn all the burners to medium. Place the mushrooms and polenta on the grill and cook, with the lid up, for a total of 10 minutes, turning once midway through. Place the grilled polenta triangles in a straight row down the middle of a platter, overlapping each slice. Cover with aluminum foil to keep warm.

6. When cool enough to handle, cut each of the grilled mushrooms into 3 or 4 slices. Add to the reduced broth-sherry sauce. Bring to a boil for about a minute, then add the parsley, butter, and lemon juice. Once the butter has melted, pour over the polenta triangles and serve.

SERVES 4

Grilled Quesadilla

This is an interesting variation on quesadillas, taught to me by my daughter's fiancé, Enriqué. The combination of crispy flour tortilla and melted cheese with crunchy fresh ingredients like lettuce, tomatoes, and onions is a winner. Betcha can't eat just one!

FOR EACH FLOUR TORTILLA (USE THE SMALL ONES, NOT THE BURRITO SIZE)
$1/2$ cup shredded cheese of your choice, such as cheddar, American, or Monterey Jack

OPTIONAL INGREDIENTS
Shredded lettuce

Diced fresh tomatoes and onions, or pico de gallo

Guacamole

Hot pepper sauce

1. Preheat the grill with all the burners on high for 10 minutes and the lid down.

2. When the grill is hot, turn all the burners to medium. Place the tortilla on the grill and spread the shredded cheese over half of the tortilla. Fold the other half over the cheese and press down slightly. Cook, with the lid down, for 2 to 3 minutes; turn and grill another 2 to 3 minutes. Keep flipping every 2 minutes or so, until the cheese is completely melted and the tortilla just begins to brown.

3. Remove from the grill and open the folded tortilla carefully. To your taste, fill the quesadilla with shredded lettuce, diced tomatoes and onions, guacamole, and hot sauce. Fold the tortilla back together again and serve immediately. *Delicioso!*

EACH QUESADILLA SERVES 1

9

Fruits and Desserts

I f most home cooks think grilling vegetables is somewhat unusual, grilling

fruits and other sweet or dessert foods may seem downright strange. Be

advised, however, that grilling fruit makes good culinary sense, especially

because there's something about the grilling process that transforms even

slightly inferior, underripe fruit into a first-rate dish. ✳ Some fruits, such as

apples and pineapples, can be used as either a dessert or a side dish, espe-

cially when paired with smoked or cured ham. The natural sweetness of the

fruit complements the saltiness of the ham perfectly. ✳ Fruits can also be

grilled in foil packets, while you eat your main dish. Simply place the fruit on a sheet of heavy-duty aluminum foil and drizzle melted butter and a little lemon juice over it. If you like, add a little sweetener or fruit liqueur, and perhaps a sprinkling of cinnamon. Bring the edges of the package together and fold them over to seal the foil. Put the packet on a warming rack or over a preheated burner that has been turned off. By the time you are ready for dessert, the fruit should be heated through. Use the grilled fruit as a topping for toasted pound cake, angel food cake, biscuits, or ice cream.

If you're up for something unusual and impressive, be sure to try the Dessert Bruschetta with Cheese and Honey (page 334). As unlikely as it sounds, the flavors are extraordinary.

Caramelized Fruit
Kebabs   328

Grilled Apple Slices   329

Grilled Bananas   330

Tropical Grilled
Bananas   330

Maple-Glazed Peaches   331

Grilled Fresh
Pineapple Spears   332

Grilled Fresh Figs
with Mascarpone
and Balsamic Syrup   333

Dessert Bruschetta
with Cheese and Honey 334

Toasted Pound Cake   334

Toasted Angel Food Cake
with Grilled Peaches
and Ice Cream   335

Grilled Peanut Butter
and Jelly Calzones   336

Grilled S'mores   337

Grilled Buñuelos with
Cajeta   338

Caramelized Fruit Kebabs

When I was experimenting with grilled fruit, this recipe came as both a surprise and a delight. Apples, peaches, and plums work best; the peaches and plums need not even be fully ripe to turn out delicious. These fruits are wonderful warm off the grill—kind of like a pie without the crust.

2 tart apples, such as Granny Smith or Fuji

3 or 4 plums

2 or 3 peaches

1/4 cup (1/2 stick) butter, or more, melted

1/4 cup sugar, or more

12 bamboo skewers, soaked in water for 30 minutes and drained

1. Preheat the grill with all the burners on high for 10 minutes and the lid down.

2. While the grill is preheating, peel and core the apples and remove the stones from the plums and peaches; then cut all the fruit into 1- to 1 1/2-inch chunks (rather than wedges). Combine the butter and sugar in a bowl and mix well. Thread the fruit chunks in turn onto the skewers, then brush liberally with the sugared butter.

3. Once the grill is hot, turn off the center burner and turn the other burners to medium. Place the skewered fruit over the center burner, close the lid, and cook for 6 to 10 minutes, turning them a few times. Serve warm off the grill.

SERVES 4

FRUIT AND SMOKE

THE DELICATE FLAVOR OF FRUIT CAN BE OVERWHELMED BY SMOKE. SAVE YOUR WOOD CHIPS FOR HEARTIER FOODS, SUCH AS BEEF, CHICKEN, OR PORK.

Grilled Apple Slices

Grilled apple slices are a wonderful accompaniment to all kinds of grilled pork dishes. Choose a cooking apple such as Rome Beauty or Granny Smith for the best texture and taste. A splash of balsamic vinegar on top of the grilled apples really enhances their flavor.

4 apples

$^1/4$ to $^1/2$ cup ($^1/2$ to 1 stick) butter, melted

2 tablespoons balsamic vinegar (optional)

1. Preheat the grill with all the burners on high for 10 minutes and the lid down.

2. While the grill is preheating, peel the apples if desired. Use an apple corer to remove the cores and seeds, then slice the apples into rounds $^1/2$ inch thick. Coat them liberally with the melted butter.

3. Once the grill is hot, turn off the center burner and turn the other burners to medium. Place the apples over the center burner, close the lid, and cook for 5 to 8 minutes, turning them a few times.

4. Serve the apples in bowls, warm off the grill, splashed with a little balsamic vinegar if desired.

SERVES 4

Grilled Bananas

Grilling softens bananas and intensifies their flavor. They are an incredible treat hot off the grill, combined with vanilla ice cream and a little chocolate sauce. Heavenly!

4 bananas, just ripe, cut in half lengthwise, with the peel still on

1. Preheat the grill with all the burners on high for 10 minutes and the lid down.

2. Once the grill is hot, turn off the center burner and turn the other burners to medium. Place the bananas, peel side down, over the center burner, close the lid, and cook for 5 to 8 minutes; then turn them cut side down and grill for another 2 minutes. Remove the peels and serve hot off the grill.

SERVES 4

Tropical Grilled Bananas

This great flavor combination is excellent with vanilla ice cream. These also make a great topping for Toasted Pound Cake (page 334).

3 tablespoons butter

1/3 cup firmly packed dark brown sugar

Juice of 2 limes

4 bananas, firm but ripe, cut in half lengthwise, with the peels still on

1. Preheat the grill with all the burners on high for 10 minutes and the lid down.

2. While the grill is preheating, melt the butter in a small saucepan over medium heat. Add the brown sugar and lime juice and stir until dissolved and smooth. Keep warm.

3. Once the grill is hot, turn off the center burner and turn the other burners to medium. Place the bananas, peel side down, over the center burner, close the lid, and cook for 5 to 8 minutes; then turn cut side down and grill another 2 minutes.

4. Transfer the bananas to a serving platter, remove the peels, and drizzle the warm sauce over them. Serve immediately.

SERVES 4

Maple-Glazed Peaches

Excellent eaten as is, right off the grill, peaches are ethereal when sliced over ice cream, especially if they're still warm!

4 fairly firm fresh ripe peaches

2 tablespoons butter, melted

2 tablespoons pure maple syrup or honey

1. Preheat the grill with all the burners on high for 10 minutes and the lid down.

2. While the grill is preheating, cut the peaches in half, remove the pits, and brush all over with the melted butter.

3. Once the grill is hot, turn off the center burner and turn the other burners to medium. Place the peach halves, skin side up, over the center burner, close the lid, and cook for 8 to 10 minutes total, turning once.

4. Serve warm, drizzled with the maple syrup.

SERVES 4

LIGHT IT UP

IF YOUR GRILLING AREA LACKS SUFFICIENT LIGHT, CONSIDER PURCHASING AN OLD-FASHIONED KEROSENE LAMP, WHICH CAN GENERATE A SURPRISING AMOUNT OF LIGHT AND IS VERY RELIABLE.

Grilled Fresh Pineapple Spears

Grilled fresh pineapple is delicious on its own, as a dessert, or as a side dish for grilled ham. To tell if a pineapple is ripe, tug on one of the leaves: If it pulls out easily, the pineapple is at its peak and ready to grill.

1 fresh pineapple

1/4 cup (1/2 stick) butter, melted

1. Preheat the grill with all the burners on high for 10 minutes and the lid down.

2. While the grill is preheating, cut the top and the bottom off the pineapple, then peel it. Cut the pineapple into quarters lengthwise and remove the tough inner core. Slice each quarter into 1 1/2-inch-thick wedges. Brush the pineapple with the melted butter.

3. Once the grill is hot, turn off the center burner and turn the other burners to medium. Place the pineapple wedges over the center burner, close the lid, and cook until lightly browned and heated through, 10 to 12 minutes total, turning once. Serve hot off the grill.

SERVES 4 TO 6

Grilled Fresh Figs with Mascarpone and Balsamic Syrup

It's good to see more supermarkets and grocery stores stocking fresh figs when they're in season. Under normal conditions, there is an early summer and a late summer crop. This is a very simple but elegant dessert—not to mention delicious.

$^1/_2$ cup balsamic vinegar

1 tablespoon light molasses

1 pint fresh figs (8 to 12), stems trimmed and cut in half lengthwise

Mascarpone cheese

1. Combine the balsamic vinegar and molasses in small heavy saucepan over medium heat, bring to a boil, and continue to boil until reduced to $2^1/_2$ tablespoons, about 10 minutes. Let cool.

2. Preheat the grill with all the burners on high for 10 minutes and the lid down.

3. With all the burners still on high, place the figs, cut side down, on the grill and cook, with the lid down, until golden, 2 to 3 minutes, turning once midway through. Use a spatula to lift the figs from the grate and transfer to a platter to cool slightly.

4. Place 2 or 3 fig halves on each serving plate. Top with about 1 tablespoon of mascarpone cheese. Drizzle with the balsamic syrup and serve immediately.

SERVES 4 TO 6

Dessert Bruschetta with Cheese and Honey

This unusual dessert was developed by Jay Harlow for *The Grilling Book*, which we coauthored in 1985. Upon first reading the ingredients, you may be put off, but by all means give it a try. The combination of flavors is outstanding!

1 loaf coarse-textured Italian or French bread

$1/2$ pound Pecorino Sardo, Asiago, fontina, or Gruyère cheese (listed in order of preference)

About $1/4$ cup extra-virgin olive oil

Honey, preferably with a strong flower or herb flavor

1. Preheat the grill with all the burners on high for 10 minutes and the lid down.

2. While the grill is preheating, slice the bread $3/4$ inch thick and slice the cheese $1/4$ inch thick.

3. Once the grill is hot, turn off the center burner and turn the other burners to medium. Place the bread over the center burner and toast the pieces on one side. Turn the bread, drizzle olive oil generously on the toasted sides, and top each piece with a slice of cheese. Close the lid and continue to cook until the cheese melts (this should take only a couple of minutes).

4. As soon as the cheese has melted, transfer the bruschetta to a platter and drizzle with honey. Serve immediately.

SERVES 6 TO 8

Toasted Pound Cake

Sliced pound cake, lightly toasted on the grill, is a delightful end-of-the meal treat. You can make your own pound cake, of course, but the ones found in the frozen food section of your grocery store are quite good, too. Serve it plain or top with fresh berries, sliced peaches, or even ice cream.

One 9-inch loaf pound cake

1/4 cup (1/2 stick) butter, melted

1. Preheat the grill with all the burners on high for 10 minutes and the lid down.

2. While the grill is preheating, slice the pound cake into uniform slices, 3/4 inch thick, and brush lightly on both sides with the melted butter.

3. Once the grill is hot, turn off the center burner and turn the other burners to medium. Place the slices of pound cake over the center burner, close the lid, and cook until lightly toasted, 6 to 10 minutes, turning once with a metal spatula. Serve the cake hot off the grill, along with your favorite topping.

SERVES 8

Toasted Angel Food Cake with Grilled Peaches and Ice Cream

This is a very pleasant combination of flavors that celebrate summer. It definitely ends dinner with a smile! *Note:* Day-old angel food cake has a little firmer texture than a fresh-out-of-the-oven cake and is easier to handle on the grill.

4 fairly firm fresh peaches

2 tablespoons butter, melted

8 slices angel food cake, about 1 inch thick

Nonstick cooking spray (preferably butter flavored)

Vanilla ice cream

1. Preheat the grill with all the burners on high for 10 minutes and the lid down.

2. While the grill is preheating, cut the peaches in half, remove the pits, and brush the halves with the melted butter.

3. Once the grill is hot, turn off the center burner and turn the other burners to medium. Place the peach halves, skin side up, over the center burner. Close the lid and

cook for 8 to 10 minutes, turning once. Transfer to a platter and loosely tent with aluminum foil.

4. Turn all the burners to low. Coat both sides of the angel food cake slices with cooking spray. Place the cake slices on the grill and toast quickly, about 45 seconds per side.

5. Place a grilled peach half and a slice of angel's food cake on each serving plate. Top with a scoop of vanilla ice cream and serve immediately.

SERVES 8

Grilled Peanut Butter and Jelly Calzones

Here's a novel dessert that will surprise and delight any youngster or like-minded adult in the crowd. Got milk?

2 tablespoons cornmeal

One 10-ounce tube premade pizza dough, available in your supermarket refrigerator case

FOR EACH CALZONE

1 to 2 tablespoons butter, melted

1 to 2 tablespoons peanut butter

1 to 3 tablespoons jam or jelly of your choice

1. Preheat the grill with all the burners on high for 10 minutes and the lid down.

2. While the grill is preheating, sprinkle the cornmeal evenly over your work surface. Open the pizza dough and unroll it on top of the cornmeal. The dough will be rectangular in shape. Cut the dough into two easy-to-manage squares. Roll out each piece of pizza dough to about an 8-inch round or square. Lightly brush both sides of each round or square with the melted butter and place on the back of two baking sheets.

3. Once the grill is hot, turn all the burners to medium. Gently slide the crusts from the baking sheets onto the grill and cook, with the lid down, until marked on the underside,

1 to 3 minutes, rotating the crusts a few times for even cooking. Don't worry if the crusts bubble; they will deflate when turned over. Transfer the crusts from the cooking grate to the back of the baking sheets, with the grilled sides facing up.

4. Spread the peanut butter and then the jelly over each pizza crust, leaving a $^1/_2$-inch border around the edges. Fold the crust in half and transfer from the baking sheet to the cooking grate. Grill until crisp, with the lid down, 2 to 4 minutes, rotating a few times for even cooking.

5. Transfer to a cutting board, cut into wedges, and serve immediately.

EACH CALZONE SERVES 1

Grilled S'mores

This is another treat sure to please the younger set—and a good number of adults, as well.

FOR EACH S'MORE

1 tablespoon marshmallow crème (such as Marshmallow Fluff)

2 squares graham crackers

1 square milk chocolate, roughly the same size as the graham cracker

Nonstick cooking spray

1. Preheat the grill with all the burners on high for 10 minutes and the lid down.

2. While the grill is preheating, assemble the s'mores by spreading the marshmallow crème on one graham square, topping with the piece of chocolate, and placing the other square of graham cracker on top.

3. Once the grill is hot, turn off the center burner and turn the other burners to low.

4. Coat both sides of the s'more with cooking spray. Open the grill and allow it to cool for about 1 minute. Place the s'more over the center burner, close the lid, and grill just until chocolate melts, about 2 minutes per side, using a spatula to flip once.

Grilled Buñuelos with Cajeta

Buñuelos are a Mexican sweet treat, often available at carnivals and fiestas. Traditionally, they are a deep-fried pastry, sprinkled with cinnamon sugar. This variation uses flour tortillas and adds a little *cajeta* (goat's milk caramel) as a surprise inside. If you find the flavor of *cajeta* too strong, substitute plain caramel sauce. These are especially good with ice cream—either vanilla or dulce de leche.

FOR EACH *BUÑUELO*

One 10-ounce jar *cajeta* or caramel sauce (you'll need 2 tablespoons for each tortilla)

2 tablespoons butter, softened

One 10-inch flour tortilla

$1^1/2$ tablespoons cinnamon sugar (made by mixing $1^1/2$ teaspoons ground cinnamon with 1 tablespoon sugar)

1. Preheat the grill with all the burners on high for 10 minutes and the lid down.

2. While the grill is preheating, place the jar of *cajeta* in a small saucepan filled with a couple inches of water. Heat over high heat until the *cajeta* is warm and easier to pour. (If you're using caramel sauce, you can skip this step.)

3. Butter both sides of the tortilla. Sprinkle the top with cinnamon sugar. Drizzle with the *cajeta*. Fold the tortilla in half and dust the outside with cinnamon sugar.

4. Once the grill is hot, turn the back burner to medium and the other burners to low. Place the *buñuelo* over the burners on low for $1^1/2$ to 2 minutes per side, just until toasted.

5. Cut into wedges and serve immediately.

EACH *BUÑUELO* SERVES 1

10

Off-the-Grill
Side Dishes

The following recipes include a few vegetable dishes, but mostly they feature complex carbohydrates, such as potatoes, beans, and rice. Because grilled food is usually seasoned intensely, with either a marinade or other spice and herb mixtures, simple sides are best, so as not to overwhelm the diner with too many competing flavors. ✳ Pasta is always welcome as a side dish, but again, keep it as simple as possible. Cooked pasta of any type can be moistened with olive oil, vegetable or chicken broth, or a sauce made from grilled tomatoes. You can add other ingredients—all types of vegetables, garlic, chopped fresh herbs, and, of course, freshly grated Parmesan—

according to a recipe or a whim. As a rule, omit meat (whether shellfish, sausage, or poultry) from pasta served as a side dish.

It's a fact of the kitchen that the most basic dishes, such as steamed rice or mashed potatoes, often require the most finesse—if only because there are so few ingredients with which to disguise a failure. With each of the following recipes, great care has been taken to give you all the information you need to ensure success, including detailed procedures and timing.

Creamy Rice and
Pea Salad 342

Savory Rice 343

Coconut-Cilantro
Basmati Rice 344

Mexican Rice 344

Risotto 345

Savory Basmati
Rice Cake 347

Wild Rice Casserole 348

Polenta 348

Orzo with Basil 350

Tabbouleh 350

Marinated Vegetable
Salad 351

Not-Your-Mother's
Coleslaw 352

Fresh Coleslaw with
Light Lemon Dressing 353

Fast Szechuan
Green Beans 354

Sautéed Lettuce
with Peas 355

Creamed Spinach 355

Tex-Mex
Black-Eyed Peas 356

Cowpoke Beans 357

Cheesy Baked
Hominy Custard 358

Boiled New Potatoes 359

Homemade French Fries 360

Potato Tart 361

Sauerkraut-and-Potato
Casserole 362

Preserved
Moroccan Lemons 363

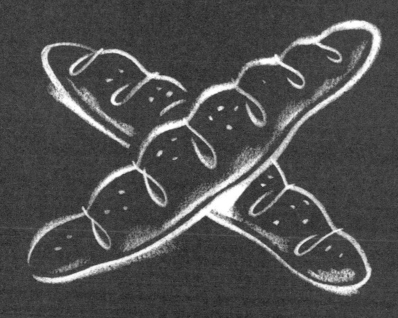

Creamy Rice and Pea Salad

Rice and peas are a timeless combination, and this salad is a classic. For a while, rice salads seemed to be losing their place on the picnic table in favor of pasta salads. However, as rice and grains have become more fashionable, rice salads have made a remarkable comeback. This salad can be made with leftover cold rice, but it is better to combine all the ingredients while the rice is still hot, then refrigerate the salad.

1^1/$_3$ cups white rice

2^2/$_3$ cups water

1 teaspoon kosher salt

^{1}/$_2$ cup mayonnaise

^{1}/$_4$ cup extra-virgin olive oil

2 tablespoons Dijon mustard

2 tablespoons red or white wine vinegar

1 tablespoon curry powder (optional)

Salt and freshly ground black pepper to taste

One 10-ounce package frozen peas (preferably baby or *petits pois*), thawed

^{1}/$_3$ cup minced green onions (white part only)

1. Rinse the rice in several changes of cold water until the water runs clear. Drain well.

2. Combine the rice, water, and salt in a medium-size saucepan, cover, and bring to a boil. Reduce the heat to medium-low and simmer until the rice is tender and the water absorbed, 15 to 20 minutes.

3. While the rice is cooking, in a small bowl, mix together the mayonnaise, olive oil, mustard, vinegar, and curry powder if desired. Set aside.

4. When the rice is done, spoon it into a large salad bowl. Add the mayonnaise dressing and mix well. Season with salt and pepper. If the rice seems a little dry, add a bit more olive oil. Gently fold the peas and green onions into the mixture. Cover and refrigerate for several hours. Alternatively, to form a salad mold, lightly oil another bowl, press the

rice salad into it, and refrigerate for at least 2 hours or overnight (though you may need to add a bit more mayo and vinegar to it the next day).

5. Serve the cold salad straight from the bowl or, if you molded it, turn it out upside down onto a bed of lettuce before serving.

SERVES 6 TO 8

Savory Rice

This is a flavorful, all-purpose side dish for almost any grilled fish—a far cry from plain steamed rice, but just as easy to make. If made ahead of time, simply take it off the heat without removing the lid. Just before serving, reheat the rice gently and fluff it with a fork. If the lid is kept on, the rice will keep for up to an hour.

1 tablespoon olive oil

1/2 cup chopped onion

2 teaspoons pressed or minced garlic

2 cups chicken or vegetable broth, or a combination of both

2 tablespoons chopped fresh parsley

1 cup long-grain rice

2 bay leaves

1. Heat the olive oil in a medium-size saucepan over medium heat, then cook the onion and garlic, stirring, until the onion is just soft. Do not brown. Add the broth, parsley, rice, and bay leaves and bring to a boil. Immediately reduce the heat to its lowest setting, cover, and cook for 15 minutes.

2. Remove from the heat and let rest for 10 minutes, without removing the lid. Just before serving, gently fluff the rice with a fork.

SERVES 4

Coconut-Cilantro Basmati Rice

Great with any Asian-inspired grilled food, this rice dish is easy to prepare and a definite cut above regular steamed rice.

One 14-ounce can unsweetened coconut milk

1 3/4 cups water

1 teaspoon kosher salt

2 cups basmati rice

1/2 cup coarsely chopped fresh cilantro

1/4 cup chopped salted dry-roasted peanuts (optional)

1. In a medium-size saucepan, combine the coconut milk, water, and salt and bring to a rolling boil. Add the rice and stir well. When the liquid boils again, cover, reduce the heat to low, and cook for 25 minutes. The rice kernels will be tender and the liquid absorbed.

2. Remove the saucepan from the heat and let stand, covered, for 10 minutes. Uncover, add the cilantro, and, using a fork, gently fluff to distribute it evenly. Sprinkle with the chopped peanuts if desired. Serve hot or warm.

SERVES 4

Mexican Rice

This is an easy way to produce a tasty rice dish, excellent with any Mexican-style grilled fish. If made ahead of time, simply move from the heat without removing the lid. Just before serving, reheat gently, and fluff with a fork. If the lid is kept on, the rice will keep fine for up to an hour.

1 tablespoon olive oil

1/2 cup chopped onion

1 cup long-grain rice

1 cup chicken or vegetable broth

1 cup tomato-vegetable juice (such as V-8)

2 teaspoons chili powder

1 teaspoon ground cumin

1 teaspoon dried oregano

1. Heat the oil in a medium-size saucepan over medium heat, then cook the onion, stirring, until just soft. Do not brown. Add the remaining ingredients and bring to a boil. Immediately reduce the heat to its lowest setting, cover, and cook for 15 minutes.

2. Remove from the heat and let rest for 10 minutes, without removing the lid. Just before serving, gently fluff the rice with a fork.

SERVES 4

Risotto

What makes Italian risotto so creamy, tender, and delicious is the rice itself. Risotto must be made with a unique, almost round short-grain rice from Italy. The only rice commonly available in this country for making risotto is Arborio; in Italy they have a choice of Arborio, Carnaroli, Nano, or Vialone. The secret of these plump little grains is that they contain sufficient starch to absorb large quantities of liquid, which in turn results in risotto's characteristic creaminess. Although risotto is at its best when served immediately, it can be kept warm in the top of a double boiler—over hot but not boiling water—for about 1 hour. *Note:* You may not need the entire amount of broth indicated; it all depends on the degree of heat at which you're cooking the risotto. Risotto that is partially covered halfway through the cooking time will absorb much less broth (sometimes no more than 2 to 3 cups).

2 tablespoons extra-virgin olive oil

2 shallots, minced

1 cup Arborio rice

$^1/3$ cup dry white wine

4 to 5 cups hot chicken broth, as needed

Kosher salt and freshly ground black pepper to taste

2 tablespoons butter (optional)

3 to 4 tablespoons freshly grated Parmesan cheese (optional)

Chopped fresh parsley for garnish (optional)

1. Warm the olive oil in a large, heavy skillet or saucepan over low heat. Add the shallots and cook, stirring, until very soft but not brown, 3 to 4 minutes. Add the rice and blend it with the shallots. Stir in the wine, raise the heat to medium-high, and cook, stirring constantly, until the wine has completely evaporated. Start adding the broth $^1/2$ cup at a time, stirring constantly. Keep the heat moderately high so that the rice absorbs the liquid but does not dry out too quickly. Continue adding the broth $^1/2$ cup at a time as the liquid is absorbed.

2. After about 20 minutes, start adding the broth $^1/4$ cup at a time. If the rice is still partly chewy, cover the pan partially and let the rice cook a little more slowly, allowing it to absorb the liquid. Keep an eye on it. The finished rice will be a creamy mass with kernels that are soft but still chewy.

3. When the rice is done, adjust the seasoning carefully with salt and pepper. Add the butter if desired, stir well, and cook until the butter is well absorbed, another 2 to 3 minutes. If you wish, stir in the Parmesan.

4. Transfer the rice to a hot serving dish, sprinkle it with parsley if desired, and serve immediately.

SERVES 4 TO 6

WARM PLATES, WARM FOOD

GET IN THE HABIT OF PUTTING SERVING PLATES IN A PREHEATED 200°F OVEN FOR 10 MINUTES BEFORE SERVING TIME. HOT FOOD ON HOT PLATES IS A SIMPLE LUXURY ANYONE CAN AFFORD.

Savory Basmati Rice Cake

With extra-long grains, a flowery, buttery aroma, and superior flavor and texture, basmati rice is well worth its premium price. Delicious when simply boiled or steamed, basmati rice is even better when prepared like this.

1 cup basmati rice

1 teaspoon kosher salt

2 tablespoons extra-virgin olive oil

Several saffron threads, pulverized between your thumb and forefinger

$^1/4$ cup chopped green onions or fresh chives

1. Place the rice in a strainer and rinse it in several changes of cold water until the water runs clear. Drain well.

2. Transfer the rice to a medium-size saucepan, add the salt, and add enough water to cover the rice by 1 inch. Bring to a boil over medium-high heat, immediately reduce the heat to medium-low, and simmer the rice, uncovered, until tender, 15 to 20 minutes. Test the rice by biting into a grain: It should not be chalky.

3. Drain the rice, rinse it under cold running water, and set aside.

4. Coat the bottom and sides of a heavy skillet (a well-seasoned cast-iron or heavy nonstick skillet works well) with the oil and warm over medium heat. Once the skillet is warm, add the rice and mix in the saffron and green onions. Cover the skillet with a clean towel and cover the towel with the lid or a large plate. Reduce the heat to low and cook the rice for 20 to 25 minutes.

5. Remove the lid and the towel from the pan. Using a flexible spatula or knife, loosen the rice from the edges of the skillet. Cover the skillet with a large, inverted serving plate (one that is an inch or so longer than the skillet) and, holding the plate in place with one hand, turn the skillet upside down. Cut the rice into wedges and serve immediately.

SERVES 4

Wild Rice Casserole

This is excellent as an accompaniment to hearty grilled fare such as roasts and game. People who know wild rice well almost always cook it in chicken broth rather than water.

Butter

2 tablespoons olive oil

$1/2$ cup chopped onion

2 cups sliced mushrooms

1 cup wild rice

3 cups chicken broth

Kosher salt and freshly ground black pepper to taste

1. Preheat the oven to 350°F. Butter the bottom and sides of a $1^1/2$-quart ovenproof casserole dish.

2. Warm the oil in a large skillet over medium-high heat. Add the onion and mushrooms and cook, stirring, until soft. Spoon them into the casserole, add the remaining ingredients, and stir to combine. Cover the dish and bake until all the liquid has been absorbed and the rice is tender, about 1 hour. Serve hot out of the oven.

SERVES 4

Polenta

Polenta—an Italian version of our cornmeal mush—is a simple and satisfying side dish. To make authentic polenta, you'll need the proper ingredients; regular cornmeal won't do because it is ground too fine. It's the coarser cornmeal, specially ground for polenta, that you want. In some Italian groceries, you'll find "instant polenta," which cooks up in a matter of minutes. It's more expensive than regular polenta but certainly a lot easier to make—and every bit as good. For a wonderful recipe for Grilled Polenta, see page 322.

7 cups water

1 tablespoon kosher salt

2 cups coarse-ground polenta cornmeal

$^1/_4$ cup ($^1/_2$ stick) butter, cut into pats

$^1/_2$ cup freshly grated Parmesan cheese

1. Pour the water and salt into a large pot—one with a handle you can grip comfortably. (You're going to be gripping it for about 20 minutes, so you might as well be comfortable.) Bring the water to a boil over high heat. Reduce the heat so that the water is at a low boil. Add the cornmeal, one handful at a time, letting it slowly sift through your fingers. Keep stirring, stirring, stirring, adding the cornmeal one handful at a time, until it is used up. Stir the polenta until it starts to pull away from the sides of the pot. Add the butter and Parmesan cheese and stir until blended.

2. Transfer the polenta to a warm platter and serve.

SERVES 6 TO 8

MICROWAVE POLENTA

$^3/_4$ cup coarse yellow cornmeal

3 cups water

$^1/_2$ teaspoon kosher salt

1 tablespoon butter

$^1/_2$ cup finely shredded mozzarella cheese

1. Combine the cornmeal, water, and salt in a microwavable bowl. Cover with plastic wrap or a glass plate and microwave on high for 8 minutes.

2. Remove from the microwave, stir, and cook on high for another 2 to 3 minutes.

3. Remove from the microwave; stir in the butter and mozzarella. Spray an 8-inch square baking pan with cooking spray, then pour in the polenta. Refrigerate until cold.

SERVES 4

Orzo with Basil

Orzo is a very small pasta, sometimes called "melon seed" pasta. This recipe somewhat resembles risotto, but is much easier to prepare. Diners of all ages love it.

2 cups chicken or vegetable broth, or a combination of both

1¹/2 cups orzo pasta

2 teaspoons dried basil

1¹/2 teaspoons olive oil

Freshly ground black pepper to taste

1. Bring the broth to a boil in a medium-size saucepan. Add the orzo and basil and return to a boil. Immediately reduce the heat to low, cover, and let simmer without disturbing for 7 minutes.

2. Turn off the heat and let the orzo sit for 10 minutes, covered.

3. Gently fluff the orzo with a fork, stir in the olive oil, and season with pepper. Can be served hot, warm, or at room temperature. Reheats well.

SERVES 4

Tabbouleh

This fresh and pungent Middle Eastern salad features a combination of bulgur (cracked wheat), diced tomatoes and red onion, mint, olive oil, and lemon juice. Its basic purpose is to serve as a counterpoint to the often hot and spicy cuisine of the Middle East. If possible, make this a day ahead of time; it improves with time in the refrigerator. This is great hot-weather fare.

2 cups vegetable broth

1 cup bulgur

2/3 cup chopped red onion

2 tablespoons extra-virgin olive oil

2 medium-size ripe tomatoes, seeded and diced

1/3 cup fresh mint, finely chopped

Juice of 1 lemon

Kosher salt and freshly ground black pepper to taste

1. In a medium-size saucepan, bring the broth and bulgur to a boil. Reduce the heat to low, add the chopped onion, cover, and simmer gently for 15 minutes.

2. Remove from the heat and let sit, covered, for 15 minutes. Do not remove the lid.

3. After 15 minutes, remove the lid and gently fluff the bulgur with a fork. Transfer to a bowl, toss with the olive oil, and put in the refrigerator to cool for about 30 minutes.

4. Remove the bulgur from the refrigerator. Add the tomatoes, mint, and lemon juice, season with salt and pepper, and toss to coat.

SERVES 4

Marinated Vegetable Salad

These crunchy vegetables make an excellent substitute for a green salad, particularly with grilled fish or a spicy dish that needs a little cooling off. The vegetables are best if they're made the night before you intend to serve them.

1/3 cup water

2/3 cup distilled white vinegar

1 teaspoon kosher salt

1 teaspoon celery seeds

1/2 teaspoon sugar

1 unwaxed European or English cucumber

2 medium-size carrots, cut into thin matchsticks

1/4 cup chopped fresh dill, mint, or parsley

1. In a small saucepan, combine the water, vinegar, salt, celery seeds, and sugar. Bring to a boil, then continue to boil for 2 minutes, stirring the mixture constantly, and remove from the heat. Set aside.

2. Score the cucumber lengthwise with a fork, repeating the action several times all the way around; the scores will give the individual cucumber slices a decorative pattern at the edges. Slice the cucumber into $1/8$-inch-thick rounds, place them in a bowl, and add the carrots.

3. Pour the warm vinegar solution over the cucumber and carrots. Add the dill and stir the vegetables. Cover and refrigerate for several hours and preferably overnight. Serve cold.

SERVES 4 TO 6

Not-Your-Mother's Coleslaw

The cumin in this recipe, inspired by one from Julia Child, takes this coleslaw out of the ordinary. It pairs nicely with Cowpoke Beans (page 357) and any traditional barbecue fare, such as ribs or brisket.

3 cups cored and finely shredded green cabbage

3 cups cored and finely shredded purple cabbage

2 carrots, finely shredded

1 red bell pepper, seeded and diced

6 green onions, white part only, minced

$1/4$ cup chopped fresh parsley

$2/3$ cup plain yogurt

$1/2$ cup mayonnaise

Juice of $1/2$ lemon

3 tablespoons white wine vinegar

1 tablespoon Dijon mustard

1 teaspoon ground cumin

Kosher salt and freshly ground black pepper to taste

1. In a large salad bowl, combine the cabbages, carrots, bell pepper, green onions, and parsley and toss to mix well.

2. In a small bowl, combine the yogurt, mayonnaise, lemon juice, vinegar, mustard, and cumin. Add the dressing to the vegetables and mix well to coat everything. Season with salt and pepper and refrigerate for at least 1 hour before serving. It will keep for 1 to 2 days, though it does become a bit soupy.

SERVES 6 TO 8

Fresh Coleslaw with Light Lemon Dressing

Most traditional coleslaw recipes are heavy on the mayonnaise and, consequently, heavy on the waistline. This is a much lighter version with bright flavors.

One 16-ounce bag preshredded coleslaw mix

1 apple, preferably Golden Delicious, peeled, cored, and finely shredded

LIGHT LEMON DRESSING

1/2 cup nonfat plain yogurt

1/2 cup lowfat sour cream

Juice of 2 lemons

2 teaspoons rice vinegar

1/2 teaspoon ground cumin

1/2 teaspoon kosher salt

1/4 teaspoon ground white pepper

1/4 teaspoon grated lemon peel

1. Combine the coleslaw mix and grated apple in a 1-gallon zippered-top plastic bag.

2. Combine the dressing ingredients in a large measuring cup, then pour over the slaw mix in the bag. Seal the bag and punch gently from the bottom up to mix the slaw and dressing. If possible, make the coleslaw an hour before the meal to give the flavors time to blend. It will keep in the refrigerator for 1 to 2 days.

SERVES 4

KIDS AND GRILLS

IF THERE ARE KIDS IN YOUR HOUSEHOLD, MAKE SURE THEY UNDERSTAND THAT THEY SHOULDN'T PLAY AROUND THE GRILL. NEVER LEAVE A HOT GRILL UNATTENDED WHEN THERE ARE CHILDREN ON THE SCENE.

Fast Szechuan Green Beans

Here's a fast and good imitation of that Chinese favorite, Szechuan green beans.

1 tablespoon toasted sesame oil

4 cups frozen green beans

2 teaspoons sesame seeds

2 tablespoons seasoned rice vinegar

1. Heat the sesame oil in a large skillet over high heat. When it begins to smoke, add the still-frozen green beans (careful—there will be some spattering). Shake the pan more or less continuously for 3 minutes or so.

2. Reduce the heat to medium, add the sesame seeds, and continue to shake the pan for another minute or so. Sprinkle the vinegar over all, give the pan another couple of shakes, and serve immediately.

SERVES 4 TO 6

Sautéed Lettuce with Peas

Even people who supposedly hate peas like them prepared in this traditional French manner. Just don't overcook the peas; they should still be bright green when served. If you can find them, buy baby peas, sometimes labeled *petits pois*.

2 tablespoons butter

2 cups shredded iceberg lettuce

One 10-ounce package frozen baby green peas

2 tablespoons minced fresh parsley

$1/2$ teaspoon sugar

Dash of ground nutmeg

Kosher salt to taste

Melt the butter in a large skillet over medium-high heat. Add the lettuce while the butter is still bubbling and cook, stirring, for 1 to 2 minutes. Mix in the frozen peas, parsley, sugar, nutmeg, and salt, reduce the heat to medium, cover, and cook for 6 to 8 minutes, just until the peas are tender and heated through. Serve immediately.

SERVES 4

Creamed Spinach

This old-fashioned dish is still popular with discerning diners. I particularly like it with grilled fish.

2 pounds fresh spinach

2 tablespoons butter

2 tablespoons all-purpose flour

1 cup half-and-half or light cream

$1/2$ teaspoon dry mustard

$1/8$ teaspoon ground nutmeg

Salt and freshly ground black pepper to taste

1.   Wash the spinach in several changes of cold water and drain well. Remove the stems from the spinach. In a large pot, bring about 1 inch of water to a boil, add the spinach, cover, and steam until the leaves are limp, 3 to 5 minutes. Drain well, grabbing handfuls of it and squeezing out the excess water. Chop the leaves, drain again, and set aside.

2.   Melt the butter in a medium-size heavy saucepan over medium heat. Add the flour, 1 tablespoon at a time, stirring constantly with a wooden spoon or wire whisk. Cook for 2 to 3 minutes, but do not let it brown. Add the half-and-half and stir continuously until it boils and then thickens. Increase the heat slightly if necessary. Stir in the mustard, nutmeg, and salt and pepper. Add the chopped spinach, mix well, and adjust the seasonings. Serve immediately.

SERVES 4 TO 6

Tex-Mex Black-Eyed Peas

There is something about the characteristic flavor of black-eyed peas that complements most grilled foods, particularly those with a Southwestern or Mexican accent.

1 tablespoon vegetable oil

1 small onion, minced

2 garlic cloves, pressed

One 10-ounce package frozen black-eyed peas

$^1/_2$ cup chicken broth

2 teaspoons chili powder

$^1/_2$ teaspoon ground cumin

Kosher salt and freshly ground black pepper to taste

Chopped fresh parsley for garnish (optional)

Warm the oil in a medium-size saucepan over medium-high heat. Add the onion and garlic and cook, stirring, until the onion is softened, about 4 minutes. Add the black-eyed peas, broth, chili powder, and cumin and mix well. Reduce the heat to medium and cook until the peas are just tender, about 15 minutes. Season with the salt and pepper. Serve the peas hot, garnished with parsley if desired.

SERVES 4

Cowpoke Beans

Beans go well with most grilled meats, but they have a special affinity for red meats. Add some cornbread and coleslaw and you have a great-tasting, rustic meal—the kind that tastes best eaten out-of-doors.

1/2 pound sliced bacon

2 medium-size yellow onions, minced

3 cloves garlic, pressed

Three 15-ounce cans pinto beans, rinsed and drained

One 12-ounce bottle or can beer

1 cup chicken or beef broth

One 28-ounce can peeled whole tomatoes, with their juice

2 to 3 tablespoons chili powder, to your taste

1 tablespoon ground cumin

1 teaspoon dried oregano

Kosher salt and freshly ground black pepper to taste

1. Cook the bacon in a Dutch oven until crisp; then drain on paper towels, crumble, and set aside.

2. Drain off all but 2 tablespoons of the bacon grease in the Dutch oven. Add the onions and garlic and cook, stirring until the onions are softened, about 4 minutes. Add the remaining ingredients, stir, and bring to a boil. Reduce the heat to low and simmer the beans, uncovered, for about 30 minutes.

3. Serve hot, with the crumbled bacon sprinkled on top.

SERVES 6 TO 8

Cheesy Baked Hominy Custard

This custard is delicious paired with grilled pork or ham.

1/4 cup (1/2 stick) butter

1/4 cup all-purpose flour

1 cup milk, heated just until bubbles form around the edge of the pan (do not boil)

Pinch of cayenne pepper or 2 shakes of Tabasco sauce

1 cup finely shredded cheddar cheese

One 15.5-ounce can hominy, drained

1 large red bell pepper, seeded and diced

One 4-ounce can chopped green chiles, undrained

4 large eggs

Butter and cornmeal

1. Preheat the oven to 375°F.

2. Melt the butter in a medium-size heavy saucepan over medium-high heat. Using a wooden spoon or wire whisk, stir in the flour and blend until smooth, 2 or 3 minutes. Slowly add the scalded milk, stirring constantly. Continue to stir for 2 to 3 minutes, until the mixture is thick and smooth. Add the cayenne, cheese, hominy, red pepper, and chiles and stir until the cheese has melted.

3. Remove from the heat and allow the mixture to cool for about 5 minutes. While it's cooling, beat the eggs in a small bowl. Spoon about 1/4 cup of the cooled hominy mixture into the beaten eggs and stir together, then pour them back into the saucepan and mix well.

4. Generously grease a 2-quart baking dish with butter or margarine and dust it with cornmeal. Pour the hominy mixture into the dish and bake until the custard has set, 40 to 45 minutes. Serve hot out of the oven.

SERVES 4

SPIDERS AT THE GRILL

SPIDERS, ATTRACTED TO THE SMELL OF AN ADDITIVE USED IN GAS, SOMETIMES GET LODGED IN A GRILL'S TUBING. IF YOU'RE HAVING TROUBLE LIGHTING YOUR GRILL, SPIDERS COULD WELL BE THE PROBLEM. CONSULT YOUR OWNER'S MANUAL TO LEARN HOW TO CLEAN OUT THE TUBES.

Boiled New Potatoes

Tender, boiled new potatoes, served with nothing more than a little butter and chopped dill, can be found in just about every grill restaurant in this country and in Europe. The little ones (about the size of a pullet egg) are the first choice; the larger new potatoes may not be quite as attractive on a plate, but they're still great eating.

About 20 new potatoes

Kosher salt

2 to 6 tablespoons butter, to your taste

1/4 cup chopped fresh dill

1. Scrub the potatoes under cold running water, but do not peel them. Place them in a pot, cover with about 2 inches of water, and sprinkle in some salt. Cover, bring to a boil, and continue to boil until a sharp knife easily pierces their center. The cooking time depends on the size of the potatoes: 3-inch potatoes will take 20 to 25 minutes.

2. Drain the potatoes, toss them with the butter and dill, and serve hot.

SERVES 4

Homemade French Fries

French-fried potatoes, or *pommes frites* as the French call them, are delicious with almost any grilled fare—especially steaks, chops, and fish. Double frying is the secret to achieving the best results.

4 large brown-skinned baking potatoes (about 1 per person)

4 cups vegetable oil, preferably peanut

Kosher salt and freshly ground black pepper to taste

1. Scrub the potatoes under cold running water, but do not peel them. Using a sharp knife or a food processor, cut the potatoes into uniform, $^3/_8$-inch-square sticks 3 to 4 inches long.

2. In a deep, heavy pot, heat the oil to 300°F. Add the potatoes to the hot oil, in about 3 separate batches, frying each batch for 4 to 5 minutes. Use a long-handled fork to keep the potatoes from sticking together as they cook. The goal is to partially cook or soften the potatoes, not brown them. While the potatoes cook, line a cookie sheet with several layers of paper towels.

3. With a slotted spoon, transfer the potatoes to the cookie sheet and let drain. If you will be serving the potatoes later the same day, let them sit at room temperature for up to 4 hours. Otherwise, cover them loosely and refrigerate overnight.

4. A few minutes before serving time, reheat the oil—this time to 375°F. Divide the partially cooked fries into 3 batches and fry each batch until it turns light golden brown, about 3 minutes. Remove the potatoes from the oil with a slotted spoon and drain on paper towels.

5. Transfer to a basket, sprinkle with salt and pepper, and serve immediately.

SERVES 4

Potato Tart

French in origin, this potato tart represents rustic farmhouse cooking at its best. Serve it with any grilled meat.

4 large baking potatoes

3 tablespoons olive oil

5 tablespoons butter

4 cloves garlic, pressed

1/4 cup chopped fresh tarragon or 1 tablespoon dried tarragon

Kosher salt and freshly ground black pepper to taste

Chopped fresh parsley for garnish (optional)

1. Wash and peel the potatoes, then slice into 3/16-inch-thick rounds, as evenly as possible. Put the potatoes in a bowl of cold water until you're ready for the next step (or they will turn brown).

2. Heat the oil and 2 tablespoons of the butter in a large heavy skillet with a lid. Add the garlic and cook for 30 seconds. Remove the pan from the heat.

3. Drain the potato slices on paper towels and blot dry. Chop 2 more tablespoons of butter into small bits. Add the potato slices to the pan, arranging them in layers of overlapping, concentric circles. Sprinkle each layer with a little of the tarragon, chopped butter, and salt and pepper. When all the potatoes have been arranged in the pan, press them down firmly with a lid or plate so that they hold together a bit.

4. Cover the skillet and cook the potatoes over medium heat for 5 minutes. Remove the lid and continue to cook for 15 minutes or so; lower the heat if you think the potatoes on the bottom are about to burn.

5. Loosen the potatoes with a metal spatula or knife, so they will flip out of the skillet more easily. Cover the skillet with a large inverted plate (one that's larger than the skillet by a couple of inches), hold the plate in place with one hand, and carefully turn the skillet upside down. Add the remaining tablespoon of butter to the skillet, let it melt, then ease the potatoes, brown side up, back into the pan. Cook the potatoes for another 15 minutes over medium heat, to brown the other side of the tart.

6. Using the same method as in step 5, flip the potato tart onto an inverted serving plate, sprinkle with parsley if desired, cut into wedges, and serve immediately.

SERVES 4

Sauerkraut-and-Potato Casserole

This is a hearty side dish, great with any type of grilled pork, ham, or sausage. If you want to make the dish less salty, rinse the sauerkraut after draining it. Also, please get the sauerkraut sold in bags as opposed to cans—there really is a taste difference.

3 or 4 large baking potatoes, scrubbed, peeled, and sliced $1/2$ inch thick

4 strips bacon

1 medium-size onion, thinly sliced

2 pounds sauerkraut, drained and rinsed

2 carrots, sliced 1 inch thick

$3/4$ cup beer, chicken broth, or a mixture of the two

1 teaspoon caraway seeds

Freshly ground black pepper to taste

1. Boil the potato slices in a large pot of salted water until just tender, about 10 minutes. Drain well.

2. In a large skillet or Dutch oven, cook the bacon until crisp, and drain on paper towels. Discard all but 1 tablespoon of the bacon grease in the pan. Add the onion slices and cook, stirring, over medium heat until softened, about 3 minutes. Add the potato slices, sauerkraut, carrots, beer, caraway seeds, and pepper and toss together lightly. Cover and cook until the carrots are tender, about 15 minutes.

3. Spoon the mixture into a serving dish, crumble the bacon over the top, and serve.

SERVES 4 TO 6

Preserved Moroccan Lemons

Preserved lemons are a Moroccan specialty. There's nothing quite like them and, hence, no substitute. Traditionally used in lamb and vegetable *tagines* (Moroccan stews), preserved lemons are an excellent accompaniment to all types of grilled fish. Once I learned how easy they are to make at home, I've never been without them.

2 lemons

$^1/_3$ cup coarse sea salt

4 black peppercorns

2 bay leaves

$^1/_2$ cup fresh lemon juice

1. Scrub the lemons and dry them. Cut each into 8 wedges, place in a small bowl, and toss with the salt, peppercorns, and bay leaves.

2. Transfer the mixture to a half-pint glass jar with a lid. Pour the lemon juice over the top of the lemon wedges. Close the jar tightly and allow the lemons to "marinate" for 7 days at room temperature, shaking the jar each day to make sure the liquid and spices are evenly distributed.

3. After a week, the lemons will be ready to use. Store any leftovers in the refrigerator. Keeps indefinitely.

Measurement Equivalents

Please note that all conversions are approximate.

Liquid Conversions

U.S.	METRIC
1 tsp	5 ml
1 tbs	15 ml
2 tbs	30 ml
3 tbs	45 ml
1/4 cup	60 ml
1/3 cup	75 ml
1/3 cup + 1 tbs	90 ml
1/3 cup + 2 tbs	100 ml
1/2 cup	120 ml
2/3 cup	150 ml
3/4 cup	180 ml
3/4 cup + 2 tbs	200 ml
1 cup	240 ml
1 cup + 2 tbs	275 ml
1 1/4 cups	300 ml
1 1/3 cups	325 ml
1 1/2 cups	350 ml
1 2/3 cups	375 ml
1 3/4 cups	400 ml
1 3/4 cups + 2 tbs	450 ml
2 cups (1 pint)	475 ml
2 1/2 cups	600 ml
3 cups	720 ml
4 cups (1 quart)	945 ml
	(1,000 ml is 1 liter)

Weight Conversions

U.S./U.K.	METRIC	U.S./U.K.	METRIC
1/2 oz	14 g	7 oz	200 g
1 oz	28 g	8 oz	227 g
1 1/2 oz	43 g	9 oz	255 g
2 oz	57 g	10 oz	284 g
2 1/2 oz	71 g	11 oz	312 g
3 oz	85 g	12 oz	340 g
3 1/2 oz	100 g	13 oz	368 g
4 oz	113 g	14 oz	400 g
5 oz	142 g	15 oz	425 g
6 oz	170 g	1 lb	454 g

Oven Temperature Conversions

°F	GAS MARK	°C
250	1/2	120
275	1	140
300	2	150
325	3	165
350	4	180
375	5	190
400	6	200
425	7	220
450	8	230
475	9	240
500	10	260
550	Broil	290

Index

A

Anchovy(ies)
- -Garlic Butter, 295
- Sauce Niçoise, 73
- *Tonnato* Sauce, 149–50

Angel Food Cake, Toasted, with Grilled Peaches and Ice Cream, 335–36

Appetizers
- Asparagus Wrapped in Provolone and Prosciutto, 24
- "Barbecued" Oysters, 34
- Bruschetta with Shaved Parmesan, 18
- Cheese-Stuffed Grape Leaves, 22
- Exotic Grilled Oysters–Two Ways, 35–37
- Fresh Ginger–Garlic Chicken Satay, 42
- Garlicky Skewered Shrimp, 32
- Gorgonzola Toasts, 20
- Grilled Cheese on a Skewer, 21
- Grilled Chicken "Sashimi," 40–41
- grilled crudités, serving, 18
- Grilled Garlic Bread, 17
- Grilled Oysters with Fresh Ginger Vinaigrette, 34–35
- Grilled Pizza, 16
- Grilled Scallop Ceviche, 27–28
- Grilled Shrimp Cocktail, 30–31
- Hoisin-Chili Pork Satay, 44
- Hot Peanut-Sesame Beef Satay, 43
- Lamb Riblets with Garlic and Rosemary, 46
- Marinated Mushrooms and Cherry Tomatoes, 25–26
- Mixed Grilled Vegetables with Feta Cheese Dip, 26–27
- Mussels Bordelaise, 33
- Prosciutto and Basil-Wrapped Lemon Shrimp, 31
- Raclette in a Bowl, 23
- Red Wings, 39–40
- Rumaki, 38–39
- Scallops on Endive with Pickled Ginger, 29
- Skewered Chicken Livers with Fresh Lime and Cilantro, 37–38
- Spicy Asian Lamb Chops, 45
- Tomato-Basil Bruschetta, 19

Apple(s)
- –Asian Pear Sauce, 251
- -Cabbage Coleslaw, 92–93
- Caramelized Fruit Kebabs, 328
- Fresh Coleslaw with Light Lemon Dressing, 353–54
- -Lime Marinade, Spicy, 141
- and Onion Sauce, 261
- Slices, Grilled, 329

Apricot Nectar and Guinness Marinade, 232

Argentine Squirt Sauce, 207

Artichoke Sauce, 222

Arugula, Caramelized Onions, Mushrooms, and Chèvre, Hanger Steaks with, 193–94

Asian Lamb Chops, Spicy, 45

Asian Pear–Apple Sauce, 251

Asian-Style Barbecue Marinade, 272

Asparagus
- Grilled Lemon-Sherry, 283
- Grilled Marinated, 282
- Wrapped in Provolone and Prosciutto, 24

B

Bacon
- Pancetta-Wrapped Grilled Quail, 163
- Rumaki, 38–39
- -Wrapped Spicy Barbecued Shrimp, 103

Bananas, Grilled, 330

Bananas, Tropical Grilled, 330–31

Barbecue(d)
- Catfish Sandwiches, 52–53
- Chicken, Old-Fashioned, 121–22
- Country-Style Pork Ribs, 248
- Dry Rub, Spicy, 114
- Marinade, Asian-Style, 272
- Pork Tenderloin, 257–58
- Rub, 247
- Shrimp, Bacon-Wrapped Spicy, 103
- Spareribs, Authentic, 246

"Barbecued" Oysters, 34

Basil
- Dressing, Fresh, 84–85
- -Mustard Sauce, 240
- Orzo with, 350
- Pesto, 314

Basil (*cont.*)
  and Prosciutto-Wrapped Lemon
    Shrimp, 31
  Skewered Plum Tomatoes with
    Garlic and, 312
  -Tomato Bruschetta, 19
Basting, tools for, 205
Basting Sauce, Beer and Chili, 203
Basting Sauce, Sweet, Hot, and Sour,
  208–9
Bean(s)
  Black, and Corn Salsa, 185
  Black, and Red Pepper Puree,
    Salmon Fillets with, 62–63
  Cowpoke, 357–58
  Green, Fast Szechuan, 354
  Salade Niçoise with Grilled Tuna,
    87–89
  Tuscan White, Grilled Tuna with,
    84–85
  White, Roast Leg of Lamb with,
    218–19
Béarnaise Sauce, 181–82
Beau Monde Turkey Breast, 151
Beef
  Beefsteak with Salsa Verde, 174–75
  Boneless Chuck Roast with
    Bourbon and Coke, 204–5
  Bourguignon, Skewered, 202–3
  Brisket, Real Tasty, 208–9
  buying, 165, 178
  Chateaubriand with Green
    Peppercorn Sauce, 172–73
  Chateaubriand with Honey
    Mustard Glaze, 173–74
  choice, about, 165
  Chuck Roast, Sherry and Garlic
    Marinated, 206
  Chuck Roast with Argentine
    Squirt Sauce, 207
  Chuck Wagon Chuck Roast, 203–4
  The Classic Burger, 209–10
  Fajitas, Chili-Rubbed, with
    Peppers and Onions, 190–91
  Filet Mignon Steaks, Marinated,
    with Hidden Wasabi Jolt,
    170–71

Filet Mignon with Grilled
  Marinated Mushrooms, 168–69
Flank Steak, Everybody's Favorite,
  196–97
Flank Steak, Red Rooster–Soy
  Marinated, 197–98
flank steak, slicing, 199
Flank Steak, Spicy, 198–99
Flank Steak Sandwiches with
  Grilled Bell Peppers and Onions,
  199–200
Flat Iron Steaks with Black, White,
  and Green Peppercorns, 194–95
Hanger Steaks with Caramelized
  Onions, Mushrooms, Chèvre,
  and Arugula, 193–94
judging doneness, 166
Kebabs, Tried-and-True Marinated,
  201
Liver Steaks, Grilled, 214
London Broil, Garlic-Studded, 184
London Broil with Black Bean and
  Corn Salsa, 185–86
London Broil with Sherried
  Mushrooms, 186–87
marinating, 165–66, 171
Porterhouse Steak for Two with
  Cambozola Butter, 179
prime, about, 165, 178
Rib-Eye Steaks with Chili Butter,
  178
Ribs, Short Ribs of, Savory, 213
Ribs, Sweet, Hot, and Sour Basted,
  212
Ribs, The Commissioner's Best, 211
Satay, Hot Peanut-Sesame, 43
Satay, Indonesian-Style, 189–90
select, about, 165
serving sizes, 174
Skirt Steak with Tequila Marinade,
  195
Standing Rib Roast with
  Horseradish Sauce, 182–83
Steak, Vietnamese-Style Sliced, in
  Lettuce Leaf Wraps, 192–93
Steaks with Roquefort Butter,
  175–76

Strip Steaks with Grilled Potato
  Skins, 176–77
T-Bone Picante, 180
Teriyaki, with Green Onions and
  Mushrooms, 188
Whole Tenderloin of, with
  Béarnaise Sauce, 181–82
Beer, Bratwurst in, 274
Beer and Chili Basting Sauce, 203
Beer Can Chicken, 113–14
Beets, Grilled Whole, with Fresh
  Ginger-Orange Sauce, 284
Blackberry and Lavender Marinade,
  227
Black-Eyed Peas, Tex-Mex, 356–57
Blue Thai Prawns with Green Curry
  Dipping Sauce, 104
Bockwurst, Grilled, with Sauerkraut,
  Applesauce, and Cornbread,
  275
Bourbon and Coke Marinade, 204–5
Bourguignon Marinade, 202
Bratwurst in Beer, 274
Brazilian Mixed Grill Fish Soup, 50–51
Bread(s)
  Bruschetta with Shaved
    Parmesan, 18
  Dessert Bruschetta with Cheese
    and Honey, 334
  Garlic, Grilled, 17
  Gorgonzola Toasts, 20
  Grilled Cheese on a Skewer, 21
  Raclette in a Bowl, 23
  Tomato-Basil Bruschetta, 19
Brined Spring Chicken, 115
Bruschetta, Dessert, with Cheese
  and Honey, 334
Bruschetta, Tomato-Basil, 19
Bulgur
  Tabbouleh, 350–51
Buñuelos with *Cajeta*, Grilled, 338
Burgers
  Chicken, 143–44
  The Classic, 209–10
  cooking, tip for, 210
  Lamb Patties with Mozzarella and
    Mint, 237

Lamb Souvlaki, 235–36
Pork, Chinese-Style, 273
Portobello Mushroom, 299
Sage Turkey, 156
Veggie Cheesy, 317–18
Burnt-End Sandwiches, 269–70
Butter
Anchovy-Garlic, 295
Cambozola, 179
Chili, 178
Chili-Lime, 71–72
Chipotle, 37
Fresh Herb, 135
Lemon Beurre Blanc, 69
Lemon-Caper, 55
Lime-Chili, 286
Roquefort, 175–76

C

Cabbage
-Apple Coleslaw, 92–93
Fresh Coleslaw with Light Lemon
Dressing, 353–54
Grilled Chinese-Style Chicken
Salad, 138–40
Not-Your-Mother's Coleslaw,
352–53
Cake, Angel Food, Toasted, with
Grilled Peaches and Ice Cream,
335–36
Cake, Pound, Toasted, 334–35
Calzones, Grilled Peanut Butter and
Jelly, 336–37
Cambozola Butter, 179
Caper(s)
-Lemon Butter, 55
-Lemon Sauce, 239
Salsa Verde, 174–75
Caraway-Coriander Rub, 77
Caribbean Skewered Pork with Garlic
and Fresh Lime, 264
Caribe Sauce, 91
Carrots, Buttered Grilled, 285
Catfish Sandwiches, Barbecued,
52–53
Ceviche, Grilled Scallop, 27–28
Ceviche Marinade, 28

Cheese
-and-Sausage Quesadillas, 276
Asparagus Wrapped in Provolone
and Prosciutto, 24
Bruschetta with Shaved
Parmesan, 18
Cambozola Butter, 179
Cheesy Baked Hominy Custard,
358–59
Chicken Breasts Marsala, 130
Chicken Breasts with Chèvre and
Yellow Pepper Puree, 132–33
Dijon-Mascarpone Sauce, 266
Feta, Dip, 26–27
Flattened Whole Chicken Boursin,
117
Fontina, Marinated Eggplant with
Tomatoes and, 289–90
Gorgonzola Toasts, 20
Grilled, on a Skewer, 21
Grilled Fresh Figs with
Mascarpone and Balsamic
Syrup, 333
Grilled Quesadilla, 324
Grilled Veal Saltimbocca, 241–42
Hanger Steaks with Caramelized
Onions, Mushrooms, Chèvre,
and Arugula, 193–94
and Honey, Dessert Bruschetta
with, 334
Lamb Patties with Mozzarella and
Mint, 237
Light Lemon Sauce, 54
Mediterranean Dressing, 118
Microwave Polenta, 349
Polenta, 348–49
Raclette in a Bowl, 23
Roquefort Butter, 175–76
-Stuffed Grape Leaves, 22
-Stuffed Peppers, Grilled, 304–5
Tomatoes Stuffed with Duchess
Potatoes, 316–17
Veggie Cheesy Burgers, 317–18
Chicken
Barbecued, Old-Fashioned, 121–22
Beer Can, 113–14
best types, for grilling, 109

Breasts, Boneless, with Fresh Herb
Butter, 135
Breasts, Pesto, 129
Breasts Marsala, 130
Breasts with Chèvre and Yellow
Pepper Puree, 132–33
Breasts with Thai Lemongrass
Marinade, 131–32
Burgers, 143–44
Chickalone, 133–34
Chimichurri, 119–20
defrosting, 110, 121, 123
Flattened, Dijonaise, 116
Flattened Whole, Boursin, 117
in Fresh Herb Marinade, 127–28
Grilled, Fajitas, 136–37
Grilled, "Sashimi," 40–41
Grilled Curried, 126–27
grilling, tips for, 106
Jamaican Jerked, 120–21
judging doneness, 108–9
Livers, Skewered, with Fresh Lime
and Cilantro, 37–38
marinating, 108
Mediterranean, 118–19
Red Wings, 39–40
Rumaki, 38–39
safe handling of, 110, 121, 134
Salad, Grilled Chinese-Style,
138–40
Satay, Fresh Ginger-Garlic, 42
Southwestern, 124
Spring, Brined, 115
Tandoori, 122–23
Teriyaki, Skewered, 137–38
Thighs, Spicy Apple-Lime, 141
Thunder Thighs, 140
whole, flattening, 108
Whole Roast, with Lemon and
Garlic, 111
Wings, Hot and Spicy Chinese,
142–43
in Zinfandel Marinade with
Grilled Onions and Mushrooms,
125–26
Chilean Sea Bass with Minted Pea
Sauce, 70–71

Chile peppers
  Bacon-Wrapped Spicy Barbecued
    Shrimp, 103
  Cheesy Baked Hominy Custard,
    358–59
  Chipotle Butter, 37
  Chipotle Marinade, 251–52
  Mint Chimichurri Sauce, 226
  Veracruz Sauce, 59–60
Chili Butter, 178
Chili-Lime Butter, 71–72, 286
Chili Rub, 191
Chili-Rubbed Beef Fajitas with
    Peppers and Onions, 190–91
Chimichurri Marinade, 119–20
Chimichurri Sauce, Mint, 226
Chinese Chicken Wings, Hot and
    Spicy, 142–43
Chinese Cornish Game Hens, Sweet,
    158–59
Chinese Marinade, Hot and Spicy, 142
Chinese Marinade, Sweet, 158
Chinese-Style Chicken Salad, Grilled,
    138–40
Chinese-Style Marinade, 138–39
Chinese-Style Pork Burgers, 273
Chipotle Butter, 37
Chipotle Marinade, 251–52
Chocolate
  Grilled S'mores, 337–38
Choucroute, Grilled, 278
Cilantro
  -Coconut Basmati Rice, 344
  -Lime Butter, Roast Sweet
    Potatoes with, 308–9
  Sauce, Fresh, 66
  Skewered Chicken Livers with
    Fresh Lime and, 37–38
Cocktail Sauce, Mexican-Style, 30
Coconut-Cilantro Basmati Rice, 344
Coke and Bourbon Marinade, 204–5
Coleslaw
  Apple-Cabbage, 92–93
  Fresh, with Light Lemon Dressing,
    353–54
  Not-Your-Mother's, 352–53
Coriander-Caraway Rub, 77

Corn
  and Black Bean Salsa, 185
  on the Cob, Good Old, 285–86
  on the Cob with Lime-Chili Butter,
    286–87
Cornish Game Hens
  grilling, tips for, 109–10
  Herbed Mustard, 157
  Sweet Chinese, 158–59
Cowpoke Beans, 357–58
Cucumber(s)
  -Dill Sauce, 64
  Garlic Yogurt, 154–55
  Marinated Vegetable Salad, 351–52
  Spears, Minted Grilled, 287–88
  Tzatziki Sauce, 235–36
  -Yogurt Sauce, 94–95
Cumin Turkey Breast Tenders in Pita,
    154–55
Cured Pork Tenderloin with
    Rémoulade, 254–55
Curried Chicken, Grilled, 126–27
Curry, Green, Dipping Sauce, 104
Curry Dry Rub, 126–27
Custard, Cheesy Baked Hominy,
    358–59

D

Desserts
  Caramelized Fruit Kebabs, 328
  Dessert Bruschetta with Cheese
    and Honey, 334
  Grilled Apple Slices, 329
  Grilled Bananas, 330
  Grilled *Buñuelos* with *Cajeta*, 338
  Grilled Fresh Figs with
    Mascarpone and Balsamic
    Syrup, 333
  Grilled Fresh Pineapple Spears, 332
  Grilled Peanut Butter and Jelly
    Calzones, 336–37
  Grilled S'mores, 337–38
  Maple-Glazed Peaches, 331
  Toasted Angel Food Cake with
    Grilled Peaches and Ice Cream,
    335–36
  Toasted Pound Cake, 334–35

  Tropical Grilled Bananas, 330–31
Dijonaise Marinade, 116
Dijon-Mascarpone Sauce, 266
Dijon Mustard Slather, 255
Dijon Mustard–Slathered Pork
    Tenderloin, 255–56
Dill-Cucumber Sauce, 64
Dill Sauce, Creamy Fresh, 229–30
Dip, Feta Cheese, 26–27
Dipping Sauce, Green Curry, 104
Dipping Sauce, Sake, 99–100
Dipping Sauce, Spicy Ginger, 61
Dressings
  Fresh Basil, 84–85
  Fresh Ginger Vinaigrette, 35
  Lemon-Ginger, 86
  Lemon-Sherry Vinaigrette, 283
  Light Lemon, 353–54
  Mediterranean, 118
  Niçoise Vinaigrette, 87–88
  Peanut-Lime, 139–40
Duck
  Breasts, Peking, 160–61
  Breasts with Tuscan Rub, 162
  grilling, 110
  Quartered Duckling with Fig and
    Green Olive Sauce, 159–60

E

Eggplant
  Grilled Ratatouille, 319–20
  Grilled Thyme, 289
  Grilled Whole, 288
  Marinated, with Tomatoes and
    Fontina Cheese, 289–90
  Mixed Vegetable Brochettes,
    318–19
  Stacks, Grilled, with Udon
    Noodles and Fresh Cilantro
    Sauce, 291–93
  Tomato, and Pepper Mélange,
    290–91
Endive, Scallops on, with Pickled
    Ginger, 29
Escarole, Grilled, 294
Escarole, Wilted, and Halibut with
    Light Lemon Sauce, 56–57

F

Fajita Marinade, 136
Fajitas, Chili-Rubbed Beef, with
  Peppers and Onions, 190–91
Fajitas, Grilled Chicken, 136–37
Fennel, Grilled, with Anchovy-Garlic
  Butter, 295
Fig and Green Olive Sauce, 159
Figs, Grilled Fresh, with Mascarpone
  and Balsamic Syrup, 333
Fish
  Barbecued Catfish Sandwiches,
    52–53
  best types, for grilling, 72
  buying, 47–48
  Chilean Sea Bass with Minted Pea
    Sauce, 70–71
  Fresh Tuna Fish Sandwiches,
    89–90
  Grape Leaf-Wrapped Dover Sole,
    53
  Grilled, Sandwiches, 90–91
  Grilled Tuna with Homemade
    Tartar Sauce, 80–81
  Grilled Tuna with Tuscan White
    Beans, 84–85
  Grilled Whole Salmon, 67–68
  grilling, tips for, 48, 50, 55
  Halibut with Lemon-Caper Butter,
    54–55
  Halibut with Wilted Escarole and
    Light Lemon Sauce, 56–57
  judging doneness, 48
  Piquant Swordfish Brochettes,
    76–77
  Red Snapper à la Veracruz, 59–60
  rinsing, 82
  Salade Niçoise with Grilled Tuna,
    87–89
  Salmon Fillets with Black Beans
    and Red Pepper Puree, 62–63
  Salmon Steaks with Cucumber-
    Dill Sauce, 64–65
  Scallop and Salmon Brochettes,
    97–98
  Sea Bass with Lemon Beurre
    Blanc, 68–69
  Seared Fresh Tuna Salad with
    Lemon-Ginger Dressing, 86–87
  Seared Tuna Steaks with Mango
    Salsa, 81–82
  serving sizes, 65
  Shark Steaks with Chili-Lime
    Butter, 71–72
  Soup, Brazilian Mixed Grill, 50–51
  Spicy Salmon Skewers with Udon
    Noodles and Fresh Cilantro
    Sauce, 65–67
  Swordfish Brochettes with Lemon
    and Garlic Marinade, 75
  Swordfish Steaks with Sauce
    Niçoise, 72–73
  Swordfish with Black and White
    Sesame Crust, 74
  Tacos, 92–93
  Tonnato Sauce, 149–50
  Tuna Steaks with Green Olive
    Tapenade, 83
  Tunisian Tilapia with Pita, 77–79
  Vietnamese-Style Lettuce-
    Wrapped Marlin, 57–59
  Whole, Lebanese-Style Salt-
    Grilled, 94–95
  Whole "Camp-Style" Trout, 79
  Whole Snapper with Spicy Ginger
    Dipping Sauce, 60–61
Fruit. See also specific types
  grilling, in foil packets, 325–26
  Kebabs, Caramelized, 328
Fruity Mexican Marinade, 147

G

Game birds
  best types, for grilling, 109–10
  defrosting, 110, 121, 123
  Duck Breasts with Tuscan Rub, 162
  Grilled Pheasant, 164
  grilling, tips for, 106
  Herbed Mustard Cornish Game
    Hens, 157
  judging doneness, 108–9
  marinating, 108
  Pancetta-Wrapped Grilled Quail,
    163
  Peking Duck Breasts, 160–61
  Quartered Duckling with Fig and
    Green Olive Sauce, 159–60
  safe handling of, 110, 121, 134
  Sweet Chinese Cornish Game
    Hens, 158–59
  whole, flattening, 108
Garlic
  -Anchovy Butter, 295
  -and-Rosemary Rack of Lamb,
    224–25
  Bread, Grilled, 17
  Cucumber Yogurt, 154–55
  and Fresh Lime Marinade, 264
  Garlicky Grilled Tomatoes, 313
  Garlicky Skewered Shrimp, 32
  -Ginger Marinade, 153, 198
  -Ginger Marinade, Fresh, 42
  and Ginger Sake Marinade, 170
  Grilled, 296
  and Lemon, Whole Roast Chicken
    with, 111
  and Lemon Marinade, 75
  -Rosemary Marinade, 46
  Rub, Wet, 211
  Salsa Verde, 174–75
  Scampi Marinade, 102
  -Sherry Marinade, 206
  -Studded London Broil, 184
  and Wine Marinade, 32
  -Yogurt Sauce, 77
gas grills
  accessories for, 8–10
  BTU heat levels for, 2–3
  buying considerations, 2–4
  cooking times, 5–6
  direct cooking on, 4–5
  general guidelines for, 6
  history of, 1–2
  indirect cooking on, 4–5
  safety considerations, 6–8
  wood chips, flavors of, 10–12
  wood chips, using, 243–44
Ginger
  Dipping Sauce, Spicy, 61
  -Garlic Marinade, 153, 198
  -Garlic Marinade, Fresh, 42

Ginger (*cont.*)
    and Garlic Sake Marinade, 170
    Grilled Chicken "Sashimi," 40–41
    -Lemon Dressing, 86
    -Orange Sauce, Fresh, 284
    Pickled, Scallops on Endive with,
      29
    -Sake Marinade, 189–90
    Vinaigrette, Fresh, 35
Glaze, Honey Mustard, 173–74
Glaze, Maple-Sherry, 271
Gorgonzola Toasts, 20
Grape Leaf–Wrapped Dover Sole, 53
Grape Leaves, Cheese-Stuffed, 22
Greek Butterflied Leg of Lamb with
    Lemon and Oregano, 220
Greek-Style Marinade, 230–31
Green Beans
    Fast Szechuan, 354
    Salade Niçoise with Grilled Tuna,
      87–89
Greens. *See also* Cabbage; Lettuce
    Creamed Spinach, 355–56
    Grilled Escarole, 294
    Halibut and Wilted Escarole with
      Light Lemon Sauce, 56–57
    Hanger Steaks with Caramelized
      Onions, Mushrooms, Chèvre,
      and Arugula, 193–94
Guinness and Apricot Nectar
    Marinade, 232

H

Halibut with Lemon-Caper Butter,
    54–55
Halibut with Wilted Escarole and
    Light Lemon Sauce, 56–57
Ham. *See also* Prosciutto
    Grilled Choucroute, 278
    steaks, grilling, tip for, 272
    Steaks with Grilled Fresh
      Pineapple Spears, 272
    Whole, Cured, on the Grill, 271
    Whole, Fresh, 270
Herb(ed). *See also specific herbs*
    Fresh, Butter, 135
    Fresh, Marinade, 128, 259

Mediterranean Dressing, 118
Mustard Cornish Game Hens, 157
Mustard Marinade, 157
Potatoes, Skewered, 307
Provençal Marinade, 112
Salsa Verde, 174–75
Hoisin (sauce)
    -Chili Marinade, 44
    -Chili Pork Satay, 44
    Drizzling Sauce, 41
    Hot-and-Sweet Marinade, 250
    Marinade, Spicy, 253
    Peking Sauce, 160–61
    Sweet-and-Sour Marinade, 249
Hominy Custard, Cheesy Baked,
    358–59
Honey-Glazed Winter Squash en
    Brochette, 311
Honey Mustard Glaze, 173–74
Horseradish Sauce, 183

I

Indonesian-Style Beef Satay,
    189–90

J

Jamaican Jerked Chicken, 120–21
Jamaican Jerked Pork Tenderloin,
    256–57
Japanese-Style Grilled Oysters, 36

L

Lamb
    buying, 216
    Chops, Spicy Asian, 45
    Chops with Blackberries and
      Lavender, 227
    Chops with Creamy Fresh Dill
      Sauce, 229–30
    Chops with Fresh Mint Sauce,
      228–29
    Chops with Mint Chimichurri
      Sauce, 226–27
    fell membrane on, 216
    judging doneness, 216
    Kebabs with Spicy Yogurt
      Marinade, 233–34

Leg of, Butterflied, Marsha's
    Miracle, 221
Leg of, Greek Butterflied, with
    Lemon and Oregano, 220
Leg of, Roast, with White Beans,
    218–19
overcooked, texture of, 215
Patties with Mozzarella and Mint,
    237
Rack of, Garlic-and-Rosemary,
    224–25
Rack of, Little Debbie's, 223–24
Riblets with Garlic and Rosemary,
    46
Shanks in Guinness and Apricot
    Nectar, 232
Shish Kebabs, Mediterranean,
    234–35
Shoulder Chops, Marinated Greek,
    230–31
Souvlaki Burgers, 235–36
spring, about, 216
Tenderloin with Artichoke Sauce,
    222–23
USDA certification for, 216
Lavender and Blackberry Marinade,
    227
Lebanese-Style Salt-Grilled Whole
    Fish, 94–95
Leeks, Whole, Grilled, 296–97
Lemongrass Marinade, Thai, 131
Lemon(s)
    Beurre Blanc, 69
    -Caper Butter, 55
    -Caper Sauce, 239
    Ceviche Marinade, 28
    Dressing, Light, 353–54
    and Garlic, Whole Roast Chicken
      with, 111
    and Garlic Marinade, 75
    -Ginger Dressing, 86
    -Lime Marinade, 92–93
    Preserved Moroccan, 363
    Sauce, Light, 54
    Sauce Niçoise, 73
    -Sherry Vinaigrette, 283
    and White Wine Marinade, 76

-Wine Marinade, 97
Lettuce
    Leaf Wraps, Vietnamese-Style
        Sliced Steak in, 192–93
    Salade Niçoise with Grilled Tuna,
        87–89
    Sautéed, with Peas, 355
    -Wrapped Marlin, Vietnamese-
        Style, 57–59
Lime(s)
    -Apple Marinade, Spicy, 141
    Ceviche Marinade, 28
    -Chili Butter, 71–72, 286
    -Cilantro Butter, Roast Sweet
        Potatoes with, 308–9
    Fresh, and Cilantro, Skewered
        Chicken Livers with, 37–38
    Fresh, and Garlic Marinade, 264
    Fruity Mexican Marinade, 147
    -Lemon Marinade, 92–93
    Mexican Marinade, 262
    -Peanut Dressing, 139–40
Liver(s)
    Chicken, Skewered, with Fresh
        Lime and Cilantro, 37–38
    Rumaki, 38–39
    Steaks, Grilled, 214
Lobster Tails, Grilled, 96

M

Mango Salsa, 81–82
Maple-Glazed Peaches, 331
Maple-Sherry Glaze, 271
Marinades
    Apple-Lime, Spicy, 141
    Asian, Spicy, 45
    Asian-Style Barbecue, 272
    Blackberry and Lavender, 227
    Bourbon and Coke, 204–5
    Bourguignon, 202
    Ceviche, 28
    Chimichurri, 119–20
    Chinese, Hot and Spicy, 142
    Chinese, Sweet, 158
    Chinese-Style, 138–39
    Chipotle, 251–52
    Dijonaise, 116

Dijon Mustard Slather, 255
Fajita, 136
for fish, tip for, 76
Flank Steak, The Best Ever, 196
Garlic and Fresh Lime, 264
Garlic and Wine, 32
Ginger and Garlic Sake, 170
Ginger-Garlic, 153, 198
Ginger-Garlic, Fresh, 42
Ginger-Sake, 189–90
Greek-Style, 230–31
Guinness and Apricot Nectar, 232
Herb, Fresh, 128, 259
Herbed Mustard, 157
Hoisin, Spicy, 253
Hoisin-Chili, 44
Hot-and-Sweet, 250
Hot Red, 39–40
Lemon and Garlic, 75
Lemon and White Wine, 76
Lemon-Lime, 92–93
Lemon-Wine, 97
Marsala, 130
Mediterranean, 234
Mexican, 262
Mexican, Fruity, 147
Orange-Tomato, 57–58
Peanut, Spicy, 265
Peanut-Sesame, Hot, 43
Pomegranate, 223
for poultry, tip for, 108
Provençal, 112
Red Rooster-Soy, 197
Red Wine and Soy, 213
Red Wine and Thyme, 25
Rosemary-Apple, 268
Rosemary-Garlic, 46
Sake, 99–100
Scampi, 102
Sherried Kebab, 201
Sherry-Garlic, 206
Sherry-Soy, 199–200
Southwestern, 124
Sriracha, 140
Sweet-and-Sour, 249
Tandoori, 122–23
Tequila, 195

Teriyaki, 137–38
Thai Lemongrass, 131
Toasted Sesame, Spicy, 65–66
Tuscan Rub, 162
used as baste or sauce, 143
Vietnamese-Style, 192
Yogurt, Spicy, 233
Zinfandel, 125
Marlin, Vietnamese-Style Lettuce-
    Wrapped, 57–59
Marsala Marinade, 130
Marsala Sauce, 152, 241–42
Mediterranean Dressing, 118
Mediterranean Lamb Shish Kebabs,
    234–35
Mediterranean Marinade, 234
Mexican Fiesta Turkey, 146–47
Mexican Marinade, 262
Mexican Marinade, Fruity, 147
Mexican Pork Strips, Skewered,
    262–63
Mexican Rice, 344–45
Mexican-Style Cocktail Sauce, 30
Mexican-Style Grilled Oysters, 36–37
Mint(ed)
    Chimichurri Sauce, 226
    Grilled Cucumber Spears, 287–88
    Lamb Patties with Mozzarella and,
        237
    Pea Sauce, 70
    Sauce, Fresh, 228
    Spicy Asian Marinade, 45
    Tabbouleh, 350–51
Mushroom(s)
    Caramelized Onions, Chèvre, and
        Arugula, Hanger Steaks with,
        193–94
    and Cherry Tomatoes, Marinated,
        25–26
    Chicken in Zinfandel Marinade
        with Grilled Onions and, 125–26
    Grilled Marinated, 168–69,
        297–98
    Mixed Grilled Vegetables with
        Feta Cheese Dip, 26–27
    Mixed Vegetable Brochettes,
        318–19

Mushroom(s) (*cont.*)
    Portobello, Burgers, 299
    "Ragout," Grilled Polenta with,
      322–23
    and Raspberry Sauce, 259–60
    Sherried, 186–87
    Skewered Beef Bourguignon,
      202–3
    Teriyaki Beef with Green Onions
      and, 188
    Tofu Kebabs, 321–22
Mussels
    Bordelaise, 33
    Brazilian Mixed Grill Fish Soup,
      50–51
Mustard
    -Basil Sauce, 240
    Dijon, Slather, 255
    Dijonaise Marinade, 116
    Dijon-Mascarpone Sauce, 266
    Honey, Glaze, 173–74
    Marinade, Herbed, 157

N

Niçoise Vinaigrette, 87–88
Noodles
    Grilled Chinese-Style Chicken
      Salad, 138–40
    Udon, and Fresh Cilantro Sauce,
      Grilled Eggplant Stacks with,
      291–93
    Udon, and Fresh Cilantro Sauce,
      Spicy Salmon Skewers with,
      65–67

O

Olive(s)
    Green, and Fig Sauce, 159
    Green, Tapenade, 83
    Salade Niçoise with Grilled Tuna,
      87–89
    Veracruz Sauce, 59–60
Onion(s)
    and Apple Sauce, 261
    Caramelized, Mushrooms, Chèvre,
      and Arugula, Hanger Steaks
      with, 193–94

Chili-Rubbed Beef Fajitas with
    Peppers and, 190–91
Flank Steak Sandwiches with
    Grilled Bell Peppers and,
    199–200
Green, and Mushrooms, Teriyaki
    Beef with, 188
Green, Oriental Grilled, 301
and Mushrooms, Grilled, Chicken
    in Zinfandel Marinade with,
    125–26
Skewered Beef Bourguignon,
    202–3
Slices, Grilled, 301–2
White, Kebabs with Rosemary and
    Balsamic Vinegar, 300
Orange(s)
    Ceviche Marinade, 28
    -Ginger Sauce, Fresh, 284
    -Tomato Marinade, 57–58
Oriental Grilled Green Onions, 301
Orzo with Basil, 350
Oysters
    "Barbecued," 34
    Exotic Grilled, –Two Ways, 35–37
    Grilled, Japanese-Style, 36
    Grilled, Mexican-Style, 36–37
    Grilled, with Fresh Ginger
      Vinaigrette, 34–35

P

Pancetta-Wrapped Grilled Quail, 163
Parsley
    Mint Chimichurri Sauce, 226
    Salsa Verde, 174–75
Pasta. *See also* Noodles
    Grilled Chinese-Style Chicken
      Salad, 138–40
    Orzo with Basil, 350
Peaches
    Caramelized Fruit Kebabs, 328
    Grilled, and Ice Cream, Toasted
      Angel Food Cake with, 335–36
    Maple-Glazed, 331
Peanut Butter
    Hot Peanut-Sesame Marinade, 43
    and Jelly Calzones, Grilled, 336–37

Peanut-Lime Dressing, 139–40
Peanut Sauce, 189
Peking Sauce, 160–61
Spicy Peanut Marinade, 265
Pea(s)
    Black-Eyed, Tex-Mex, 356–57
    Grilled Chinese-Style Chicken
      Salad, 138–40
    and Rice Salad, Creamy, 342–43
    Sauce, Minted, 70
    Sautéed Lettuce with, 355
Peking Duck Breasts, 160–61
Peking Sauce, 160–61
Peppercorn, Green, Sauce, 172–73
Peppercorns, Black, White, and Green,
    Flat Iron Steak with, 194–95
Pepper(s). *See also* Chile peppers
    Bell, and Onions, Grilled, Flank
      Steak Sandwiches with,
      199–200
    Cheese-Stuffed, Grilled, 304–5
    Eggplant, and Tomato Mélange,
      290–91
    Grilled, 302
    Grilled Chicken Fajitas, 136–37
    Grilled Eggplant Stacks with Udon
      Noodles and Fresh Cilantro
      Sauce, 291–93
    Grilled Ratatouille, 319–20
    Marinated Roasted, 303
    Mixed Grilled Vegetables with
      Feta Cheese Dip, 26–27
    Mixed Vegetable Brochettes,
      318–19
    and Onions, Chili-Rubbed Beef
      Fajitas with, 190–91
    Red, Puree, Salmon Fillets with
      Black Beans and, 62–63
    Tofu Kebabs, 321–22
    Yellow, Puree, 132–33
Pesto, 314
Pesto Chicken Breasts, 129
Pesto Tomatoes, Grilled, 314
Pheasant, Grilled, 164
pheasant, grilling, 110
Pineapple
    Fruity Mexican Marinade, 147

Grilled Tacos al Pastor, 251–52
Spears, Fresh, Grilled, 332
Spears, Fresh, Grilled, Ham Steaks
    with, 272
Pizza, Grilled, 16
Polenta, 348–49
    Grilled, with Mushroom "Ragout,"
        322–23
    Microwave, 349
Pomegranate Marinade, 223
Pork. See also Ham; Sausage(s)
    Baby Back Ribs, 246–47
    Brochettes, Spicy Hoisin, 253
    Burgers, Chinese-Style, 273
    Burnt-End Sandwiches, 269–70
    buying, 244
    Caribbean Skewered, with Garlic
        and Fresh Lime, 264
    Chops, Hot-and-Sweet, with
        Asian Pear–Apple Sauce, 250
    Chops, Sweet-and-Sour, 249
    Grilled Choucroute, 278
    Grilled Tacos al Pastor, 251–52
    judging doneness, 244
    Loin, Rolled, Roast Florentine, 267
    Loin Normandy, 268
    Loin with Dijon-Mascarpone
        Sauce, 266
    Ribs, Country-Style, Barbecued,
        248
    Satay, Hoisin-Chili, 44
    Skewered, with Spicy Peanut
        Marinade, 265
    Spareribs, Authentic Barbecued,
        246
    Strips, Skewered Mexican, 262–63
    Tenderloin, Cured, with
        Rémoulade, 254–55
    Tenderloin, Dijon
        Mustard–Slathered, 255–56
    Tenderloin, Jamaican Jerked,
        256–57
    Tenderloin Barbecue, 257–58
    Tenderloin of, with Mushrooms
        and Raspberries, 259–60
    Tenderloin with Apples and
        Onions, 260–61

Potato(es)
    -and-Sauerkraut Casserole, 362
    "Baked," on the Grill, 305–6
    Duchess, Tomatoes Stuffed with,
        316–17
    Homemade French Fries, 360
    New, Boiled, 359
    Raclette in a Bowl, 23
    Salade Niçoise with Grilled Tuna,
        87–89
    Skewered Herbed, 307
    Skins, Grilled, 306
    Skins, Grilled, Strip Steaks with,
        176–77
    Sweet, Roast, with Cilantro-Lime
        Butter, 308–9
    Tart, 361–62
    Wedges, Rosemary, 307–8
Poultry. See Chicken; Game birds;
    Turkey
Pound Cake, Toasted, 334–35
Prawns, Blue Thai, with Green Curry
    Dipping Sauce, 104
Prosciutto
    Asparagus Wrapped in Provolone
        and, 24
    and Basil-Wrapped Lemon
        Shrimp, 31
    Grilled Veal Saltimbocca, 241–42
    -Wrapped Turkey Brochettes with
        Marsala Sauce, 152
Provençal Marinade, 112

Q

Quail, Grilled, Pancetta-Wrapped, 163
quail, grilling, 110
Quesadilla, Grilled, 324
Quesadillas, Sausage-and-Cheese, 276

R

Raclette in a Bowl, 23
Raspberry and Mushroom Sauce,
    259–60
Ratatouille, Grilled, 319–20
Red Rooster–Soy Marinade, 197
Red Snapper à la Veracruz, 59–60
Rémoulade Sauce, 254–55

Rice
    Basmati, Cake, Savory, 347
    Basmati, Coconut-Cilantro, 344
    Mexican, 344–45
    and Pea Salad, Creamy, 342–43
    Risotto, 345–46
    Savory, 343
    Sticky, Perfumed, 58
    Wild, Casserole, 348
Risotto, 345–46
Roquefort Butter, 175–76
Rosemary
    -and-Garlic Rack of Lamb,
        224–25
    -Apple Marinade, 268
    -Garlic Marinade, 46
    Potato Wedges, 307–8
    Rolled Pork Loin Roast Florentine,
        267
Rubs
    Barbecue, 247
    Chili, 191
    Coriander-Caraway, 77
    Dry, Curry, 126–27
    Dry, Hot-and-Sweet, 180
    Dry, Salt-and-Cumin, 154
    Dry, Spicy Barbecue, 114
    Wet Garlic, 211
Rumaki, 38–39

S

Sage Turkey Burgers, 156
Sake
    -Ginger Marinade, 189–90
    Marinade, Ginger and Garlic, 170
    Marinade/Dipping Sauce, 99–100
    Scallops, Skewered, 99–100
Salad
    Apple-Cabbage Coleslaw, 92–93
    Chicken, Grilled Chinese-Style,
        138–40
    Creamy Rice and Pea, 342–43
    Fresh Coleslaw with Light Lemon
        Dressing, 353–54
    Marinated Vegetable, 351–52
    Not-Your-Mother's Coleslaw,
        352–53

Salad (cont.)
  Salade Niçoise with Grilled Tuna,
    87–89
  Seared Fresh Tuna, with Lemon-
    Ginger Dressing, 86–87
  Tabbouleh, 350–51
Salad dressing. See Dressings
Salmon
  Fillets with Black Beans and Red
    Pepper Puree, 62–63
  and Scallop Brochettes, 97–98
  Skewers, Spicy, with Udon
    Noodles and Fresh Cilantro
    Sauce, 65–67
  Steaks with Cucumber-Dill Sauce,
    64–65
  Whole, Grilled, 67–68
Salsa
  Black Bean and Corn, 185
  Mango, 81–82
  Verde, 174–75
Salt-Grilled Whole Fish, Lebanese-
  Style, 94–95
Sandwiches. See also Burgers
  Barbecued Catfish, 52–53
  Burnt-End, 269–70
  Cumin Turkey Breast Tenders in
    Pita, 154–55
  Flank Steak, with Grilled Bell
    Peppers and Onions, 199–200
  Fresh Tuna Fish, 89–90
  Grilled Fish, 90–91
  leftover steak, 198
  Pork Tenderloin Barbecue, 257–58
  Tunisian Tilapia with Pita, 77–79
"Sashimi," Grilled Chicken, 40–41
Satay
  Beef, Hot Peanut-Sesame, 43
  Beef, Indonesian-Style, 189–90
  Chicken, Fresh Ginger-Garlic, 42
  definition of, 43
  Pork, Hoisin-Chili, 44
Sauces. See also Salsa
  Apple and Onion, 261
  Argentine Squirt, 207
  Artichoke, 222
  Asian Pear–Apple, 251

Basil-Mustard, 240
Basting, Beer and Chili, 203
Basting, Sweet, Hot, and Sour,
  208–9
Béarnaise, 181–82
Caribe, 91
Cilantro, Fresh, 66
Cocktail, Mexican-Style, 30
for cold leftover steak, 169
Cucumber-Dill, 64
Cucumber-Yogurt, 94–95
Dijon-Mascarpone, 266
Dill, Creamy Fresh, 229–30
Dipping, Green Curry, 104
Dipping, Sake, 99–100
Dipping, Spicy Ginger, 61
Drizzling, 41
Fig and Green Olive, 159
Garlic Cucumber Yogurt, 154–55
Garlic-Yogurt, 77
Ginger-Orange, Fresh, 284
Green Peppercorn, 172–73
Horseradish, 183
Lemon, Light, 54
Lemon Beurre Blanc, 69
Lemon-Caper, 239
Marsala, 152, 241–42
Mint, Fresh, 228
Mint Chimichurri, 226
Minted Pea, 70
Mushroom and Raspberry,
  259–60
Niçoise, 73
Peanut, 189
Peking, 160–61
Pesto, 314
Rémoulade, 254–55
Tartar, Homemade, 80–81
Tonnato, 149–50
Tzatziki, 235–36
Veracruz, 59–60
White, 100–101
Sauerkraut
  -and-Potato Casserole, 362
  Applesauce, and Cornbread,
    Grilled Bockwurst with, 275
  Grilled Choucroute, 278

Sausage(s)
  -and-Cheese Quesadillas, 276
  Bratwurst in Beer, 274
  Flattened Turkey with, 145–46
  Grilled Bockwurst with
    Sauerkraut, Applesauce, and
    Cornbread, 275
  Grilled Choucroute, 278
  Grilled Italian, with Polenta, 277
Scallop(s)
  Brazilian Mixed Grill Fish Soup,
    50–51
  Creamed Grilled, on Sourdough
    Toast, 100–101
  on Endive with Pickled Ginger, 29
  Grilled, Ceviche, 27–28
  and Salmon Brochettes, 97–98
  Skewered, with Bay Leaves, 98–99
  Skewered Sake, 99–100
Scampi Marinade, 102
Sea Bass with Lemon Beurre Blanc,
  68–69
Sesame, Black and White, Crust,
  Swordfish with, 74
Shark Steaks
  Brazilian Mixed Grill Fish Soup,
    50–51
  with Chili-Lime Butter, 71–72
Shellfish
  Bacon-Wrapped Spicy Barbecued
    Shrimp, 103
  "Barbecued" Oysters, 34
  Blue Thai Prawns with Green
    Curry Dipping Sauce, 104
  Brazilian Mixed Grill Fish Soup,
    50–51
  buying, 47–48
  Creamed Grilled Scallops on
    Sourdough Toast, 100–101
  Exotic Grilled Oysters–Two Ways,
    35–37
  Garlicky Skewered Shrimp, 32
  Grilled Lobster Tails, 96
  Grilled Oysters with Fresh Ginger
    Vinaigrette, 34–35
  Grilled Scallop Ceviche, 27–28
  Grilled Shrimp à la Scampi, 102

Grilled Shrimp Cocktail, 30–31
grilling, 48, 50
judging doneness, 48
Lemon, Prosciutto and Basil-
    Wrapped Shrimp, 31
Mussels Bordelaise, 33
Scallop and Salmon Brochettes,
    97–98
Scallops on Endive with Pickled
    Ginger, 29
Skewered Sake Scallops, 99–100
Skewered Scallops with Bay
    Leaves, 98–99
Sherried Kebab Marinade, 201
Sherried Mushrooms, 186–87
Sherry-Garlic Marinade, 206
Sherry-Maple Glaze, 271
Sherry-Soy Marinade, 199–200
Shrimp
    Bacon-Wrapped Spicy Barbecued,
        103
    Blue Thai Prawns with Green
        Curry Dipping Sauce, 104
    Brazilian Mixed Grill Fish Soup,
        50–51
    Cocktail, Grilled, 30–31
    Garlicky Skewered, 32
    Grilled, à la Scampi, 102
    Lemon, Prosciutto and Basil-
        Wrapped, 31
Side dishes, off-the-grill
    Boiled New Potatoes, 359
    Cheesy Baked Hominy Custard,
        358–59
    Coconut-Cilantro Basmati Rice,
        344
    Cowpoke Beans, 357–58
    Creamed Spinach, 355–56
    Creamy Rice and Pea Salad,
        342–43
    Fast Szechuan Green Beans, 354
    Fresh Coleslaw with Light Lemon
        Dressing, 353–54
    Homemade French Fries, 360
    Marinated Vegetable Salad,
        351–52
    Mexican Rice, 344–45

Microwave Polenta, 349
Not-Your-Mother's Coleslaw,
    352–53
Orzo with Basil, 350
Polenta, 348–49
Potato Tart, 361–62
Preserved Moroccan Lemons, 363
Risotto, 345–46
Sauerkraut-and-Potato Casserole,
    362
Sautéed Lettuce with Peas, 355
Savory Basmati Rice Cake, 347
Savory Rice, 343
Tabbouleh, 350–51
Tex-Mex Black-Eyed Peas, 356–57
Wild Rice Casserole, 348
skewered foods, tip for, 32
S'mores, Grilled, 337–38
Snapper, Whole, with Spicy Ginger
    Dipping Sauce, 60–61
Sole, Dover, Grape Leaf-Wrapped,
    53
Soup, Fish, Brazilian Mixed Grill,
    50–51
Southwestern Chicken, 124
Southwestern Marinade, 124
Spinach, Creamed, 355–56
Squash
    Grilled Ratatouille, 319–20
    Grilled Zucchini, 310–11
    Mixed Grilled Vegetables with
        Feta Cheese Dip, 26–27
    Mixed Vegetable Brochettes,
        318–19
    Summer, Grilled, 309–10
    Winter, Honey-Glazed, en
        Brochette, 311
Sriracha Marinade, 140
Sweet Potatoes, Roast, with
    Cilantro-Lime Butter, 308–9
Swordfish
    with Black and White Sesame
        Crust, 74
    Brochettes, Piquant, 76–77
    Brochettes with Lemon and Garlic
        Marinade, 75
    Steaks with Sauce Niçoise, 72–73

T

Tabbouleh, 350–51
Tacos, Fish, 92–93
Tacos al Pastor, Grilled, 251–52
Tandoori Chicken, 122–23
Tandoori Marinade, 122–23
Tapenade, Green Olive, 83
Tart, Potato, 361–62
Tartar Sauce, Homemade, 80–81
Tequila Marinade, 195
Teriyaki Beef with Green Onions and
    Mushrooms, 188
Teriyaki Marinade, 137–38
Teriyaki Turkey Breast, 148
Tex-Mex Black-Eyed Peas, 356–57
Thai Lemongrass Marinade, 131
Thunder Thighs, 140
Thyme and Red Wine Marinade, 25
Thyme Eggplant, Grilled, 289
Tilapia, Tunisian, with Pita, 77–79
Tofu, Grilled Marinated, 321
Tofu Kebabs, 321–22
Tomato(es)
    -Basil Bruschetta, 19
    Cherry, and Mushrooms,
        Marinated, 25–26
    Cherry, en Brochette, 315
    Cowpoke Beans, 357–58
    Eggplant, and Pepper Mélange,
        290–91
    and Fontina Cheese, Marinated
        Eggplant with, 289–90
    Garlicky Grilled, 313
    Grilled Cheese-Stuffed Peppers,
        304–5
    Grilled Pesto, 314
    Grilled Ratatouille, 319–20
    Mexican-Style Cocktail Sauce, 30
    Mixed Grilled Vegetables with
        Feta Cheese Dip, 26–27
    Mixed Vegetable Brochettes,
        318–19
    -Orange Marinade, 57–58
    Plum, Skewered, with Garlic and
        Basil, 312
    Stuffed with Duchess Potatoes,
        316–17

Tomato(es) (*cont.*)
  Tabbouleh, 350–51
  Tofu Kebabs, 321–22
  Veracruz Sauce, 59–60
tongs, buying, 21
Tonnato Sauce, 149–50
Tortillas
  Chili-Rubbed Beef Fajitas with
    Peppers and Onions, 190–91
  Fish Tacos, 92–93
  Grilled *Buñuelos* with *Cajeta*, 338
  Grilled Chicken Fajitas, 136–37
  Grilled Quesadilla, 324
  Grilled Tacos al Pastor, 251–52
  heating, 93
  Peking Duck Breasts, 160–61
  Sausage-and-Cheese Quesadillas,
    276
  Skewered Mexican Pork Strips,
    262–63
Trout, Whole "Camp-Style," 79
Tuna
  Fish, Fresh, Sandwiches, 89–90
  Grilled, Salade Niçoise with, 87–89
  Grilled, with Homemade Tartar
    Sauce, 80–81
  Grilled, with Tuscan White Beans,
    84–85
  Seared Fresh, Salad with Lemon-
    Ginger Dressing, 86–87
  Steaks, Seared, with Mango Salsa,
    81–82
  Steaks with Green Olive Tapenade,
    83
  Tonnato Sauce, 149–50
Tunisian Tilapia with Pita, 77–79
Turkey
  best types, for grilling, 109
  Breast, *Beau Monde*, 151
  Breast, Teriyaki, 148
  Breast Tenders, Cumin, in Pita,
    154–55

  Brochettes, Ginger-Garlic, 153
  Brochettes, Prosciutto-Wrapped,
    with Marsala Sauce, 152
  Burgers, Sage, 156
  defrosting, 110, 121, 123
  Flattened, with Sausage, 145–46
  grilling, tips for, 106
  judging doneness, 108–9
  marinating, 108
  Mexican Fiesta, 146–47
  safe handling of, 110, 121, 134
  Tonnato, 148–50
  whole, flattening, 108
  Whole Roast, 144–45
Tuscan Rub Marinade, 162
Tzatziki Sauce, 235–36

V

Veal
  buying, 216
  Chops, Grilled, with Lemon-Caper
    Sauce, 239
  Chops with Basil-Mustard Sauce,
    240–41
  judging doneness, 216
  overcooked, texture of, 215
  Paprika Chops with Sour Cream
    and Chives, 238
  Saltimbocca, Grilled, 241–42
Vegetable(s). *See also specific types*
  grilling, guidelines for, 280
  Mixed, Brochettes, 318–19
  Mixed Grilled, with Feta Cheese
    Dip, 26–27
  Salad, Marinated, 351–52
  Veggie Cheesy Burgers, 317–18
  Veracruz Sauce, 59–60
Vietnamese-Style Lettuce-Wrapped
    Marlin, 57–59
Vietnamese-Style Marinade, 192
Vietnamese-Style Sliced Steak in
    Lettuce Leaf Wraps, 192–93

Vinaigrette
  Fresh Ginger, 35
  Lemon-Sherry, 283
  Niçoise, 87–88

W

Wasabi
  Japanese-Style Grilled Oysters, 36
  Paste, 170–71
Wild Rice Casserole, 348
Wine, Marsala
  Marinade, 130
  Sauce, 152, 241–42
Wine, Red
  Bourguignon Marinade, 202
  and Soy Marinade, 213
  and Thyme Marinade, 25
  Zinfandel Marinade, 125
Wine, White
  and Garlic Marinade, 32
  Greek-Style Marinade, 230–31
  -Lemon Marinade, 97
  and Lemon Marinade, 76

Y

Yogurt
  -Cucumber Sauce, 94–95
  Garlic Cucumber, 154–55
  -Garlic Sauce, 77
  Marinade, Spicy, 233
  Tandoori Marinade, 122–23
  Tzatziki Sauce, 235–36

Z

Zinfandel Marinade, 125
Zucchini
  Grilled, 310–11
  Grilled Ratatouille, 319–20
  Mixed Grilled Vegetables with
    Feta Cheese Dip, 26–27
  Mixed Vegetable Brochettes,
    318–19